THE
Skyhawk
YEARS

The A-4 Skyhawk in Australian Service 1968–1984

PETER GREENFIELD
DAVID PREST

Avonmore Books

The Skyhawk Years
The A-4 Skyhawk in Australian Service 1968–1984

Peter Greenfield and David Prest

ISBN: 978-0-6457004-1-1

First published 2023 by Avonmore Books
Avonmore Books
PO Box 217
Kent Town
South Australia 5071
Australia

Phone: (61 8) 8431 9780
www.avonmorebooks.com.au

 A catalogue record for this
book is available from the
National Library of Australia

Cover design & layout by Diane Bricknell

Editing by Andy Wright, Wright Stuff Editing and Proofreading

In publishing this title Avonmore Books is grateful for the support of the Fleet Air Arm Association of Australia and the sponsors and supporters listed in the preface. Thanks to the Robert Garratt of the Seapower Centre and the John Hopton Collection for assistance with Skyhawk images.

The squadron badges of VC724 and VF805 are reproduced with the kind permission of the Department of Defence.

Dust jacket photographs:
Front: Touchdown by Skyhawk 874 from VF805 on the deck of HMAS Melbourne circa mid/late-1970s. (Seapower Centre)
Back: TA-4G trainers of VC724 at Nowra in the mid-1970s. (John Hopton Collection)

CONTENTS

'The Sandblowers'
This original painting by RG Smith was presented to the RAN by the Douglas Aircraft Corporation.

FOREWORD

The authors, Lieutenant Peter Greenfield and Chief Petty Officer David Prest, who later served as a Flight Lieutenant engineer in the Royal Australian Air Force, have done me the honour of asking me to write this foreword, despite my 'hands on' involvement being only for the first quarter of the timespan of Royal Australian Navy (RAN) Skyhawk operations.

I guess their request could be justified in that I was the first RAN Skyhawk squadron Commanding Officer and, as a Royal Navy (RN) trained Air Warfare Instructor (AWI), together with my erstwhile Qualified Flying Instructor colleague Lieutenant Commander Grahame King, and our tame United States Navy (USN) exchange pilot, Lieutenant Mike Gump, defined and implemented the Operational Flying School syllabus of training, which remained substantially unchanged over the operational life of the RAN Skyhawks.

The lead author of this book, Peter Greenfield, began his Skyhawk training after I had left the squadron but, clearly, embraced and put into practice the concepts that we, the first instructors, wished to instil. His ability as a Skyhawk pilot is exemplified by his having been awarded a 'Subsunk' by exercise umpires after what I believe to have been the only time an RAN Skyhawk pilot identified a 'hostile' snorting submarine during an exercise and simulated an attack with a Sidewinder missile.

Of course, none of the training, or subsequent operational flying, would have been possible without the dedicated and professional competence of aircraft maintainers such as David Prest. I consider there has not been sufficient acknowledgement of these men, who often worked late into the night, if not all through it, to provide aircraft on the line to meet the often-ambitious flying programmes drawn up by the senior pilots! Skyhawks would not have flown, but for them.

The chapters of this book give a detailed account of all aspects of RAN Skyhawk operations in the RAN over the period of the life of this remarkable aircraft. In that regard, I must say the authors have done superb justice to the aircraft, the aircrews, the maintainers and others who contributed to the 'Skyhawk Years'. The operational commanders who tasked the Skyhawk squadrons could not have been anything other than impressed by how their needs were met.

I think it appropriate in this foreword to look at the history of RAN fighter aircraft from the late 1940s to the early 1980s.

The first RAN fighter was the single-seat, 2,500-hp Bristol Centaurus-powered Hawker Sea Fury FB.11 (fighter-bomber), purchased to operate from the straight-deck carrier HMAS

Sydney. This was a wonderful aircraft to fly, particularly for a young Sub-Lieutenant Da Costa, who couldn't believe he was being paid to do so after completing his Fighter Operational Flying School in 1956 (on 805 Squadron as it happened!). *Sydney* had ceased operating aircraft by that time, so I did not have an opportunity to carry out challenging straight-deck landings. The Sea Fury was a good weapons platform for its day, having a gyro gunsight, and was armed with 4 × 20-mm cannon, 3-inch rockets and free-fall bombs.

The arrival of HMAS *Melbourne* in 1955 saw the introduction of the Sea Venom FAW.53 (fighter, all-weather), crewed by a pilot and an observer radar operator, and powered by a de Havilland Ghost turbojet engine rated at 4,950-lb thrust. The night-fighter intercept business was a challenge on a dark night. With the navigation lights of the evading 'target' turned off, the 'fighter' pilot, guided by the observer's interpretation of the AI Mk.17 radar, had to fly the aircraft to a stabilised position at gun-firing range 200 yards astern of the target. The night deck landing afterwards was marginally more relaxing, but not noticeably! In the ground-attack role, the Sea Venom had 4 × 20-mm cannon, and 3-inch rockets. It had, however, unlike the Skyhawk, a gyro gunsight.

And so, the RAN came to the A-4G Skyhawk, powered by a Pratt & Whitney J52-P8A turbojet engine rated at 9,300-lb thrust. The aircraft could be armed with a range of bombs, rockets, 2 × 20-mm cannon and Sidewinder air-to-air missiles and was equipped with a pilot-operated ground-avoidance radar. I flew the Hawker Hunter swept-wing fighter in the RN's AWI training course at RN Air Station Lossiemouth. It was wonderful to fly – a classic jet aircraft – but it was very limited in its ground-attack capability. On the other hand, the Skyhawk looked like the very capable attack aircraft that it was. It was a delight to fly and a good deck-landing aircraft to boot. Who could ask for more? Well, I suppose a gyro gunsight would have improved things, but we coped. The USN had found it to be the most capable carrier-borne attack aircraft in its inventory throughout the war in Vietnam, and the RAN purchased our version in that same time period. We could not have chosen better for a light fleet carrier such as *Melbourne*, and this was demonstrated for a good many years.

Sydney carried out operations in Korea in the early 1950s, but *Melbourne* was never required to operate its fighter aircraft in a 'hot' war. However, throughout the ship's operational life, it was a visible and successful deterrent force in the Australian sphere of interest. This was particularly relevant during the worrying Indonesian Confrontation. There can be little doubt that 'peace' in South-East Asia was largely maintained because of the state of training and operational performance of *Melbourne*'s attack and air-defence aircraft. This is the true value of naval flag-waving port visits.

Sadly, the Skyhawk era came to a premature end when our sole carrier was paid off without replacement. The 'powers that be' decided (incorrectly, in my view) there was not a role for the now land-based Skyhawks in support of the Australian Defence Force (ADF), and so the remaining, very capable, aircraft were passed over 'the Ditch' to the Royal New Zealand Air

Force (RNZAF). It was a bitter pill to swallow when Australia then paid the RNZAF to base a squadron of Skyhawks at Naval Air Station Nowra to support the ADF!

I commend this book to those who have an interest in, or have been involved in any way with, the RAN Skyhawk story. It is also a valuable resource for any person interested in, or writing about, Australian military aviation history.

Commodore John Da Costa RAN (Rtd)

PREFACE AND ACKNOWLEDGMENTS

This book is dedicated to the Skyhawk pilots and maintainers who are sadly no longer with us.

The book came about via discussion on the 'Book of Faces' between a small group of people who flew and fixed the Skyhawks flown by the Royal Australian Navy (RAN). 'Wouldn't it be nice if we had a book like *Buccaneer Boys*, about us who flew and fixed the Skyhawks?' 'Yep, we are all getting older and soon we won't remember.'

So, two of us, the self-appointed authors, had a private discussion and decided to make it happen. Between us, one a retired maintainer and the other a retired pilot, we divided up the tasks along the lines of 'I'll do the engineers' and 'I'll do the pilots.' Easy to say, but a lot harder to achieve in practice, particularly as we live in different hemispheres.

The obvious place to start was with the Fleet Air Arm Association of Australia, whose offices have been incredibly helpful. Not only did they broadcast our appeals multiple times, but they made their own archival resources available to us (including the incredible file maintained by Phil Thompson). One Skyhawk pilot, John Bartels, has always been a keen photographer and made his private collection available to us. He also maintains a list of Skyhawk pilots and their last known points of contact.

A key contributor was our own 'Mr Skyhawk', Commodore John Da Costa RAN (Rtd). He has made the first contribution with an essay never previously seen in Australia. Not only that, but when we approached him cap in hand with our request for him to write the foreword, he graciously agreed to do so.

Flying and fixing is very much a chicken and the egg situation. Without maintainers, there are no aircraft to fly. Without pilots, there are no broken aircraft to fix and then fly. Our skills are interdependent.

The two squadrons that operated the Skyhawks in RAN service were VF805 and VC724. VF805 was the operational unit that went to sea as part of the carrier air group aboard HMAS *Melbourne*, our hard-worked aircraft carrier. VC724 was the support squadron that trained the pilots, kept them current, trained the maintainers, kept them working hard, and supported the fleet operating around the shores of Australia. The aircraft and the people were interchanged regularly.

The squadrons were small in terms of numbers, both of aircraft and personnel. The backbones of each were the senior pilots and senior maintainers who had accumulated years of experience. The junior pilots and junior maintainers were trusted to do their jobs to the best of their ability. In our humble opinion, all these people, who flew and fixed the Skyhawks between the years of 1968 and 1984, did extremely well.

We would like to acknowledge the people who helped us both to achieve this book. The contributors whose stories bring this book to life are listed in detail in Annex B. There are many others though who helped us bring the book to fruition.

Firstly, Marcus Peake, the webmaster at the Fleet Air Arm Association of Australia, who seems to be a walking encyclopedia of knowledge. He has found answers to obscure questions, published requests for stories multiple times, and offered us more help when it came to the difficult question of what to do with this huge effort.

Stuart Harwood, the manager and senior curator of the Fleet Air Arm Museum, was somebody that Marcus pointed us at. In conversations with him, we discovered that squadron-level documentation had been forwarded to him for safekeeping. These included squadron diaries, authorisation sheets, and squadron linebooks. Although the desire is to digitise these important records, finding the funds to achieve this is a problem. Nevertheless, Stuart had helpful volunteers who perused records to provide us answers to our questions. The turnaround time was remarkable.

Commander Craig Castle RAN at the Navy Office, who answered our questions about publishing, forwarded us the name of Lieutenant Commander Des Woods. Remarkably, Marcus knows him as well, and some of the detail of the project Des recently completed, *Flying Stations II*. So, our thanks to both those gentlemen.

Captain Richard Parry, a colleague of 23 years at our mutual former employer, and a fellow retiree here in Penang, is an ardent amateur military historian. He volunteered to proofread the chapters as I finished them. Each week he sent me (Peter) pages of finely detailed corrections which have made my writing clearer, more readable or both. Many thanks for your painstaking work, Richard.

Finally, I wish to acknowledge my patient wife of 31 years, Pam, who has put up with my focus on producing this book. She has had a bit of practice; my PhD took eight years, a huge effort, while I held down a demanding job. Pam made sure I did not get bogged down, diverted me when I needed to be diverted and ensured I ate when I should.

I (Dave) would like to acknowledge my wife Margaret who very patiently waited for me to solicit submissions from maintainers for the book – through the 'HMAS Nirimba', 'VF805/ VC724 Skyhawk Squadrons', 'A-4G Scooterphiles' and 'HMAS Melbourne II' Facebook pages – then compile them into a reasonable order date wise for inclusion in the book. Despite that, the dog still managed to get its evening walks, which, of course, broke my fixation on the task.

We have tried very hard to be accurate, to acknowledge that everyone is expressing their memories in their own way, from a perspective of nearly 50 years. Any mistakes you may perceive are not theirs, but ours in our production.

Along the road to publishing, there is a thing called pre-printing costs. These costs are borne by the authors, to enable the publisher to setup the publishing process. Being retirees, the authors sought help with these. After the original attempt to source a grant failed, we turned to the Fleet Air Arm Association of Australia, who launched a crowd funding appeal.

There were two categories: "Supporters" who offered $200 or more, and "Sponsors" who offered $500 or more. Amazingly, the money was raised within three weeks and has made the publishing of this book a possibility. The authors gratefully acknowledge the generosity of the Sponsors and Supporters who are listed below.

Peter 'Purps' Greenfield and David Prest

SPONSORS
John DaCosta
James Caldwell
Murray Coppins
Ian Gibson
Peter Greenfield
Marcus Peake
David Prest
Phil Thompson

SUPPORTERS
John Bartels
Mark Binskin
Clive Blennerhassett
Rosalie Callan
Keith Johnson
Stephen Shugg
Graham Winterflood

GLOSSARY

Note: The terms in this glossary only apply to the Skyhawk era, i.e., from 1967 to 1984 and therefore may not be applicable either side of that period.

A-4	The Skyhawk's designation. The RAN had A-4G single-seat and TA-4G two-seat aircraft.
AED	Air Engineering Department. On HMAS *Melbourne*, manned by the ship's technical birdies. Responsible for servicing the aircraft tow-tugs (modified coal mine machinery tugs), aircraft engine oil and hydraulic oil analysis (for detecting degrading engines and contaminated aircraft hydraulic oil systems), repair of aircraft equipment, the LOX Bay, and assistance to embarked squadrons if required.
AEO	Aircraft Engineering Officer
AIM-9	The Sidewinder anti-aircraft missile.
Aircraft Series/Bureau Number/Side Number	The RAN series number which identifies a particular aircraft and type. The Skyhawk series number was N13. All Skyhawks had a Bureau Number which was allocated to the aircraft when accepted by the USN from the manufacturer. The RAN Skyhawks also had side numbers. The Skyhawk with the side number '887' had its series number as N13 and its Bureau Number as 154908, i.e., Skyhawk 887 was N13-154908. The Bureau Number would be referred to for spare parts usage/identification.
Aircraft Handler	The branch responsible for the movement of aircraft while at sea. Also responsible for the upkeep of the hangars on *Melbourne* and providing the Flight and Hangar Deck Fire Party.
Air Refuelling Store	A self-contained refuelling system consisting of an extendable and retractable fuel hose, an expanding drogue with an internal fuel nozzle receptacle, a fuel transfer pump and fuel lines housed at the rear of a 300-gallon fuel tank capable of being jettisoned. The ARS was carried on the centreline stores rack of both the TA-4 and the A-4. Also known as a 'Buddy Store' and capable of refuelling any aircraft with a probe refuelling system.
AJB-3A	The aircraft all-attitude indicator with blue on top representing the sky and black on the bottom representing the earth, that revolved around itself in yaw, commonly called the Abba Jabba.
ALO	Aircraft Electrical Officer. Became Weapons Electrical Engineering Officer or WEEO.
AMCO	Aircraft Maintenance and Control Office on each squadron where all aircraft records are kept and maintained and from where maintenance tasks are delegated.
AMP	Assisted Maintenance Period
ARF	Aerial refuelling. Where a receiver aircraft uses its probe to receive fuel from a tanker.
Artificer	A fully trained and certified sailor in a technical trade. The training usually consisted of 3.5 years of full-time training followed by 1.5 years on-the-job training and being awarded a Certificate of Completion of an Apprenticeship by the Navy. Not all technical sailors had the same high level of training as an Artificer or a Mechanician. Both titles have been superseded and the length and expanse of current technical training significantly reduced. The Artificer was nicknamed a 'Tiffy'. An Artificer 3rd Class was equivalent to a Leading Seaman, an Artificer 2nd Class equivalent to a petty officer and an Artificer 1st class equivalent to the chief petty officer. The Chief Artificer was the head of maintenance on a squadron.
ASU/B Hangar	Aircraft Servicing Unit. Located in B Hangar.
ATA	Air Technical Aircraft. A sailor trained in airframe systems and engine maintenance. One of the four arms of aircraft maintenance in the Fleet Air Arm and Skyhawk Maintenance, the others being ATWL, ATWO and ATC.
ATC	Air Traffic Control
ATC	Air Technical Communications. Sailors trained in the maintenance of the aircraft communication systems including radar.
ATCO	Air Traffic Control Officer
ATD	Air Training Department. The on-base training unit for technical aircraft trades.
ATWL	Air Technical Weapons Electrical. A sailor trained in the maintenance of the aircraft's electrical systems.
ATWO	Air Technical Weapons Ordnance. A sailor trained in the maintenance of the armament systems and aircraft weapons.
AVGAS	Aviation gasoline. High octane, highly explosive and requires special stowage on a carrier. Note: HMAS *Melbourne* was only fitted with AVGAS stowage in the 1969 refit.
AVCAT	Aviation Carrier Turbine fuel. Often referred to as JP5 and contains additives to reduce the fire, biological and static electricity risks.
AWI	Air Warfare Instructor. The instructor for tactics and fighting.
B Tanks	Underwing 150-gallon fuel tanks carried on the A-4/TA-4

Banner	An aerial gunnery target made of closely woven mesh net towed behind an aircraft. The hits were keenly counted, and hotly disputed by the pilots.
Base WOD	The Warrant Officer Disciplinarian in charge of discipline on an RAAF base.
BDU33	Bomb Dummy Unit 33. A 25-pound cast-iron or machined steel unit with the flight characteristics of a Mk.82 Bomb. The BDU33 replaced the Mk.76 series used in the early 1970s.
Beecroft Range	The air-to-ground gunnery range near Point Perpendicular near Jervis Bay.
BITS	Back In The Saddle. The flying programme immediately after long leave.
Bolter	When an aircraft misses the arrestor wires and has to fly off the carrier.
Buddy Store	The air refuelling store of 300-gallon capacity carried on the centreline rack of both the A-4 and the TA-4. See also, Air Refuelling Store.
Buffett	The shaking/shuddering motion of an aircraft as it approaches its inability to fly.
CAA	Chief Aircraft Artificer. The most senior technical person on a squadron.
CAG	Carrier Air Group.
CAP	Combat Air Patrol. A flight orbiting a designated point to provide air defence.
CARQUAL	First sorties to the deck to qualify new pilots for carrier operations.
CBGLO	Carrier Borne Ground Liaison Officer, or 'Ceeballs'. The Army provided a Liaison Section – consisting of one artillery major, one sergeant and one private – assigned to the CAG.
CDRE	Commodore
C Mech	Chief Mechanician
Charlie time	When the carrier was ready to conduct aircraft recovery operations and the waiting aircraft commenced flying a circuit ahead of the ship, prior to individual landings.
Chief	Chief Petty Officer
CMDR	Commander
CMDR(A)	Commander (Air). Commonly referred to as 'Wings', head of the Air Department.
CO	Commanding Officer. On an NAS invariably referred to (very respectfully) as 'the Boss'.
Cold Shot	When the catapult does not function with enough power to 'throw' the aircraft off the ship to enable it to fly.
CPO	Chief Petty Officer. In the hierarchy of petty officer, leading seaman and seaman. One rank lower than a warrant officer.
Crabs	Derogatory name for people employed by the RAAF. See also RAAFies. The term was derived from the material selected for the original RAF uniform in 1918.
CSD	Constant Speed Drive. Installed on the front of the engine to supply constant electrical power no matter what speed the engine is doing.
CVS	USN designation for a conventionally powered fixed-wing carrier performing the anti-submarine role.
DDG	A guided-missile destroyer.
DDL	Dummy Deck Landing. An area marked on the runway at Albatross equivalent to the ships flight deck area.
Delmar	The Delmar Target was an aerial gunnery target system which provided a radar and visual indication of its position so a ship could shoot at it. Originally flown on the Sea Venom, it was transferred to the Skyhawk.
DLP	Deck Landing Practice. Landing practice aboard the carrier for qualified pilots.
EO	Engineering Officer. See also MEO and FDEO.
FAK	Fly Away Kit. A collection of spare parts and servicing equipment thought to be needed when a squadron goes on detachment away from its home base.
FCLP	Field Carrier Landing Practice. A term adopted by the RAN after the introduction of American aircraft. Used to train pilots for carrier landings. See also MADDL.
FCU	Fuel Control Unit. The device that controls/meters fuel to a jet engine.
Fitting Out, Wharf	One of the wharves at Garden Island Naval Base in Sydney.
Flash Message	An extremely high priority message that requires instant compliance.
FMP	Fleet Maintenance Party. A shore organisation that assists the crew with maintenance beyond the ship's own capability.
FMLP	Field Mirror Landing Practice. See also FCLP.
FOX 1	Brevity code used by a pilot to indicate a shot taken with guns.
FOX 2	Brevity code used by a pilot to indicate the launch of an AIM-9 Sidewinder missile.
FOX 3	Brevity code used by a pilot to indicate the launch of a radar-guided missile. Not used by RAN Skyhawks.
FRU	Fleet Requirement Unit, a squadron which provides aircraft to support the fleet in exercises, equipment calibration, gunnery shoots, etc.

G	Gravity, the force acting on a body with 1g being the normal force. The Skyhawk could 'pull' 8G.
Galley	Naval term for a kitchen.
GCA	Ground Controlled Approach. A high-definition radar operated by a specially trained ATCO to 'talk down' a military aircraft in bad weather.
Goofers	A spot where people could watch the antics of pilots trying to land on the carrier. The favoured spot was on top of the island as the catwalks around the flight deck were out of bounds during flight operations.
GTC-85	The ground start cart. See also huffer. A small jet engine that produced a lot of air to start the A-4.
Gyro	Gyroscopic device used to provide heading information to the flight instruments.
HC723	The utility helicopter squadron which flew Wessex, Hueys, and Kiowas.
Heads	Naval term for the toilets.
Hi-Lo-Hi	Flying profile where the transit is flown at a high altitude, the attack is performed at a low altitude and the return to base is at a high altitude.
HMS	Her/His Majesty's Ship. Given to all Royal Navy ships or establishments that are commissioned, i.e., formally authorised to be activated.
HMAS	Her/His Majesty's Australian Ship. Given to all Royal Australian Navy ships or establishments that are commissioned, i.e., formally authorised to be activated.
HMAS *Albatross*	Fleet Air Arm base at Nowra in New South Wales commonly referred to as *Albatross* or just *'tross*.
HMAS *Melbourne*	A modified Majestic-class aircraft carrier with an angled flightdeck, steam catapult, mirror sight and other modifications to bring it up to operating second-generation carrier-borne aircraft. Originally not fitted with any AVGAS stowage.
HMAS *Nirimba*	The RAN's premier technical training base from 1953 for all aircraft technical training. In 1956, *Nirimba* became the RAN Apprentice Training Establishment (RANATE) for the training of all Navy apprentices. The training course was initially four years full-time then reduced to three and-a-half years full time with graduates (MOBIs) becoming Artificer 3rd Class or leading seaman equivalents. From 1972, all those who commenced Navy apprentice training time had their training shortened to two years through the removal of 'the unnecessary width and depth' of training that had previously been taught. Graduates of the shortened training (Muppets) graduated as able seamen. *Nirimba* was decommissioned in February 1994, having trained some 13,000 men and women from the RAN and other nations.
HMAS *Penguin*	RAN base on Middle Head in Sydney. Originally the site of the Navy hospital but is now a training base.
HMAS *Sydney*	A Majestic-class straight-deck aircraft carrier but was not modified like HMAS *Melbourne* was.
Hold Back Unit	The device (like a dumbbell with a tapered section) that is fitted between the aircraft and a restraining cable that will break at a certain pressure enabling the catapult to develop full power during the launch.
Hot End Inspection	The 'hot end' of a jet engine is where the fuel is burnt, and which requires an internal inspection for deterioration after a specific engine operating hour.
Howdah	The hydraulically raised control box adjacent to the catapult track. Controlled the catapult launch process.
Hueys	UH-1 Iroquois helicopters - Vietnam vintage.
Huffer	The GTC-85 ground starting unit. Basically a little jet engine that produced a lot of hot air to start the A-4s.
IFP	Instrument Flying Practice. Usually under the 'bag' in a trainer to practice an essential flying skill.
IRT	Instrument Rating Test. An annual ride for all pilots where they were subjected to various manoeuvres to demonstrate their skill and proficiency at flying solely by reference to the flight instruments.
J52	The model name of the Pratt & Whitney jet engine that powers the A-4/TA-4 Skyhawk.
J Hangar	The hangar where both jet squadrons stored and maintained their aircraft.
JBMR	Jervis Bay Missile Range. This facility utilised the Jervis Bay airfield and radar facilities nearby on the coastal ridge to operate pilotless aircraft, notably the Jindivik target drone.
LCDR	Lieutenant Commander
Leading Seaman	A naval rank that approximates to a corporal in the Army and the RAAF. The rank badge is a fouled anchor on the sleeve of the uniform. Can also be called a leading hand/killick and is abbreviated as 'LS'.
LEUT	Lieutenant. Pronounced 'L'tenant', never 'lootenant' (US military), 'leftenant' (Army) or 'LT' (Hollywood).
LOX	Liquid Oxygen. J Hangar had a large tank to store liquid oxygen, replenished at intervals by a LOX tanker. HMAS *Melbourne* had an onboard LOX generating plant run by specially qualified stokers, supervised by an aircraft maintainer.

LP2	The life preserver worn by A-4 pilots, later superseded by the Hi-speed Mae West, with a metal breast plate and attached to the torso harness.
LSO	Landing Safety Officer. A pilot specially trained to observe and grade a carrier, or FCLP, approach and landing. There is always an LSO present on the LSO platform for every approach to the ship.
MAY DAY	A radio call by a pilot for immediate attention in a situation that threatens life.
Mechanician	A technical sailor whose previous technical competence followed by shortened trade training is awarded a trade certificate and so became the equivalent of an Artificer. Not all technical sailors had the same higher level of training as an Artificer or a Mechanician. A superseded rank.
Mess	The living accommodation on a ship and ashore. Messing, the act of eating, is performed in a cafeteria.
Military Power	The maximum power developed by a military jet engine.
Mils	A very accurate measurement of angle that was set on the gunsight of the A-4.
NAS	Naval Air Squadron, i.e., 724 NAS.
NAS Nowra	Naval Air Station Nowra. Strictly speaking, not HMAS *Albatross*, but the user unit of. This is because large shore establishments are commissioned ships. See also RANAS.
NATOPS	Naval Air Training and Operations Procedure Standardisation - the flying operations 'bible' for the A-4/TA-4 aircraft.
NAVEX	Navigational Exercise. Normally capitalised in the FLYPRO, a jolly enjoyed by experienced pilots but feared by students.
Nowra	The town, on the Shoalhaven River, closest to HMAS *Albatross*.
OFS	Operational Flying School. Where budding fighter pilots learnt their deadly trade.
Onboard	The term used when naval personnel have crossed the brow of a ship or through the gate of a shore establishment.
OOW	The Officer of the Watch who is in charge of the ship when afloat or on a major vessel, alongside.
OpOrder	Operational Order. The plan of events generally for an operation/exercise. Most often a thick document which must be held by all units participating. Often amended by signal.
PAN	Possible Assistance Needed. A radio call by a pilot indicating a problem that is not immediately life threatening.
PAR	Progressive Aircraft Rework. The aircraft is subjected to deep maintenance at a level beyond that performed on the squadron. For the Skyhawks, the organisation doing such work was Qantas, supervised by SAMR.
Pedro	The Naval term used for the rescue helicopter that sits off the carrier when flying during daylight hours.
PO	Petty Officer.
POMTP	Petty Officer Marine Technical Propulsion. A ship's engineering sailor responsible for the ship's engines and auxiliary services, e.g., the LOX bay.
Port Side	The left-hand side of a ship or aircraft when viewed from behind.
PP	Preservation Phase is the storage level of preservation required when an aircraft is not flown regularly and is in storage. There were three PP phases – 1, 2 and 3 – with the amount of preservation taking place according to the time in storage.
Puckapunyal	An Army base in Victoria.
Pussers	The term for the Navy derived from a ship's Purser.
Pylons	Faired protrusions under the wing which are used to carry drop tanks or weapons. They need plumbing for fuel and bleed air, and wiring for electrical control of weapons release and jettison mechanisms. On the ground they have a red-flagged safety pin inserted to make the pyrotechnic charges safe.
QFI	Qualified Flying Instructor
RAAF Butterworth	An RAAF Base near Penang in Malaysia until 1988 when it became Royal Malaysian Air Force Base Butterworth.
Rabbits	The term where sailors collect items, not necessarily legally.
Rate of Roll	Rotation around the longitudinal axis. In an aircraft, it is expressed in degrees per second.
Refit	A term used when a ship goes into a long period of maintenance in a dockyard.
RN	Royal Navy
RNAS	Royal Naval Air Station
RANAS	Royal Australian Naval Air Station. See also NAS.
Rimpac	Rim of the Pacific Naval exercise held between multiple navies to test and train interoperability. Designated by two digits to indicate the year in which it was held.
Runway	Albatross had two runways which were numbered in the direction of take-off/landing: 08/26 was the East/West runway and 03/21 was the North/South runway.

S-2 Tracker	The fixed-wing anti-submarine aircraft operated off the carrier.
SAG	Surface Action Group. Ships designated to interdict with opposing warships.
SAMR	Superintendent of Aircraft Maintenance and Repair. The technical/airworthiness authority for the Skyhawk and other naval aircraft. Now renamed NASPO and relocated to RANAS Nowra.
SBLT	Sub-Lieutenant
Sea King	A large twin-engine naval anti-submarine/utility helicopter.
Sea Venom	A post Second World War second-generation jet aircraft superseded by the A-4.
Self Maintenance Period	Where the carrier docks for maintenance using only the crew's resources.
SFA	Short Field Arrest. A landing into the approach-end wire on a runway with the hook extended.
Sick Bay	A ship's medical centre.
Side Number	A three-digit number, e.g., 886, permanently painted on the side of the aircraft, on the nose section, to easily identify a particular aircraft as opposed to its longer bureau number. Carried on from the Royal Navy Fleet Air Arm and similarly used in the USN.
Silver Jubilee	The Queen's 25th anniversary of her ascension to the throne.
Six	The position directly behind an aircraft, the six o'clock position.
Skill Grades	A technical sailor's skill level. Either Skill Grade 3 or Skill Grade 4 depending on training and courses attended.
SMP	Self Maintenance Period
SP	Senior Pilot. Deputy to the CO, and they worked very hard also.
Sponson	A platform on the side of a naval ship mainly built to hold a defensive gun, but often repurposed, e.g. the aircraft maintenance documentation sponson on the *Melbourne*.
Stand down	This can mean a temporary cessation of work as well as the end of the working day. Only grocers and shop keepers, etc., have 'Completion of Business'.
Starboard	The right-hand side of a ship/aircraft when viewed from behind.
Strike Progression	The term used on the flight schedule for a section or division of aircraft to make an opposed flight to a target.
Suspended Servicing	When the normal servicing regime is stopped, and a modified servicing regime is implemented e.g. Preservation Phased (PP) servicing.
TACAN	A military Tactical Air Navigation aid that transmitted bearing and range information decoded in a simple receiver and displayed to a crew. It was carried in a black weatherproof dome on the upper masthead of HMAS *Melbourne* and the Adams-class DDGs. Owing to EMCON policy, it was rarely turned on. Ashore, TACAN beacons were on every military airfield and there were air portable mobile TACANs as well.
T-Bird	Colloquial name for the two-seat TA-4G.
Tiffy	A sailor trained at HMAS *Nirimba*, the Apprentice Training Establishment. Known as an Artificer and can be of various ranks, i.e., Tiffy 3, 2, 1 and Chief Tiff/Tiffy.
Trap	Common reference to an arrested landing, afloat, or, less often, ashore.
Trim	A check and adjustment to ensure an engine reaches its rated performance after maintenance. A noisy and lengthy process performed adjacent to J Hangar or tied down on the catapult aboard ship. Also, the action by a pilot to reach stabilised and balanced flight.
UA	Unusual Attitude. Where the aircraft unintentionally departs from straight and level/planned flight to an attitude that is not normal, e.g. an uncommanded spinning.
USN	United States Navy
Watchkeeping	The system of hourly based shifts or 'watches' of four hours duration used on naval ships.
WEEO	Weapons Electrical Electronics Officer. The officer responsible for all operations and operational electrical and electronic maintenance and weapons electrical personnel. ALOs were redesignated WEEOs in the 1980s.
Wessex	The naval anti-submarine and utility helicopter constructed by Westland.
Williamtown	The RAAF base north of Newcastle. The main base for the Mirage, then F/A-18C/D Hornets and now the F-35. Almost universally known as 'Willytown'.
WOATA-4	Warrant Officer Air Technical Aircraft Skill Grade 4
Workup	A period where ships, after a maintenance period, strive to become fully operational and work the crew into a cohesive group.
XO	Executive Officer. Second in command of a unit or ship. Deals with more of the day-to-day aspects of running the unit in order to free up the CO.
Zuni Rocket	A 5-inch diameter, unguided, folding fin, rocket used in air-to-ground operations with a maximum speed of 2,599 km/hr.

Chapter 1

1945–67: ROLE, TESTING AND PURCHASES

Naval aviation after the Second World War was one of the most rapid evolving areas of the military. The evolution from piston-engine aircraft to early jets, and then the subsequent leaps and bounds in jet technology, meant the ships from which they flew also had to evolve. Higher landing speeds, heavier aircraft and an increasing range of capabilities led to innovations like mirror-landing aids and angled flight decks. The aircraft carrier was the new capital ship, replacing the battleship, and the greatest means of force projection from the sea. With *Sydney* and *Melbourne* (and *Vengeance*), Australia had a front-row seat and was well placed to benefit from all that carrier aviation had to offer. Competing interests and budget realities were always at play, however, but, as usual, the Navy made it work.

The stated roles for the A-4G Skyhawk for the Royal Australian Navy (RAN) were:

(a) Fleet Air Defence

(b) Maritime Strike

(c) Close Air Support of troops

To achieve this, the first eight A-4Gs were ordered with all four wing stations wired to support AIM-9 Sidewinder air-to-air missiles. The subsequent purchase of eight second-hand and refurbished A-4Fs were upgraded to the same standard as the earlier new aircraft, and were also known as A-4Gs.

The A-4Gs replaced the de Havilland Sea Venoms which were two-seat all-weather fighters with an air-to-air radar operated by an observer. Their role was certainly fleet air defence, so it was logical to pass this on to the replacement aircraft.

The question is: from where did these roles originate? The best resource appears to be a book derived from a PhD thesis by Dr David Shackleton AO (Vice Admiral RAN Rtd), *The Impact of the Charles F Adams Class Guided Missile Destroyers on the RAN*. The book is a learned work, and the depth of research allows for astounding detail. It was published by the RAN's Sea Power Centre.

In the beginning, a Defence Review in 1947 established Australia had a degree of responsibility for the area covered by Australia, New Zealand and Malaya (ANZAM). The official realisation was that this ANZAM area needed to be linked to a joint and coordinated force for Commonwealth defence.

It should also be realised that the RAN, through the efforts of Sir Victor Smith, was developing a plan for a fleet including two aircraft carriers to be operated as an Australian force. That came to fruition, as we know, through the arrival of HMAS *Sydney* with the 20th Carrier Air Group, the operation of HMAS *Vengeance* on loan from the Royal Navy (RN) and, finally, the arrival of HMAS *Melbourne* in 1956 with a modern air group of Gannets and Sea Venoms.

Further to this was the development of the Malayan Emergency in 1948 that resulted in a recognition of the communist threat to the north. The Emergency, although the responsibility of the United Kingdom's armed forces, resulted in considerable effort on the part of Australia and New Zealand to supply forces to assist. The Royal Australian Air Force (RAAF) deployed Lincoln bombers and Dakota transports in 1950 and, in 1955, the 2nd Battalion, Royal Australian Regiment, was deployed. The RAN sent destroyers and the aircraft carriers throughout the period 1955–63, principally by attachment to the Commonwealth Strategic Reserve.

In the midst of this, in 1953 the Defence Review of 1947 was reviewed and reassessed. This became known as the 'long haul', with the threat being assessed as communist aggression to the north. It was considered that, if Malaya should fall, much of Australia would be open to air attack. The Dutch East Indies was in turmoil with the Dutch reducing their armed forces and conceding to Indonesian nationalism. This was to result in the armed forces of the new nation being supplied with Soviet equipment during the decade to follow.

As a result of this assessment, the roles of the Services were redefined. The RAN was to be focussed on anti-submarine warfare, with the Fleet Air Arm (FAA) being reduced to one carrier and five front-line squadrons. The RAAF was assigned its role with a weighting of its defence effort towards air protection at sea within range of land-based aircraft. In hindsight, this was a poor decision with no thought for possible consequences.

In effect, the RAN was hamstrung by a lack of resources with neither UK nor Australian shipyards able to build adequate ships to support a Fleet Air Arm. So too was the RAAF hampered by the loss of the aviation industry built up during the Second World War.

It seemed to the RAN that the only recourse would be a missile-armed ship to provide air defence; this thinking began in 1956. The Australian Naval Board began exploring the possibility of buying a ship armed with surface-to-air guided missiles (SAGM). Somebody recognised that the RAAF, with its then current equipment, was clearly unable to provide air cover over a body of ships to the north of Australia.

The RN had recognised that the clear threat to any formed body of its ships was the Sverdlov-class cruisers fielded by the Soviets. When the Soviet Union offered one to the Indonesians, there was a clear surface threat to add to the air threat.

The RN had decided to issue a specification for a nuclear-capable strike bomber to counter the threat. This became the Blackburn NA.39, later to be called the Buccaneer. It was first taken to sea in 1959 and developed into an S.2 version with upgraded engines. It was very capable, but, unfortunately, too big and too heavy to operate from a Majestic-class aircraft carrier like

Melbourne. In concert with the strike bomber, the Fairey Gannet had been reconstructed as an airborne electronic warning (AEW) aircraft with early experiments at linking data to the fleet's operations rooms. The observers, however, were trained as airborne radar-intercept controllers to assist the Sea Venom and Scimitar fighters of the era.

The doctrine developed was to find and destroy a hostile aircraft despatched to find the fleet before it could broadcast its data. The Gannet AEW would be positioned along the threat axis at a far enough range to not betray the position of the fleet. Fighters would then be vectored to the shadower when it was detected. This was expressed as 'hack the shad', as taught to the Author Peter Greenfield in Junior Officer Operations and Weapons courses in the UK in the early 1970s.

The RN was designing and building a class of ships, the elegant-looking County-class destroyers, to carry an SAGM, the Sea Slug. In a similar timescale, the United States Navy (USN) was developing the Charles F Adams-class of guided-missile destroyers (DDG). Unlike the County-class, the Adams-class was steam powered and fitted with a two-arm Tartar missile launcher. The Australian Naval Board explored the possibility of acquiring either class of ships, and which was preferable.

Clearly, the tactics of the Second World War, where the main body of the fleets was protected by a screen of anti-air gunnery ships, and airborne fighters kept outside the screen to break up raids, had evolved by the late 1950s. The new development was a concept of the main body being protected by a screen of missile-armed anti-air ships with capable search radars, with an outer screen of fighters guided by airborne controllers.

Prime Minister Menzies had, in 1957, expressed a policy designed to align Australia with the USA in actions within South-East Asia. Although the RN was still actively involved in Malaya–Borneo, the British Government was progressively whittling down the existing forces and bent on reducing expenditure. This had resulted in a force reduction in terms of the number of aircraft carriers, very few new destroyers and a reduction in the number of cruisers. On the other hand, the USA was actively building up its forces. These were factors the Australian Naval Board had to consider as it was deciding on the missile-armed ships.

In 1960, the choice was made; the Adams-class was selected and negotiations began to cost and procure two ships. Funds were very tight, hence a decision was reached to shut down the FAA by 1963. The appointment of John Gorton as Minister for Navy in 1958 was probably the most satisfactory event to happen for the RAN. The Australian Naval Board considered the RAN needed submarines, minesweepers, air-defence ships and the money to retain the FAA. Gorton was sympathetic, appeared to understand the deficiencies and needs of the RAN, and determined to do something about it. He asked questions, absorbed the details and fought for a solution.

He was behind the choice of the Charles F Adams-class ships but unable to sway the government in the question of the FAA's future. The real issue was the replacement of HMAS *Melbourne* in order to operate bigger, faster and heavier aircraft at sea. Gorton, himself a fighter pilot during

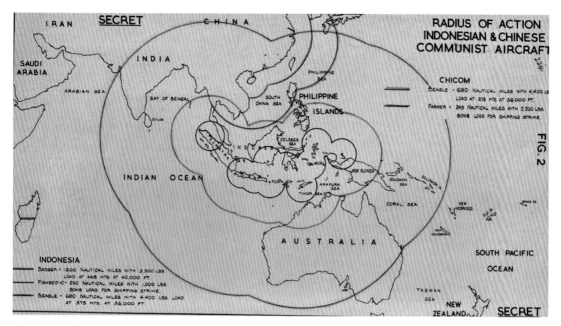

A secret Air Threat Assessment Map, undated but circa 1960s. (FAAAoA)

the Second World War, clearly understood the RAAF was unable to provide any air defence at ranges further than 400 miles from its bases.

By 1962, the Indonesians had received *Badger, Beagle* and *Fishbed* aircraft from the Soviets; their navy was operating five Skory-class destroyers and six Whiskey-class conventional submarines. A Sverdlov cruiser was reportedly on the way, as were 12 Komar-class guided-missile fast gunboats, armed with two *Styx* missiles apiece. The threat to the RAN was huge and it was almost the case that the waters of the Indonesian archipelago were denied.

In view of the considerable submarine threat, HMAS *Melbourne,* and the life of the FAA, was extended with a new buy of Wessex anti-submarine helicopters. A purchase of 14 Grumman S-2E Tracker anti-submarine aircraft was funded to replace the Gannets. In practice, though, an air-defence gap was being imposed on the RAN when it desperately needed a solution to a very real problem. A trial was arranged, during an exercise with the USN in the South China Sea in 1965, in which a Douglas A-4B Skyhawk was flown to *Melbourne* by Lieutenant Commander 'Chas' Ward from USS *Bennington*. The American ship was a small aircraft carrier by American standards, but still bigger than *Melbourne. Bennington* was classified as a CVS, tasked with anti-submarine duties. Its aircraft were carried for the prosecution of an undersea threat. However, it had a detachment of Skyhawks on board for air defence. After some touch and goes, Ward lowered his hook and arrested. The aircraft drew considerable interest from the 'birdies' and no doubt it was manoeuvred around the flight deck and taken up and down on the lifts. It was also 'zapped' with a red kangaroo painted adjacent to its Bureau Number (reportedly, that kangaroo was still there when the aircraft was spotted in the graveyard at Davis-Monthan years later). Ward was then launched to return to *Bennington*.

A USN A-4B from the USS Bennington lands on HMAS Melbourne in May 1965, with a Wessex helicopter in the background. (AWM)

Petty Officer Ronald M Forbes paints a red kangaroo motif onto the fuselage of the visiting USN A-4B. (AWM)

In October 1965, the purchase of eight A-4Es and two TA-4Es was announced. The Chief of the Staff Committee, an RAAF officer at the time, opined that it seemed 'an excessive price to pay to see out the remaining years of HMAS *Melbourne*'s life and to retain naval aviation.' There was a price to pay, however; the necessary refit to modify *Melbourne* to receive the new aircraft did not include updated search-and-direction radars, or improvements to the Air Operations Room. It meant *Melbourne* would always have to be accompanied by one of the new DDGs to provide those services.

The Minister for Navy, Mr Frederick Chaney, noted that the A-4s would be delivered in 1967, and that *Melbourne* would be capable of operating them after refit in 1968. Although it was not a withdrawal from the policy of providing land-based air defence of the fleet, he noted that 'the Skyhawks will provide the carrier with a proven counter against hostile reconnaissance aircraft and a limited strike capability against surface force attack in convoy operations.'

And so it was that the Skyhawks of VF805 were given the role of fleet air defence, maritime strike and, because a Carrier Borne Ground Liaison Officer was always on board, they inherited the role of close air support of troops.

One last little observation: the ten Skyhawks, officially A-4Gs, cost the RAN A$18,400,000 or A$1,840,000 each. The second buy was probably a little cheaper because they were second-hand and ex-Vietnam airframes. By comparison, the RAAF was authorised to order 24 F-111Cs at a cost of A$112,000,000 or A$4,600,000 each. They were delivered ten years late and at ten times the price. They were undoubtedly, however, a superb weapons system.

In terms of cost-benefit, the reader can draw their own conclusions.

One further anecdote from Dr Shackleton. The first DDG to have the Naval Tactical Data System (NTDS) fitted and worked up was HMAS *Perth*. During an air-defence exercise with the RAAF after the ship's return from the USA, the attackers mounted a force of 12 F-111s. These aircraft delivered a coordinated attack, each at the same time and from different directions. The NTDS failed at the crucial moment and the RAAF gloated over its success. The ship's Weapons Electrical Engineering Officer, who thoroughly understood the design and function of the NTDS, merely pointed out the system was saturated in the attack. He alluded to the manual input of data and said the system would have functioned better if allowed to work in full automatic.

Commodore John Da Costa found the following letter in his files and the authors are grateful for his contribution. It is noted it was written to the editor of *Skyhawk News* in 2006 and subsequently printed in that periodical. John was a member of that organisation at the time.

Dear Editor,

While browsing through some old photo slides a few days ago, I came upon the enclosed shots of a USN A-4 which may be of interest.

They were taken by me on the flight deck of HMAS *Melbourne* in May 1965 somewhere in South-East Asian waters. The occasion was the first, ever, A-4 deck-landing and cat shot from *Melbourne* and was a very significant event for the RAN as it was the final word to the doubters in the Australian defence arena (light blue uniforms) that the Skyhawk could operate from our carrier. The Navy had researched the options then available for a light-attack/fighter-type aircraft, compatible with *Melbourne*, to replace the ageing de Havilland Sea Venom two-crew night-fighter and the Skyhawk was the clear winner. There were those in Defence, however, who (for various reasons, but believed by me to be a matter of policy) were making life difficult and so a demonstration of fact was arranged with the USN.

Melbourne was exercising with USS *Bennington* at the time and a cross-deck operation was arranged. The aircrew, engineers and catapult teams of both ships got their heads together and many computations of gross weight and steam pressure, to ensure adequate end-speed off the cat, were made, checked and re-checked. Any suggestion of it having been a marginal operation would have been a major set-back to the re-equipment programme so you will appreciate that everybody involved added a few extra knots of catapult end-speed, just to be sure. The A-4 driver's name was LCDR Charles Ward USN and, although I do not know just what end-speed was achieved, his short statement, broadcast after he had recovered from the cat shot acceleration ('Holy S—!'), says it all.

I regret that I do not have a shot of the aircraft at the end of the cat stroke in my photographs ... perhaps I was too overwhelmed to remember to press the shutter release! Little did I know at the time that I would subsequently land the first RAN Skyhawk (A-4G model) on *Melbourne*.

Regards,

John Da Costa

A montage of photo slides taken by John Da Costa of LCDR Ward's visit to HMAS Melbourne. (John Da Costa)

The first aircraft was handed over on 26 July 1967 at the Douglas factory. Vice Admiral Allen Shinn USN, in the presence of Mr Donald Douglas, ceremonially handed over the aircraft logbooks to Rear Admiral GJ Crabb RAN. In the meantime, our two first Skyhawk pilots, Lieutenant Commander John Da Costa and Lieutenant Grahame King were in training with VA125 at Naval Air Station Lemoore in California.

The aircraft were brought home in November 1967. The ship carried 14 S-2E Trackers, ten Skyhawks, their associated spares, and the two trailers of the Weapons System Trainer. HMAS *Melbourne* offloaded the Skyhawks and spares by barge and lighter in Jervis Bay. Alongside the SAR Wharf at HMAS *Creswell*, the aircraft were craned ashore for loading onto semi-trailers for the road journey to HMAS *Albatross*. The Trackers were offloaded later in Sydney, trucked to de Havilland Australia at Bankstown and then flown to Nowra.

The handover ceremony at the Douglas factory on 26 July 1967. (FAAAoA)

The whole process was repeated in July 1971 with the second Skyhawk buy of eight pre-loved A-4Es and two TA-4Es, renovated to the modification state of the A-4F (the USN typed the aircraft as A-4Gs), for a very good price. The E-model carried additional electronics in a camel hump behind the cockpit. The equipment and the hump were not required so were never fitted. This buy gave a total fleet of 20 aircraft, sufficient to provide for two squadrons: VF805 as the front-line squadron and VC724 as the second-line squadron.

A Skyhawk is craned onto the wharf at HMAS Creswell from a navy barge, with HMAS Melbourne visible in the background. (Seapower Centre)

Chapter 2

1967–68: INITIAL INSTRUCTOR TRAINING

The de Havilland Sea Venoms were old, dating back to their acquisition in 1956, and showing their age. A new aircraft required new skills, so the Navy sent John Da Costa and Grahame King to California for the necessary training. Lieutenant Commander Da Costa was an Air Warfare Instructor and Lieutenant King a Qualified Flying Instructor.

An Australian view of USN Skyhawk training at NAS Lemoore, circa 1967

I would like to take you back to January 1967 at Naval Air Station (NAS) Lemoore, California. The Vietnam War was placing great demands on United States Navy (USN) carrier air groups and, to keep up with the demand for A-4 Skyhawk pilots, the very large VA125 was running a continuous RAG (Replacement Air Group) training schedule. Other squadrons at Lemoore were running similar high-intensity programmes for the other USN attack aircraft types.

Enter, stage left, two Royal Australian Navy (RAN) pilots (Lieutenant Commander John Da Costa and Lieutenant Grahame 'Dusty' King). We were in the United States for five months for A-4 RAG training plus additional special flying and other training in preparation for our return to Australia, as Commanding Officer (CO) and Senior Pilot respectively, to (re)commission 805 Squadron with A-4G/TA-4G Skyhawks, and to conduct the first RAN Skyhawk Operational Flying School course. The G-model was unique to the RAN; except for electronic warfare gear, it had the latest A-4F avionics, radar and weapons-delivery systems, and the J52P8A engine, but was wired for four AIM-9B Sidewinder air-to-air missiles on wing stations, interchangeable with the normal attack weapons fit. The RAN had selected the Skyhawk as its replacement 'fighter' as, out of all naval aircraft then available and capable of operating from a light fleet carrier (20,000 tons/24 knots on a good day), it undoubtedly had the best all-round capability in both the attack and (with extra Sidewinders) fighter roles.

To put the Lemoore scene into the perspective of we RAN pilots, I should remind you where we were coming from. Dusty and I had similar flying backgrounds – in my case, almost 2,000 flight hours (1,100 jet) and 460 deck-landings. Our carrier experience was in 1950s-era de Havilland Sea Venom subsonic all-weather fighters, having the dual role of air defence (4 × 20-mm cannon) and attack (cannon and unguided 3-inch air-to-ground rockets). Dusty was a Qualified Flying Instructor and Instrument Rating Examiner, and I was a graduate of the Royal Navy's Air Warfare Instructor Course. Neither of us had much experience in the attack role. We had been raised with more of a 'fighter' philosophy; we had a lot to learn!

But perhaps the greatest difference was that we were coming from such a relatively small naval aviation community, quite at home with our one carrier and naval air station with our squadrons of 6–10 aircraft and commanding officers of lieutenant commander rank. The culture shock hit us between the eyes on day one!

Here we were at NAS Lemoore, having to travel about ten miles to get from admin/accommodation to the squadrons/ops area. The flight line of VA125 alone had a line-up of 100 Skyhawks each morning, ranging from the 'ancient' A-4B (by then relegated to the tanker role only) right through to the latest version (TA-4F); one needed a map to find the allocated aircraft! The field had parallel 14,500-foot concrete runways. The CO of VA125 was a four-ring captain and both the Executive Officer and Operations Officer were commanders. There was an enormous A-4 RAG student population ranging from ensigns straight out of flight school to ex-anti-submarine warfare (ASW), and other, pilots of commander rank just busting to get a piece of the action in Vietnam. Add to that group two 'Aussies' with strange accents (described by some as 'Limey' which, we made sure they became aware, was about as insulting as they could get to an Australian) and some colloquial language differences which, at first, led to some hilarious social misunderstandings in mixed company (e.g., using the Aussie slang word 'screw', as in 'having a screw (look) over the balcony'!). We were looking down the barrel of a potential disaster, both personally and for the RAN, if we couldn't handle the situation.

Well, as you well know, Fleet Air Arm personnel are usually unfazed by unusual situations and, of course, such was the case with us. In fact, the 'culture shock' was reduced to negligible proportions by the outstanding hospitality, courtesy and downright friendliness extended to us (and also to the non-aviator RAN personnel at Lemoore – Air Engineering Officer Lieutenant Jim Lamb and his team of maintainers were attached to VA125 for technical training/experience on Skyhawks and equipment). I fondly recall Commander Bob Reynolds, the Operations Officer, and his wife, who took us into their home as though we had been life-long friends. Other officers and their families also entertained us at home and, of course, in the 'O' Club bar or restaurant, we were never without friendly company. One officer (casually met in the 'O' Club bar), who was deploying to Vietnam, handed us his car keys with only the simple proviso that we leave them with the club manager before we returned to Australia! Much of this was said to have been done in repayment for hospitality received during visits to Australia. The maintenance 'troops', we were told, were treated just as magnificently by their opposite numbers.

My observations are: firstly, I was proud that Australian hospitality had left such a good impression; secondly, it is beyond doubt that any such hospitality was more than amply repaid, often to the detriment of our health (sore heads); and thirdly, I am sure the friendliness and hospitality would have occurred anyway and was not necessarily related to any perceived 'repayment obligation'. Apart from the innate hospitality of individual Americans, I believe our reception had quite a lot to do with the fact we were paying our way and were not just yet another group of US 'aid recipients' draining the US taxpayers' purse. Australia was doing its bit in Vietnam and was paying cash for its A-4s to be built, and for all training carried out in the USA, and this seemed to be well known to all VA125 personnel. Those facts alone seemed to have generated an enormous degree of goodwill towards us and there seemed to be a consequent determination to not only make sure we felt welcome but that we were not 'short-changed' in any way. There is no question both objectives were achieved; in my view, we certainly got more (in training value) than was paid for by the Australian Government, not to mention the training 'rabbits' that found their way into Jim Lamb's boys' unaccompanied baggage!

The A-4 RAG syllabus of training was entirely attack orientated and fully met that aspect of our needs. Highlights for me were the 'Sandblower' low-level navigation and attack exercises over much of Nevada and Arizona and the weapons-training deployment to Fallon, Nevada (where I was snowed upon for the first time in my life, even though it was in a desert!).

There was, of course, no 'fighter' phase of the USN A-4 RAG, so special arrangements were made for a one-week A-4E/TA-4F deployment to Yuma, Arizona, for air-to-air gun attacks on towed banner targets, ground-controlled interception training, and Sidewinder firings against parachute flare targets. Our USN instructors were two pilots who had had experience in the A-4 fighter role when deployed in USN ASW carriers. We were also accompanied by a team of RAN ordnance technical sailors for hands-on experience loading and arming A-4 air-to-air weaponry.

Having had considerable air-to-air experience in the RAN using gyro gunsights (and thinking we were pretty good at this fighter stuff), Dusty and I were somewhat deflated to find we were now similarly placed to First World War fighter pilots as we tried to get shells to hit the banner using the Skyhawk's 'fixed' gunsight! We also had a problem getting adequate ranging information when firing Sidewinders against a stationary flare target. The gunsight problem was never fully resolved in the RAN as the low priority (!) project to retrofit a modern gyro gunsight had not reached fruition before the aircraft was retired from RAN service. Sidewinder ranging proved less of a problem. After training using 'captive' missiles and APG-53A radar/Mk.I eyeball for air-to-air ranging, pilots became reasonably proficient at getting themselves into the Sidewinder firing bracket. 'Live firings' were conducted against a TONIC heat-source target towed by a Jindivik drone at the Jervis Bay Missile Range.

Additional extracurricular training was arranged in the use of the CP-741 bombing computer (which at the time was fitted in some TA-4F aircraft in VA125) and in maintenance test-flying procedures in preparation for the flight testing of our A-4Gs after delivery to Australia later that same year.

An impressive new (for us) professional concept was heavily dumped in our laps (literally) with our introduction to the 5–6-centimetre-thick A-4 NATOPS Manual. Up to that point we had only known aircraft 'Pilot's Notes' – small notebook-sized publications containing essential aircraft operating details, checklists and emergency procedures – designed to fit into the leg pocket of a flying suit. Much of the technical material conveniently brought together for aviators in the NATOPS Manual had only been obtainable for earlier RAN aircraft by researching the various maintenance manuals for the aircraft type. NATOPS (Naval Air Training and Operating Procedures Standardization) was a great advance, as far as we were concerned, and we were very happy with the concept.

Day and night carrier qualifications were carried out on the 'duty carrier', the modified Essex-class USS *Kearsarge*, off San Diego. Field mirror landing practice (mirror-assisted dummy deck landings) and carrier qualifications (CARQUALS) in the Skyhawk reintroduced us to the Landing Safety Officer (LSO), 'a deck landing aid' which had not been used in the RAN since the introduction of the angled flight deck and mirror. We were convinced by our experience in the USN that the RAN would be well advised to re-introduce the 'batsman' concept for Skyhawk operations from HMAS *Melbourne* because of the enhanced safety factor, particularly at night, when recovering an aircraft which had an approach speed some ten knots faster than the aircraft it was to replace (the RAN S-2E Tracker aircrew training with the Royal Canadian Navy at the time also favoured the re-introduction of an LSO, so it happened, with good results!). I learned two things during CARQUALS: firstly, that the Skyhawk was an excellent deck-landing aircraft despite its narrow undercarriage; and, secondly, through the courtesy of some very understanding USN instructor pilots after we had completed night CARQUALS on a particularly black and rainy night with cloud cover down to circuit height, the other use for safes in USN officers' cabins, i.e., keeping the scotch safe in (officially) 'dry' USN ships!

In summary, the Skyhawk training we received entirely met our needs and it set us up well to plan and conduct RAN Skyhawk courses in Australia. We had only one criticism regarding our training, but I hasten to add the criticism was in respect to the training philosophy of the time and not its quality.

From the earliest days of (pre-simulator) flying training in the RAN (and, of course, the Royal Australian Air Force), the training philosophy was based on briefings, trust and periodic in-flight testing. By that I mean that once a pilot was assessed by his instructor as being safe for solo, thereafter he was briefed for each exercise or mission (or given dual instruction if appropriate) and sent off to carry out the exercise alone. Constant in-flight supervision was not considered necessary, or desirable (except for periodic standardisation checks), and this approach engendered in the student both a sense of confidence and an obligation to carry out each sortie precisely as briefed. Our experience was that the trust implicit in such a philosophy was rarely found to be misplaced. Of course, if that trust was abused, the transgressor was 'jumped upon' very heavily.

On the other hand, the training philosophy in vogue in the Skyhawk RAG in 1967 was entirely the opposite. No scheduled flights were carried out, whether by an ensign straight from flight school or by experienced USN aviator 'students', without there being an instructor pilot in the aircraft or in an accompanying Skyhawk. Of course, this also applied to us. We understood at the time that the rule had been handed down 'from above' because of a number of fatal aircraft accidents during RAG training and was, apparently, an attempt to reduce the risk of recurrences, given the need to minimise the training losses of pilots and aircraft in the light of Vietnam requirements. I have no idea whether or not that philosophy continued after May 1967.

Given our training backgrounds, we were perhaps oversensitive to the direct supervision applied to every sortie. Our concern was not so much that 'Big Brother' was watching our every move in case we might make a mistake, but that there was no implicit trust that we (and other student pilots) would conduct missions safely and as briefed. We felt somewhat demeaned (professionally) by the experience, whatever the reasons behind it. In the event, we were determined not to transport that particular training philosophy back to the RAN. We never had cause to regret that decision – the RAN's flying safety record remained excellent by world navy standards.

And so began a long and successful relationship between the Skyhawk and the RAN, prematurely brought to an end by the 'paying off' of HMAS *Melbourne*. I confess to bias, but I have no doubt that relationship resulted in a period during which the RAN possessed, in the form of embarked Skyhawk aircraft, the most capable and visible regionally based deterrent in South-East Asian waters. I am proud to have been part of that story.

I was fortunate enough to go on from command of the Skyhawk Operational Flying School squadron (805/724) to command VF805, the front-line squadron, became the officer commanding the air group and, later, Commanders (Air) of NAS *Nowra* and HMAS *Melbourne*. I retired from the Navy in 1989 with the rank of Commodore. Dusty King also had command of a Skyhawk squadron and retired from the Navy as a Commander. I have lost contact with him in recent years.

John Da Costa

This book is about the flyers and the fixers. So, as one would expect, when the pilots were sent to the USA to learn about flying the Skyhawk, the maintainers were also sent. After all, it was an American aircraft and the Americans do everything differently. The A-4 was significantly different to the Sea Venom. We are fortunate to have this contribution from one of the original fixers, Jim Lee. Jim had originally joined in 1951 as an 18-year-old naval airman recruit. By November 1964, he was an instructor with the Air Training Department at HMAS *Albatross*, teaching airframes and engines at both the basic and advanced levels.

MAINTAINING THE SKYHAWK

That was a most interesting period and I spent a lot of time reading aircraft manuals and magazines to keep ahead of those senior sailors on my course. One particular article caught my eye in May 1965; it was about a US Navy A-4D Skyhawk from USS *Bennington* demonstrating deck landings, handling procedures and catapult take-offs from *Melbourne*. In further reading of the article, it mentioned the RAN would be getting eight A-4G and two TA-4G Skyhawks.

In February 1966, I was lucky enough, with George Parker, Bob Willis, Barry Heron, Ian Ferguson, John Harris, and 12 others, to be posted with our families for 14 months to HMAS *Waratah* in the US for overseas training. We initially went to Marine Corps Air Station El Toro, and later to Naval Air Station Lemoore, both in California, to undertake Skyhawk training. Bob Willis and I were to be trained up to be A-4 instructors on airframes and engines. The USN assisted us getting accommodation and, as cars were cheap, we all ended up buying one to make travelling around easy. After a relatively short time, the six Chiefs were moved to Hanford in California and the USN Air Maintenance Training Group Base for hands-on training. I applied for and received my US license, which involved driving on the wrong side of the road, which was a real experience. We returned to Australia in March 1967.

On return to HMAS *Albatross* in March, I again joined the Air Training Department, this time for two years to instruct in the airframe and engines of the A-4 Skyhawk.

In January 1971, it was time for me to go to 805 Squadron, as the Chief Mechanician Airframes and Engines Senior Supervisor in charge of aircraft maintenance, for two years. During this posting, HMAS *Melbourne* and 805 Squadron went to Exercise *Rimpac 1971*. During the exercise, aircraft 887 suffered undercarriage problems and performed an emergency landing on its drop tanks after taking a short-field arrest. The aircraft remained at Barbers Point until repaired and serviceable to fly.

A posting to 724 Squadron occurred in January 1973 where I was to be again the CAA/Senior Supervisor in charge of aircraft maintenance for two years. In November 1975, I was promoted to Warrant Officer Air Technical Aircraft (WOATA) and awarded Skill Grade Four.

With the promotion to WOATA came a posting, but this time to the Aircraft Support Unit (ASU), in January 1976, and I became the warrant officer in charge of maintenance, repairs and servicing of aircraft within ASU. My additional duties were responsibility for training, investigation of defects, liaison with civilian contractors, as well as being responsible for the planning of activities within ASU.

Jim Lee

Jim continued in further postings within the Air Branch until he was discharged on 24 August 1982, completing 28 years of honourable service.

Members of the A-4 Skyhawk initial training team at NAS Lemoore, California. Jim Lee is fourth from the right, standing. (Jim Lee)

The maintainers, like all personnel who served with the Fleet Air Arm, were capable and adaptable, and renowned for using their intuition. A little snippet here about something simple, changing a wheel. It is not something as simple as changing the wheel on a car, but not at all dissimilar. Remember though, the aircraft had no parking brake. For John Hetherington, who worked his way up to Chief Petty Officer ATA (Air Technical Aircraft), it was just another day.

Main wheel change

While I was the flight line petty officer, we received a phone call that an A-4 had blown a tyre on landing on a distant runway. I gathered up all the equipment I needed – e.g., main wheel, bottle jack, maintenance tools – and, with some flight line personnel, headed out to change the tyre. On reaching the aircraft, I signalled the pilot to put his hands on his head and for him to apply the main wheel brakes. We then successfully changed the main wheel and the aircraft then went down the runway to the flight line. The American exchange pilot was astonished at what we did, i.e., change the main wheel on the strip as opposed to transport the aircraft off the runway to change the tyre.

John Hetherington

A student's journey to Skyhawks

John Da Costa began the service of the Skyhawks in the RAN almost at the same time as I was taking my first steps towards flying them. My journey began in January 1968, the 24th to be precise; I joined the RAN as a Cadet Midshipman Junior Entry, at the tender age of 16 years and five months.

I grew up in Brisbane, not far from Eagle Farm Airport. In fact, my grandmother's house overlooked the airport from the suburb of Ascot. My uncle Paul had been a Lancaster pilot who did not come home, being shot down just before the end of the Second World War. My grandmother had a sort of a shrine to his memory: a huge portrait photo of him in uniform, a squadron photograph of everybody gathered under the wings and nose of a Lancaster, and his mounted wings and medals.

The thought of flying entranced me but, at the age of eight or nine, I had no idea of how to go about it. I would sit on the roof of our house in Hamilton and watch the Sunderlands landing and taking off on Hamilton Reach. Add more hours watching the F27s and DC-3s and DC-4s flying circuits at Eagle Farm, nearly always with a propeller windmilling.

High school came and everybody had to join the cadets or sing in the choir. For want of inspiration, I joined the Army cadets. The year went fast enough, but all it taught me was that a soldier's life was damned uncomfortable. The Naval Reserve started a sea cadet unit at my school, so I transferred to that. I began to think a seagoing life would be suitable.

The recruiting office was just next door to the YMCA in Edward Street, so I sidled in there (in my school uniform) and was given all the gen about the Royal Australian Naval College at Jervis Bay. Dad and I read it all from cover to cover; Mum read it too, and there was a series of questions put to me. I was earnest about applying, but unsure whether I would be considered suitable or not. The final outcome was that I filled in the paperwork, Dad signed it, and I returned it to the recruiting office. And so, after an interview, a medical and some peculiar psych tests, I joined up.

After about a month at college, learning how to be a schoolboy in naval uniform, I was standing on the upper front verandah of my division holding a broom ready to perform my job as sweeper. It was about 0630, and my first customer was Mr Bellew, an upper classman. As I tapped at his door, I saw movement on the horizon, and then there appeared two navy-grey jets with twin booms. They came down off the ridge towards Seamans' Beach and then flattened out across the water, going very fast to my eyes.

Mr Bellew told me to speak or close my mouth, so I stammered out, 'Whose jets are those?' To which he replied, "Why the Navy's, from *Albatross*." I had discovered the Navy had aeroplanes, and they were jets.

In time, I saw the odd Dakota flying around, and strings of Hueys flying around at low level, and maybe once a Gannet.

Towards the end of term, probably mid-April, a second-year cadet started canvassing us first years about doing a gliding course over the first term leave break. I put my name down and found out it would be the second week of leave and run by the RAN Gliding Association.

I was not popular when I got home and announced I was going back in a week to do a gliding course. In fact, Mum was quite angry, but I can only understand this from the distance of many years. The course was held at Jervis Bay Airfield and, after an early breakfast, the group of us would be picked up in a Pusser's Kombi and taken up there with our packed lunches.

Time dragged in the early years at college, but somehow there was always something to do. Sometimes one had an hour to oneself and it was easy to sneak down to the beach. One day, sitting quietly on the beach, I looked up and was instantly galvanised. Way up, and only faintly audible, there were two Skyhawks twisting and turning. Now, of course, I know they were indulging in the 'Sport of Kings', air combat manoeuvres, or simply hassling, but, to me as a young cadet, it was somehow magical.

Another day, the class was gathered around the Hiroshima Lantern, while the science master demonstrated a Geiger counter. This was reportedly close to ground zero, and certainly the counter was busily clicking, but over the noise came a faint screech and, looking up at Green Patch at the end of Captain's Beach, I saw a grey Skyhawk low down over the trees and heading for the water. Transfixed, I watched it level out, and then turn right slightly to disappear around Point Perpendicular a minute or two later.

On yet another day, we were in the science classroom with big windows looking out to the bay and Point Perpendicular. As I looked out the window, a pair of Skyhawks turned hard left over the bay and swept towards the Beecroft Range. Just as suddenly, the lead aircraft broke right and up, followed by the second one 10 seconds later. I gave my attention back to the science master droning on when movement caught my eye. I glanced to the right and watched a Skyhawk plummet towards the range until a plume of smoke lanced out.

For the rest of the class, I and a few others furtively watched the Skyhawks firing rockets and dropping their practice bombs. It was fascinating, the ease with which these aircraft fired their rockets and dropped their bombs, while we cadet schoolboys listened to the science master delivering his lesson. He was, of course, totally unaware of the activities on the other side of the bay.

Peter Greenfield

Lieutenant Commander John Da Costa commissioned VF805 on 10 January 1968. Lieutenant Grahame King was the Senior Pilot, no doubt ably assisted by Lieutenant Jim Firth who was the Squadron Staff Officer, responsible for administration to Da Costa. The Aircraft Engineering Officer was Lieutenant Jim Lamb and the Aircraft Electrical Officer (ALO) was Sub-Lieutenant Reg Elphick. Lieutenant Mike Gump USN was the first exchange officer and was part of the training team for VF805 (the pilots who made up No 1 Operational Flying School can be found in the 'class photographs' in Chapter 20).

The aircraft distracting the students during their science class were in fact part of the first Operational Flying School, No 1 OFS. The pilots were learning their new trade as single-seat, fast-jet pilots. The roles the new aircraft had to perform meant a great deal of training had to be completed to perform them well.

In the meantime, HMAS *Melbourne* had entered an extended refit to allow for the operation of the new air group aircraft. The ship had been designed for the North Atlantic and sub-Arctic climates, so air conditioning of crew spaces and the Aircraft Direction Room were priority items. The refrigeration plant was expanded to provide more cold storage for food. The AVGAS tanks (for the Trackers) had never been fitted because the original air group was all gas-turbine powered. So, the dockyard had to fabricate, fit and test new AVGAS tanks, pumps and piping. The design rules for this were very stringent due to the Royal Navy's experience during the Second World War.

Chapter 3

1968–69: THE SKYHAWK GOES TO SEA

The whole point of acquiring Skyhawks, Trackers and Wessex helicopters, and refitting *Melbourne*, was to field a modern, more capable air group and deploy it to sea for extended periods. The years of training, overseas and in Australia, in the air and on the ground, for aircrew and maintainers alike, led to the first Skyhawk launch from, and embarkation on, HMAS *Melbourne*. Lieutenant Commander John Da Costa had an interesting ride on that first cat shot from the newly refurbished carrier in February 1969. It had taken a lot to get him there and it would take even more work to keep the Skyhawks at sea.

THE FIRST LAUNCH

HMAS *Melbourne* underwent a major refit required to operate the recently acquired A-4G Skyhawk and S-2 Tracker aircraft. This included an upgrade of the steam catapult [this required scavenging equipment from both HMCS *Bonaventure*, the Canadians' retired aircraft carrier, and USS *Coral Sea*].

To 'prove' the upgrade could cope with the A-4, VC724 (I was the Commanding Officer) was tasked to briefly embark an A-4 for catapult trials.

On 12 February 1969, I embarked with A-4G Skyhawk N13-154908 (side number 887) for discussions with the engineers and aviation staff and remained on board overnight.

On the 13th, I was launched. No doubt everybody involved had fingers crossed (except me, I was too busy). The cat shot felt severe, perhaps for two reasons: this was my first since launching from the longer-stroke cat on HMS *Hermes* when the Royal Navy kindly made the deck available for Skyhawk training during the carrier's visit to Australia the previous November; and/or, *Melbourne*'s steam plumbers had added some extra psi to make sure there was no chance of a 'soft shot'!

Anyway, the first thing I knew was that the APG-53A radar display had partly come out of the console, limiting the amount of right stick that was available, but allowing a climb straight ahead. I found I was unable to push the unit back into the console, so had to leave it resting on my right thigh, accepting that movement of the control column to the right was not possible and that an ejection was out of the question.

Having sorted out the immediate problem, I declared a PAN (I think, although perhaps it was a more urgent MAYDAY, too long ago to recall) and elected to divert to the Naval Air Station, necessarily using only left aileron for lateral control.

For my 'above average piloting skill and ability demonstrated in an extremely hazardous situation', I received a green endorsement (in those words) in my logbook, signed by the then Commander (Air).

The subsequent 'fix' is well described elsewhere [it was basically to provide large lugs around the radar case to prevent it moving aft under 'G' loading from the cat].

Food for thought: this was the first (and for the time being, the only) A-4 cat shot from *Melbourne*. If I had not been able to keep control of the aircraft after being launched, and neither I nor the aircraft had been recovered, can you imagine the furore in the naval technical and aviation worlds about the cause? Was it pilot error or the newly refurbished catapult, and what would have been the ramifications for our Skyhawk operations going forward?

John Da Costa

This was a year of change. Da Costa relinquished command of VF805 to Lieutenant Commander Bill Callan on 2 December 1968 and, on the same day, became Commanding Officer (CO) of VC724. His new role was to set up and run No 2 Operational Flying School (OFS) aided by Lieutenant Commander Grahame King as Senior Pilot.

On 20 January 1969, Lieutenant Commander Fred Lane became CO of VF805, relieving Bill Callan who had been in temporary command for two months. The CO changes were coincident with the reversion of VF805 to the operational control of Flag Officer Commanding HMA Fleet for the first time as a Skyhawk squadron.

On 28 August, Bill Callan took up the reins as CO VC724 and John Da Costa became CO VF805 once again. Under Callan's direction, No 2 OFS' five students completed their course. With four A-4s taken to sea by VF805, only four others and the two TA-4s were available to train the students. It must have been a scheduling nightmare for Grahame King.

There were hangar transfers because HMAS *Melbourne* had been in a tragic collision with USS *Frank E Evans* on 3 June. The ship was making its way back to Australia, after some repairs in Sembawang Dock, and would go straight into Cockatoo Dock for a new bow and further refit.

The first CO to take 805 Skyhawks to sea was Fred Lane. He was very senior and experienced. He had been on the first pilot course conducted for the Royal Australian Navy (RAN) in the United Kingdom. He flew Sea Furies in Korea and back at Royal Australian Naval Air Station (RANAS) Nowra, and then the Sea Venom.

THE FIRST EMBARKATION

Designed originally as a nuclear bomber in the early 1950s, the transonic Skyhawk was purchased by the RAN as a fighter, modified to carry four, instead of just two, AIM-9 Sidewinder heat-seeking missiles. New to RAN fighter pilots, the aircraft brought an invaluable 'buddy store' refuelling capability, an excellent computerised navigation system [an analogue doppler navigator], ground-mapping APG-53A radar and an autopilot. Unlike the Sea Fury and Sea Venom, the Skyhawk pilot could plug in a G-suit and pull much more sustained 'G' without blacking out. New Zealand Skyhawks (including some ex-RAN modified aircraft) had a better gyro gunsight and advanced bomb-aiming system, but the fixed-ring sight was sufficient for the RAN Skyhawks' brilliant anti-aircraft weapon, the Sidewinder. Intensive training produced reasonable accuracy with rockets, bombs, and strafing with the two 20-mm Colt cannons. The Skyhawk was also durable. Noting the extra demands of active service and new handling techniques demanded by anti-surface-to-air missile manoeuvres, Skyhawks with a history of flying in Vietnam were examined in detail to ensure they remained safe to fly until their designated end-of-life, 8,000 hours. Not only was that figure safe, it could be extended to 14,000 hours.

As a fighter, the RAN Skyhawk was far superior to the Sea Fury and Sea Venom. It did not have the Venom's all-weather AI Mk.17 radar, but if a Skyhawk could be manoeuvred into an approximate line astern position, even at night or in poor visibility, once the Sidewinder locked on, the enemy aircraft had much less chance of escaping. But then, while RAN aircraft dropped plenty of bombs and rockets on the enemy in Korea, no enemy bomber has ever attempted to attack any target protected by any RAN fighter, day or night.

During a 20 February 1969 armament sortie, I had the honour to fire the first RAN AIM-9 Sidewinder at a Jindivik drone-towed flare off Jervis Bay. It was dead easy, a lot easier than 20 mm air-to-air banner work Simply set the switches, point the fixed gunsight at the heat source, listen for the distinctive weapon lock-on growl in the earphones, check the range and press the fire button. The successful outcome was due, in no small measure, to the superb armourers, electricians and many others who prepared the weapon and aircraft. Also, it

A VC724 Skyhawk escorting a Jindivik on a Sidewinder firing profile exercise. Fred Lane fired the first RAN Sidewinder from a Skyhawk on 20 February 1969. (FAAAoA)

did no harm to carry an inert practice AIM-9 with an active training head on all routine flights.

It was in the strike role that the Skyhawk best showed its outstanding value. The RAN had some experience in this regard, for instance with Sea Furies and Fireflies in Korea, 1950–51. While those aircraft did well enough, when comparing performance in that kind of warfare, a brief comparison with a Korean War USN contemporary, the Douglas Skyraider, might be profitable. How did the Skyhawk and Skyraider compare with other *Melbourne*-capable aircraft like the Supermarine Seafire, Sea Fury and de Havilland Sea Venom?

I was fortunate to deck land the Seafire (Marks XV and XVII) during my OFS in the UK in March 1950. The Seafire was an excellent fighter, but never as good as the Sea Fury. Piston-engine aircraft, such as the Seafire and Sea Fury, as well as the jet-powered Sea Venom, all fell far short of both the Skyhawk and Skyraider in the strike role. Both the Sea Fury and Venom could carry a few three-inch rockets and both the Sea Fury and Firefly could even deliver a couple of 1,000-lb bombs. Unfortunately, the Sea Fury's bombs competed for the same under wing hardpoints as the drop tanks. Therefore, it was always a difficult compromise: good endurance (75 to 120 minutes) and range with just rockets, cannon and drop tanks; or limited range and time (45 to 60 minutes) from the carrier with bombs and no drop tanks.

Neither Sea Fury nor Sea Venom had the strike ability and versatility of the early Skyraider that first flew in 1945, just a year after the Sea Fury. A Skyraider with drop tanks might loiter ten hours. The Skyraider had seven hardpoints under each wing and might carry a highly varied 8,000-lb bombload, including even a 2,200-lb torpedo on its centreline rack. Skyraiders, flown by United States Navy (USN), United States Air Force and South Vietnamese squadrons, destroyed many valuable enemy targets in Korea and Vietnam, but the distinctive engine noise of the 'Sandy' RESCAP (Rescue Combat Air Patrol) was especially welcomed by downed aircrew. Jet RESCAPs were fine for the first few minutes, but the dependable 'Sandies' might hang around for an hour or two until a lumbering 'Jolly Green Giant' (Sikorsky MH-53) or other helicopter made an even more welcome quick dart. 'Sandy' duty USN Skyraiders even shot down two MiG-17s in Vietnam. If we are talking either strike or RESCAP, the Sea Fury is not on the same page.

Again, to illustrate load-carrying differences, a minimum-fuelled Skyhawk might launch from HMAS *Melbourne* carrying the near equivalent of a maximum-weight Sea Fury with its full load of fuel, bombs, rockets and all other armament. With buddy stores or other aerial refuelling, that Skyhawk could then deliver all that armament much further, much faster and with much more precision than any Sea Fury. Indeed, the RAN Skyhawk could deliver bigger bombloads faster and more accurately than most of the dedicated bombers of the Second World War.

Then there is the reliability problem. Nearly all aircraft have an idiosyncrasy or two with the potential to ruin a whole day, and they are not very useful if scattered on enemy soil or grounded for back-of-the-hangar repairs. The Seafire, for all its fighter prowess, had a narrow-tracked and delicate little undercarriage that was definitely not suited to pitching and rolling decks [admittedly not what its progenitor, the Spitfire, was designed for]. It was even less suitable than the Sea Fury in a strike or RESCAP role. With their big propeller and powerful engine, both the Sea Fury and Skyraider had a rare but nasty capability to torque stall.

The Sea Fury also had an Achilles' Heel oil cooler, under its port wing root, which, if hit, gave the pilot a standard 30–60-second warning before the big sleeve-valve engine either seized or burst into flames, or both. The Sea Venom's biggest problem was that while it had an excellent air-to-air radar and four 20-mm Hispano cannon, frustratingly, it carried no homing missile. The Skyhawk's worst behaviour was a very rare, but potentially very lethal, 'flat spin', maybe initiated by asymmetrical slat deployment, for instance at the top of a yo-yo with out-of-whack rudder.

Delivered to RANAS Nowra in 1967, the first ten Skyhawks were a breath of short-lived but lifesaving air for our Fleet Air Arm. Another ten were purchased in 1969 and delivered in 1971. After parrying potentially lethal political, and other Service, interference over the years, this versatile and capable aircraft in RAN colours was a dream realised. Slated to start exciting Skyhawk conversions in January 1968, the welcome anticipation of early days transformed into a bit of a quagmire. Failure to stay abreast of what seemed to us to be a 'pay early and pay often' system for aircraft equipment support meant that, even when solid in the dozens of production queues, an item might be arbitrarily deleted without notice because of, say, inflation or other financial fluctuation.

Then we were reminded that fresh reorders went only one way, to the back of the queue. By then, some queues were two years or more long; others 'No more orders, production ceasing in a couple of months, have a nice day.' We found ourselves replete with spare wings and engines not needed for a year or two, but no sign of any torso harness or even a boarding ladder that was needed to get into the aircraft to strap in. It took some time just to identify exactly what we did not have. After scrounging alternatives, like local hardware shop step ladders, and considerable help from sympathetic key USN people, the RAN Skyhawk No 1 OFS course finally got underway in early August 1968.

During the early *Melbourne*/Skyhawk final compatibility trials, we also had some early catapult bridle strikes and one radar screen popped out of the instrument panel during a launch, severely fouling the control column. These were resolved in jig time. During our first bombing workup, it was found the front-line squadron's entire annual live bomb allocation could be delivered in one single Skyhawk sortie. This took longer to change.

Embarking 805 Squadron on 9 April 1969 for our first Skyhawk cruise, HMAS *Melbourne* headed north. One night, during Exercise *Sea Spirit*, a surface action group (SAG) was scheduled to approach and attack the fleet. Trackers searched diligently and one made a brief sighting report before going radio silent except for an air-to-air TACAN [Tactical Air Navigation transmission]. That TACAN was tuned to a pre-briefed frequency indicating which of the four cardinal points the Tracker might orbit at 500 feet, exactly ten miles from the shadowed target. The Skyhawks launched, also radio silent except for one intermittent TACAN, and made a low-level transit in the pitch-black night to pass under the Tracker at best speed. At the right moment, the leader pulled away, turned ten degrees left, climbed and held speed at the flare drop limiting speed while Number 3 and the other two aircraft turned ten degrees right and climbed for a simulated rocket attack. The six-flare drop illuminated the SAG perfectly, two destroyers nestling close to a cargo ship. The rocketeers did the rest.

Re-forming, everybody flew home to 'Mother', highly satisfied with a novel job well done. That was the night when, despite official and unofficial briefing after briefing and increasing the 'no-go zone' from two to three miles ahead of the carrier, lighting up the darkened carrier with every possible light, automatically stopping the exercise, sounding the siren, sending warnings, and even altering away from a probable whistle down our starboard side, USS *Frank E Evans* closed, fine on our starboard bow, then made a sudden dart to starboard, directly across our bows. Lumbering along at close to 25 knots, there was not much any aircraft carrier could do to evade the collision. Had *Evans* initiated that same turn just five seconds earlier, it might have frightened the life out of a few *Melbourne* compass platform watchkeepers, but just avoided contact. Five seconds later and the destroyer would probably have rammed us amidships and sunk us both. Ten seconds later and the Americans would have maybe passed just clear astern.

The follow-up formal inquiry was a farce: little or no attention was given to *Evans*'s captain lying in bed and not on his bridge as demanded by exercise orders; neither of the two deck officers on *Evans*'s bridge had any formal night watchkeeping qualification; no identification was made of who ordered the fatal turn or why the order was given; and, after putting their ship into a dangerous situation (inside the carrier's three-mile exclusion zone), why they failed to heed *Melbourne*'s both en clair and simple code warnings.

Fred Lane

Melbourne entering Subic Bay in the Philippines in May 1969, shortly before the collision with USS Frank E Evans. (AWM)

Ashore on VC724, the Skyhawks had serviceability problems, with the squadron diary commenting that spares shortages limited availability. Nevertheless, No 2 OFS commenced training, slowly at first in April 1969 but, as more Skyhawks became available, progress sped up.

RAAF Williamtown was struck by three Skyhawks as part of an air defence exercise on 22 April. A week later, two participated in a combined flypast with Royal Australian Air Force assets to mark the retirement of the Governor-General, Lord Casey.

During the week beginning 23 June, the RAAF Staff College visited RANAS Nowra. VC724 provided both static and flying displays of Skyhawks, and Group Captain DW Colquhoun DFC AFC was given a rear seat demonstration flight. The Station Commander (Air), otherwise known as 'Wings' was Commander Norman Lee. Another Sea Venom pilot, he managed to complete conversion to the Skyhawk on 11 June.

In August, VC724 took part in Exercise *King Kong*, alongside VF805, at Tianjara. This was a close-support 'army co-operation' exercise requested by the Army. Another tasking was flying radar-calibration support for the Jervis Bay Missile Range. The RAN had adopted responsibility for the range from contractors.

By September, the squadron diary noted aircraft maintenance had been very satisfactory, resulting in high availability. This had allowed No 2 OFS to complete all but the mission sorties and field carrier landing practice prior to a deck qualification. During August, VF805 borrowed the trainers to complete Instrument Flying Practice and Instrument Rating Tests, a practice that would become the norm over the years.

The diary noted that the first Skyhawk returned from Progressive Aircraft Rework (PAR) on 14 October. The only deficiency noted was that aircraft markings did not stand up to high-speed flight. Qantas had the problem under investigation. The diary also noted that although the squadron establishment was six Skyhawks, only five were available as one was always away undergoing PAR. No 2 OFS was completed on 18 November. All five pilots graduated and all were qualified for day deck landings.

VF805 noted three of its aircraft had been found to have cracks in their wings. Two were subsequently sent to Qantas for urgent repairs and modification, while the third was retained at Qantas and expected back in the New Year. The flying included the first strikes controlled by an airborne forward air controller. These strikes were carried out at Beecroft and, for the first time, the squadron fired 5-inch Zuni rockets.

Skyhawk 886 firing a Zuni rocket. Note the corrosion control (dark paint patches) indicating the early corrosion problems. (RAN)

Chapter 4

FLIGHT DECK ENGINEERING

HMAS *Melbourne* was a traditional aircraft carrier built to a Second World War design but modified with the latest improvements prior to acceptance and commissioning into the Royal Australian Navy (RAN). These included a steam catapult, an angled deck, and a mirror-landing sight. To operate these systems, there were dedicated officers to oversee some vital positions on the flight deck. The Mirror Control Officer sat with a viewing sight at the mirror and was provided from aircrew ranks.

Melbourne had a standard displacement of 15,740 long tons (17,630 short tons), which increased to 20,000 long tons (22,000 short tons) at full load. At launch, the carrier was 213.97 metres (702 feet) long overall, but this was increased by 2.43 metres (8 feet) during a refit in 1969. The ship's beam was 24.38 metres (80 feet) and the draught was 7.62 metres (25 feet). *Melbourne*'s two propellers were driven by two Parsons single-reduction geared-turbine sets, providing 40,000 shaft horsepower, which were powered by four Admiralty three-drum boilers. The carrier could achieve a top speed of 24 knots (44 km/h) and had a range of 12,000 nautical miles (22,000 km) at 14 knots (26 km/h) or 6,200 nautical miles (11,500 km) at 23 knots (43 km/h). The ship's company averaged 1,350 officers and sailors, including 350 personnel from the embarked squadrons.

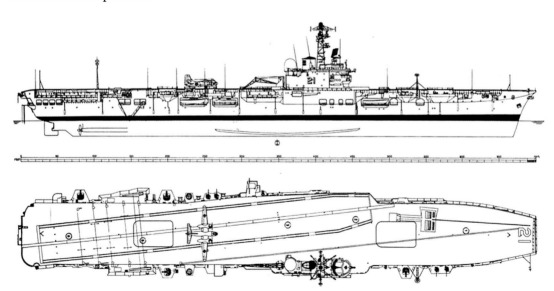

A official drawing showing the layout of HMAS Melbourne after the 1969 refit. (RAN)

HMAS *Melbourne* was originally one of six Majestic-class light fleet aircraft carriers ordered for the Royal Navy (RN) during the Second World War. These carriers were intended as 'disposable warships', i.e., to be disposed of at the end of the war or within three years of entering service.

Melbourne initially flew de Havilland Sea Venoms and Fairey Gannet aircraft until these were replaced by McDonnell-Douglas A-4G Skyhawks and Grumman S-2 Trackers in 1968. The TA-4G was unsafe to operate off the ship due to its two-seat configuration resulting in an undesirable centre of gravity (the balance of the aircraft), which prevented the aircraft launching safely if, on landing, it missed the arrestor wires and had to take off on the relatively short flight deck.

A stern view of HMAS Melbourne from the early 1970s. (AWM)

The photograph above shows:

- The 5.5-degree angled flight deck with its light-coloured dashed centreline
- The width of the landing area denoted by the two light lines either side of the centreline
- The five arrestor wires (the black lines on the flight deck)
- The catapult (the line to the left of the line of helicopters)
- The 'round down' where the aft end of the flight deck curves down (between the white horizontal line and the end of the flight deck)
- A helicopter landing spot (the white circle with a number in it)
- The droplight, the vertical line on the right end of the Admiral's Gallery
- The Landing Safety Officer platform at the left rear corner of the flight deck
- The Mirror Landing System to the left of the parked and folded Trackers

The flight deck engineers were involved with hydraulic and live steam machinery. These vital positions were filled by the Engineering Branch of the RAN. Rear Admiral Ruting provided this contribution dealing with his part in getting fixed-wing aircraft off and on the deck. Many an RAN pilot owes him their thanks for getting them off and on with never a problem.

THE CATAPULT

One of the many groups facilitating our adventurous aviators' outstanding achievements when embarked in HMAS *Melbourne* were the members of the flight deck engineering division (FDEng). This group were organisationally part of the Marine Engineering Department of the ship, although one member, a Petty Officer Electrician, was from the ship's Weapons Electrical Department.

The principal roles of the FDEng team included: operation and maintenance of the aircraft catapult; managing aviation fuels (AVGAS 140 Octane petrol for the Trackers and AVCAT jet fuel for the Skyhawks and helicopters); liquid-oxygen production and bulk storage (for the pilot's breathing system in Skyhawks); and operation and maintenance of the arrestor gear (catching aircraft on landing).

The catapult mainly consisted of two parallel steam cylinders that ran 112 feet (about 34 metres) just under the flight deck, in which the two pistons were connected to a single hook on the flight deck to which the aircraft towing strop was connected. These two pistons were propelled forward using steam pressure built up in two large cylindrical receivers located in the catapult machinery space. The receivers were charged with steam from the two boilers in the forward main propulsion engine room. Once the catapult steam system was opened up to the ship's boilers, there was a complex hydraulic control system to ensure all of the launch valves and other systems operated in a very precisely controlled order. There was also a hydraulically operated large steel-wire rope and pulley system for returning the steam pistons from their forward 'post-launch' position to their aft position ready for the next launch. All of these complex hydraulic, steam and mechanical wire systems required regular maintenance, checking and careful calibration, the responsibility of a dedicated team of 12 sailors, from senior able seaman (AB) to chief petty officer (CPO), who were all trained 'on the job' in the ship.

A senior, very experienced artificer CPO was in charge of the maintenance, training and operation, supported by two teams of five sailors (CPO/PO, leading seaman and three ABs) who would operate in two watches for extended flying operations. The catapult machinery space, where the two large steam receivers and all the hydraulics were located, was particularly hot when the catapult was operating in the tropics, despite all the steam pipes and receivers being lagged with asbestos-based insulation. This was a challenge for the operating team as the leading seaman (LS) and ABs needed to be in this space for many hours of their six-hour watch; wearing protective clothing and masks in the confined space made it even less pleasant.

The flight deck of HMAS Melbourne with the catapult track in the foreground, and a Skyhawk about to launch. The chequered tails of the VF805 A-4Gs started appearing in the mid-1970s. (Seapower Centre)

Being a steam-operated system, all these systems had to be slowly warmed to operating temperature each morning, with steam slowly bled down the two main launch cylinders via the manually operated 'track steam' valves at about 10psi until the catapult was ready to launch. With the pilots' lives at stake, there was a comprehensive range of pre-launch checks and tests conducted by the 'on watch' sailors, plus independent checks by the senior CPO, the Flight Deck Electrician (focusing on the catapult 'end speed' recorder and control systems) and the Catapult Officer. The personal responsibility placed on each of these sailors was considerable and this was reflected in the careful selection and grooming process for each individual, as well as carefully overlaid quality checking practices by each senior sailor and catapult officer, similar to those required for actual aircraft maintenance.

These checks included the Catapult Officer having to slide on a flat trolley some 30 metres up the catapult cylinders from the bow, to confirm there were no obstructions and all the fittings on the forward end of the pistons were properly secured, before the start of flying each day. For each launch series, the Catapult Officer would be given a list of the aircraft launch weights and required take-off speeds from which he consulted a set of tables and graphs based on air and steam temperatures, etc., to calculate the required steam pressure the catapult receivers were to be charged with to achieve the required aircraft end speed.

During the actual launch, the Catapult Officer would sit on the flight deck next to the catapult control station (Howdah), connected to the flight deck radio system, so he could personally check the required steam pressure had been achieved before the aircraft was launched, and to adjust the pressure for the next launch if needed. Due to the short length (about 34 metres) of the catapult, accelerating a heavy A-4G (especially with full wing tanks) to 125+ knots often resulted in the pilot receiving a very substantial acceleration on launch [the standard launch loading was 5.45G. A 'war shot' was 6G. Author Peter Greenfield experienced one of these during a weapons trial].

The on-watch catapult CPO/PO manned the launch-control system in the Howdah during all launches and actually pressed the launch button on the hand signal command of the Flight Deck Officer. His reaction time and checks on system operation were critical to a successful aircraft launch, especially when the ship was pitching into head seas.

A typical flying operations day could involve starting to warm the catapult at 3am for a 5am launch of five Skyhawks fighters and two ASW Trackers, followed by Tracker launches every four hours and Skyhawks every two hours through to midnight, when the last Tracker would be launched. If we were participating in a full international exercise, we could often be 'at 30 minutes notice' to launch all day, requiring the catapult team to operate in two watches (except for the Chief Technician and the FDEng or Catapult Officer who were 'watch on, stop on' until flying operations ceased for the day).

Being effectively the ship's main weapon, the single catapult, with many non-duplicated systems, was a single point of failure so the emphasis on careful condition and performance checks and thorough maintenance was essential. As the ship aged, this became a challenge and, for example, during the 1977 Jubilee

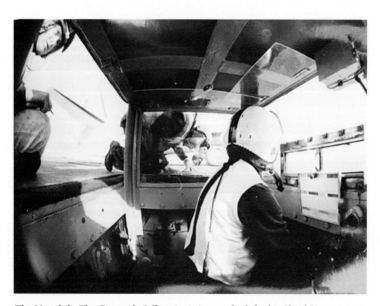

The Howdah. The Catapult Officer is sitting on the left, the Chief Operator is on the right. (RAN)

deployment to the UK, the catapult team lost much shore time and had to call on UK dockyard experience to help with a jammed main hydraulic cylinder in the launch piston recovery system. The catapult officer even missed the Queen's Fleet Review due to being ashore trying to find parts to fix this major defect.

During *Rimpac 78*, off Hawaii, *Melbourne* acquired the nickname 'Little M' after working with the 'Big E', the nuclear-powered USS *Enterprise* – the smallest and largest aircraft carriers, respectively, in operation in the world at the time. We could launch A-4Gs with one catapult almost as fast as *Enterprise* could with four catapults. With well worked-up pilots, flight deck and catapult teams, and a well warmed-up catapult, we managed to break the one-minute cycle between launches of A-4Gs. What a great team achievement!

THE ARRESTORS

At the other end of the flight deck, a similarly important aviation capability was conducted, catching the Skyhawks using the five wires of the arrestor system and their hydraulic accumulators. There was, similarly, one officer and a small team of about seven sailors under the close management of a Petty Officer Marine Technical Propulsion who participated intimately in both operation and maintenance of the equipment. During flying operations, two of the sailors were positioned below decks to observe the performance of the sheaves and accumulator systems while the PO and Arrestors Officer were in a port side flight-deck sponson just aft of the landing-signals mirror and lights. The role of the Arrestors Officer during flying operations involved carefully watching the performance of the arrestor gear on every aircraft recovery (including many sprints across the flight deck to closely inspect the arrestor wire where the aircraft hook had caught to ensure it was not damaged, then a sprint back to the deck-edge sponson before the next aircraft landed).

Between flying operations, there was much maintenance to be done on the wires, large sheaves, hydraulic cylinders and air cylinders. The shortening of the 50-mm diameter multi-strand wires, as they stretched during operations, was a major task that occupied the whole arrestors team of eight sailors, with the officer generally

Skyhawk 884 with tail hook deployed about to catch an arrestor wire. The yellow and blue chequered tail indicates this is a VC724 aircraft. (Seapower Centre)

providing the independent quality control. There was also an emergency barrier system that used hydraulically raised masts to string a net across the flight deck if the arrestor systems failed and an aircraft had to land. A single arrestor system was set up at *Albatross* to help train the pilots there, but it was quite different to the onboard system, so all training was conducted 'on the job' and thus relied heavily on the personal qualities and teaching ability of the PO in charge, and his two LS. The arrestors team also looked after the maintenance of the aircraft lifts 'in their spare time'.

The liquid-oxygen plant was a very complex, refrigeration and pressure-based technology, and was very sensitive to external environmental conditions, including ship roll and pitch accelerations. There was a small team of six sailors, led by a POMT artificer, who had undertaken a specialist course run by BOC Gases at their Sydney commercial oxygen-generation plant, with the second week undertaken operating our own plant at sea in *Melbourne* with BOC supervisors. The arrestors engineer officer also undertook this same two-week course and oversaw operations and maintenance of the plant.

The aviation fuels section comprised one PO, one LS and three ABs and operated a physically dispersed system of three AVCAT tanks with their own dedicated electric pumps and piping to the flight deck for receiving fuel from ashore or a replenishment tanker. They also supplied fuel to aircraft on deck or in the hangar, or via a long 150-mm diameter hose to an adjacent frigate during an underway replenishment. The AVGAS was stowed in a completely different water displacement system due to its highly explosive nature. The Arrestors Officer also oversaw all major AVFUELS operations, and maintenance of the systems.

In addition to the onboard naval engineering sailors who maintained the FDEng equipment, we were also heavily reliant on a small cadre of expert engineers and tradesmen at Garden Island Dockyard to undertake depot-level maintenance of the equipment. This was especially important for the catapult as few engineers had access to the data, and previous knowledge, to check the catapult steam cylinders' shape and their complex alignment when cold. After full refits of the catapult machinery, 'proving shots', using live steam from the ship's boilers, were undertaken alongside at the Garden Island wharf. The shots used a weighted steel 'box on wheels' to simulate a loaded Skyhawk; quite a splash arose when the test vehicle hit the water about 100 metres in front of the ship! The test vehicle, nicknamed 'Chloe', was then recovered from the harbour by the wharf's hammerhead crane and placed on the catapult launch site for the next test shot. The results of each shot, at varying weights and launch pressures, were carefully analysed before the catapult could be certified to launch aircraft at sea.

Trevor Ruting

Testing the catapult with 'Chloe'

In order to test the ability of the catapult to develop full steam power to throw the heaviest aircraft possible off *Melbourne*, and at the correct steam pressure for the aircraft type, 'Chloe' was developed. 'Chloe' was a steel box on aircraft wheels (Gannet wheels I was told) and was ballasted with water to vary the weight according to the aircraft type to be catapulted. On the front was painted 'Sylvester the Cat' with 'Chloe' painted on the side.

While the S-2E Tracker may have been heavier than the A-4, it didn't require the same velocity at the end of the catapult; the A-4 required it to be physically thrown off the catapult.

The A-4 required 20 knots of wind, i.e., the ship had to find wind, then head into it, for the A-4 to fly. The end speed of an A-4 was 108 knots into a 20-knot wind to get off the deck at its maximum landing weight at the end of the 97-foot catapult stroke. If the wind was a bit low, then 50 feet of height above sea level was required to remain airborne. More wind meant more weight could be carried and that the aircraft's attitude off the cat had to be carefully monitored. The Tracker had an end speed of 101–103 knots and was flying at the end of the catapult stroke. Trackers could fly when the A-4s could not get enough wind over the deck to fly.

Ray Oliver

The steel box named 'Chloe' with four Gannet wheels that was used to test the catapult. The weight could be varied by adding water inside. (Ray Oliver)

'Chloe' airborne after a test catapult launch. (George Hicks)

Chapter 5

1970: EXERCISE *BERSATU PADU*

VF805 was embarked under the command of Lieutenant Commander John Da Costa, with Lieutenant Commander Brian Dutch as Senior Pilot (SP), and Lieutenants Keith Johnson, Gary Northern, Ralph McMillan, Dave Collingridge and Ken Palmer. They only had four aircraft to fly, but the authorisation sheets show all flew often during the exercise.

So, what does Exercise *Bersatu Padu* and the FPDA (Five Powers Defence Agreement) have to do with A-4G Skyhawks? Quite a lot actually, but it is a long story. Malaya was not a colony as such, but more of a country in which Britain held great interests from early colonial times. It began with the East India Company settling on the island of Penang as a trading centre. Stamford Raffles followed with setting up Singapore as a trading port and, together with Malacca and Dinding, they became known as the Straits Settlements. When the East India Company fell on hard times following the Indian Mutiny, the British Government stepped in to take control of India and the Straits Settlements.

The Colonial Office was the agency used by the Government to provide very loose control. The government of the day provided advisors from the Colonial Office to the various rulers of the Malayan Peninsula. The British, wherever they went in the world, much preferred to govern through the rulers recognised by the 'natives'. The only place where this policy could not be applied was our own Australia.

So, the sultans still ruled in Malaya, but were given guidance by the political advisors, who were in turn directed by the Colonial Office. The system actually worked well and, as time passed, evolved into a system of self-government. Industry centred around tin mining and rubber production, which made Malaya very wealthy. With the Communist Emergency beginning in 1948, British Forces arrived back in Malaya, supplemented by Australian and New Zealand units. This was known as the ANZAM area by the time Malaya was given independence in 1957.

It had a great influence on Australian defence thinking and led to the acquisition of submarines, air-defence ships and the Skyhawks in the 1960s. It also led to the development of RAF Butterworth, which was taken over by the Royal Australian Air Force (RAAF) post-1970. A little-known feature of the assistance provided by the Royal Australian Navy (RAN) was the provision of senior officers for the fledgling Royal Malaysian Navy. This extended from the Chief of Navy down to frigate captains, the development of a training system, and a naval staff. And the Army was involved too, with the establishment of a Jungle Warfare School, an ANZAC Infantry Battalion in Johore, and the Rifle Company Butterworth (extant at Gerik to this day).

The Confrontation between Indonesia and Malaya broke out in 1963, caused by the decision of

Sarawak and Sabah to join the Federated States of Malaya. The Indonesians conducted cross-border armed incursions in Borneo and covert landings of armed parties in Johore. The British responded with force and Australia and New Zealand supported this actively.

Headquarters was in Singapore, but air defence was flown from Butterworth with co-ordination from the air defence unit in Singapore. Naval forces operated out of Singapore and the great base of Sembawang, patrolling the Malacca Straits and the southern coast of Sabah. The Royal Navy (RN) provided fixed-wing support from aircraft carriers rotating through the Far East and rotary wing support from HMS *Bulwark*.

Roll on 1965 and the leader of Singapore, Lee Kuan Yew, was unhappy with the policies espoused by the Malaysian Government in Kuala Lumpur. He broke from the federation and Singapore became independent. However, both the governments of Malaysia and Singapore recognised their defence needs remained intertwined. Concurrent with the wind down of *Konfrontasi*, a Labour Government came to power in the UK and, by 1967, their policy was to withdraw all forces east of the Suez Canal.

They did, however, realise they could not just leave a power vacuum behind. In 1968, the FPDA was discussed in terms of the military support that could be offered by Australia, New Zealand and the UK in the event of hostility arising again towards Malaysia and Singapore. A major exercise, to be known as 'Bersatu Padu' ('Complete Unity' in Malay), was planned for 1970 to demonstrate this commitment.

Fate stepped in and, in June 1970, a Conservative Government replaced Labour in the UK, with Ted Heath as prime minister. No sooner were the election results announced than Heath decided to demonstrate the UK's willingness to honour its part in the proposed FPDA. As a result, a massive logistical exercise ensued to move aircraft, troops and equipment to Malaysia and Singapore to take part in Exercise *Bersatu Padu*.

The exercise was actually three in one: an air-defence exercise over Butterworth, Singapore and the fleet at sea; a maritime exercise in the South China Sea off the east coast of Malaysia; and, finally, an amphibious assault and landing of troops to capture an airfield, and then an airlift of troops to the captured airhead.

The Royal Air Force (RAF) maintained just one squadron of English Electric Lightnings, two Shackleton maritime patrol aircraft, and a squadron of Canberra bombers in Singapore. Australia had a squadron of Mirages at Butterworth and a battalion of troops in Johore. New Zealand had a squadron of Bristol Freighters at Butterworth and an artillery unit co-located with the Australians. Both the RN and the RAN had ships established in the Far East Strategic Reserve.

The RAF mounted a vast logistical transport exercise to move the 19th Brigade, an air-portable unit, to Singapore. This required a near-unbroken chain of VC10 transports flying via Bahrain to Changi in 20 hours of flying time. Additionally, No 54 Squadron RAF ferried their Phantom FGRs to Changi. Four aircraft dashed from tanker to tanker, with three ferry tanks in 14 hours, but most moved more sedately with their tankers via Bahrain. Six Vulcan bombers also ferried out to Changi.

On hand in Singapore, the RN had HMS *Bulwark*, with Royal Marine commandoes and troop-carrying helicopters on board, and HM Ships *Fife, Euralyus, Plymouth, Chichester* and *Leopard*. The RAN had HMAS *Melbourne* with VF805 embarked, and HMA Ships *Stalwart, Duchess, Parramatta, Derwent, Stuart, Oxley, Ibis, Curlew* and *Teal*. New Zealand contributed HMNZS *Taranaki*, two of their new C-130 Hercules and a squadron of Canberra bombers. Malaysia contributed nine ships, including its flagship RMN *Hang Tuah*, and eight fast patrol boats. Singapore, newly established as an island state, could only offer a single infantry battalion.

The goal of the exercise was to seize Penarek Airstrip, a basic unpaved airfield in the Malaysian state of Terengganu, back from opposition forces via an amphibious landing, and then airlift in reinforcing troops. Air defence of the airfield could only be provided by the Skyhawks from *Melbourne* because the airfield was too far for the RAAF Mirages or RAF Lightnings to provide any cover.

The exercise was considered an expensive success by all concerned. A report was written and published and can still be found in antiquarian bookshops for a large sum of money. There were two very telling conclusions drawn, however. The reception airfields for the airlift were Butterworth and Changi (the based air defence was tasked as enemy air in the initial exercises, while the Phantoms belonged to the good guys). Without air superiority, the men and materials from Britain could not have been delivered. Only fighters from an aircraft carrier could possibly have delivered that air superiority. The other conclusion was that only HMAS *Melbourne*, with the four A-4 Skyhawks, could provide some semblance of air cover for the fleet out in the South China Sea prior to the landing.

As a result of the exercise, the FPDA was signed in 1971 in Kuala Lumpur. Administrative and operational functions were specified and set up largely in Butterworth. These exist to this day with an RAAF Air Marshal from Australia heading the Integrated Air Defence System. The deputy position alternates between Malaysia and Singapore. Regular land, sea and air exercises are scheduled on a rolling basis.

While VF805 had four of the Navy's Skyhawks embarked for this exercise, the rest, four A-4Gs and the two TA-4Gs, were working hard for VC724 to train more Skyhawk pilots. The four VF805 Skyhawks were flown hard and made the point about embarked fixed wing at sea. No doubt they heavily influenced the decision making surrounding the next purchase of ten aircraft in 1971. After all, the Defence Minister, Malcolm Fraser, was there in person observing the exercise.

After the carrier air group disembarked, Lieutenant Commander Colin Paterson assumed command from John Da Costa. There was a period of low availability of aircraft due to two hot-end inspections and three main oleo changes. Of the two engines removed for inspection, the two heat-shield blankets for the No 6 bearing were found to be in need of replacement. There was no repair scheme for these items.

The workup for the next embarkation was interrupted after the field carrier landing practice period when No 77 Squadron RAAF deployed to Nowra for a week from 17 August. VF805 replied in kind with a week's deployment to RAAF Williamtown the following week.

In September, the workup continued with extensive deck landing practice and, at the end of it, all pilots were day deck qualified, with some night qualified. To enable this, aircraft exchanges were made with VC724. Night flying was carried out by the ship in Jervis Bay during which Paterson and Lieutenant Northern completed their night landing qualification.

At this stage, there were only three Skyhawks on board, and one with Qantas awaiting rectification. Colin Paterson flew to Nowra for Exercise *Nullarbor Express*, leaving two aircraft on board. These aircraft were disembarked on 8 December, and then returned to the ship for a family day display on 10 December. On return to Nowra, all aircraft were placed in suspended service until January 1971.

Meanwhile, ashore, VC724 began training No 3 Operational Flying School (OFS), consisting of five pilots, in early January 1970. Despite aircraft availability problems, the OFS progressed well and was expected to finish in early June. All pilots were expected to go straight to VF805. Two ex-helicopter pilots joined the squadron in early January as well but needed a refamiliarisation on the de Havilland Vampire and some additional Fleet Requirement Unit flying prior to beginning No 4 OFS in July. In the event, No 3 OFS completed ahead of schedule, on 26 May, with all students graduating at a high standard.

Commander Norm Lee completed a two-week familiarisation course on the Skyhawk. He subsequently flew Captain Dollard RAN, Commanding Officer (CO) HMAS *Albatross*, on a familiarisation flight. On 8 June, a long-range navex was flown by Lieutenant Commander John Park USN and Lieutenant Errol Kavanagh, covering 2,000 miles in four hours and 40 minutes without air refuelling. No 4 OFS commenced on 6 July.

VC724's aircraft serviceability fluctuated throughout the next few months. Despite this, progress continued with No 4 OFS, which completed on 11 December with all students achieving satisfactory results.

The life of a maintainer on VC724 was always interesting, especially as you sorted out the 'this is how you do it by the book' as opposed to 'this is how we do it on the squadron.'

ENGINE REMOVAL

In August 1970, I had just finished a Skyhawk course run by Paddy Linton and pupils (Peter Welsh, Ben Link and others) on the Friday and joined VC724 on the Monday as a young Artificer 3rd Class (aka Tiffy 3, a leading seaman equivalent). I had a head full of knowledge but no real aircraft maintenance skills. As I entered the Skyhawk maintenance and storage hangar, J Hangar, after lunch, I was asked by an Artificer 2nd Class (a Tiffy 2 and a Petty Officer equivalent) who needed help in the removal of an engine out of a Skyhawk. He was by himself and I knew from the previous week's course that we needed to have at least four others (approximately six all up) to perform the task successfully. My 'We need more people' was met by his 'It's all right, I have done this before.' I then became the person who would wind the engine out using a speed-brace device attached to the extraction frame on the engine transport trolley. 'What do you want me to do?' asked I to his 'Just wind it out and tell me if it gets hard to wind.' What could go wrong with that?

So, I start to wind and, almost immediately, 'It's hard to wind.' With that, he darts between both fuselage side ports, to the underside of the engine to the hell hole at the back under the engine. 'It's okay,' he says, 'Keep winding as it must be misaligned a bit.' I wind half a turn and tell him, 'It's still tight.' He again does the inspection of all access points, finds nothing wrong and tells me 'Keep winding,' which I do. 'It's still tight,' repeats I to his 'Keep winding' and, as I do, there is an almighty bang and winding then becomes extremely easy.

Within a day or two, I'm standing in front of a row of commanders, lieutenant commanders and lieutenants, and none of them are wearing a happy face as I tell my story of what happened. It seems that while a still-connected hydraulic line could withstand 3,000 psi of internal pressure, it couldn't withstand the mechanical advantage I had over it. Also, there were some electrical wires that resisted my mechanical advantage for a while. Then there was the slight matter of the constant-speed drive (CSD) that was bolted to the front of the engine. The CSD was hidden behind a close-fitting door that had managed to fall down from its propped open position during the engine removal. The CSD door locking mechanism managed to get itself embedded in the oil tank of the CSD until my mechanical advantage overcame it, tearing a hole in the CSD. All these things appeared to happen all at once with the bang that was heard throughout the hangar. From memory, the Tiffy 2 was transferred from the squadron very soon after the inquiry.

DELMAR TARGET SERVICING

Shortly after arriving on the squadron in 1970, I was given a couple of tasks, with one being to get the hangar queen in a condition to fly. It was a good job I could burrow myself into without being too distracted, but always seeking the advice from the chiefs on the squadron. The other task was to get the aerial target system, the Delmar target system, serviceable. It was a towed target with 20,000 feet of 0.05-inch Suzuki 'piano wire', with a breaking strain of 1,200 lbs (strong in tension and, from experience, when it broke, it was in a sheared way that left a very sharp and vicious spike), in a carrier that was attached to the aircraft centre rack. The wire was wound around a reel that was situated longitudinally with the wire feeding out the centre of the carrier to the target. The target, about two metres long, cylindrical, with a diameter of about 300 mm, had four fins, of which two held flares that were fired by the pilot to give the ship's gun crews a visual target to shoot at. The cylinder body held a number of steel spheres which the ship's radar could lock on to provide a target for radar-directed guns. The target was wound out and retracted by the pilot.

A young David Prest and a rudder power pack. (David Prest)

I had to wind on the piano wire and proceeded to do so without the safety guard for the reel. I momentarily caught my finger between the wire and the reel, which gave me a significant fright and I quickly installed the guard as I only needed one of those frights in my life. Lesson learnt.

David Prest

The Delmar was a target system which had been flown on the Sea Venom. It was used to provide a high-speed target for ships firing at aerial targets. It was red for visual gunnery and radar reflective for radar-controlled shoots. This meant the service could be provided by day or night if the target could be observed by the ships. It was a given it would be fitted to the

A red Delmar Target with its grey launcher on the centreline rack of a Skyhawk. (David Prest)

Skyhawk. However, it was rarely fitted to a single seat A-4. Most often, it was fitted to a TA-4 with the pilot controlling the Delmar via a specially fitted control panel.

1970 snapshot

The carrier air group embarked on 9 February. During this period the ship and air group conducted Exercise *Sea Rover*, visited Sattahip, Hong Kong and Osaka for Expo '70, then conducted Exercise *Bersatu Padu*. The air group disembarked on 14 July. It embarked again on 26 October for Exercise *Swan Lake* off Western Australia, disembarking on 8 December.

CO VF805 was Lieutenant Commander John Da Costa from 28 July 1969 to 17 July 1970. From 20 July, it was Lieutenant Commander Colin Paterson.

The pilots for the four A-4s on strength were Dutch, McMillan, Palmer, Northern, Collingridge and Johnson. On 15 July, Paterson and Sub-Lieutenant Peter Cox joined, and McMillan departed. Collingridge posted off on 25 September, with Peter McNair and John Hamilton joining on 1 October.

CO VC724 was Lieutenant Commander Bill Callan from 28 August 1969 to 21 July 1970. The SP was Lieutenant Commander Grahame King until 21 July 1970 when he became CO VC724. Lieutenant Commander Park USN came in as SP from that date.

The Skyhawk fleet stood at ten: two TA-4Gs and eight A-4Gs.

Chapter 6

1971: TRAINING AND GROWING THE A-4 FLEET

The year of 1971 kept *Melbourne* alongside in a long refit until August. The Captain, GJ Willis, took the ship to sea for a long weekend in late July to prove the machinery, clean the ship and give the long-suffering crew a taste of what they joined for. In late August, they started working up the air group, which consisted of four A-4s, six Trackers and six Wessex. While a relatively quiet year in terms of getting the Skyhawks to sea, training, of course, continued and, the type having proved itself in a short time, the size of the fleet doubled.

The dreaded CSD servicing

As part of a CSD (constant-speed drive) service I performed, I had to give the aircraft a run while the electricians checked it was putting out the correct amount of electrical power. I knew from a previous experience that the bayonet connection of the filling plug, although seemingly in the correct place, was difficult to seat and therefore liable to pop out. If the filling plug popped out, the silicon fluid would be sucked into the engine and produce white smoke out the tailpipe. Therefore, I triple-checked its security and then ran the engine for the electricians to confirm the CSD was producing the correct power. While doing so, I was watching the young man who was the fire guard and noticed he had a puzzled look on his face as he looked towards the back of the aircraft. Realising something was wrong, I quickly shut the engine down and, yes, the filling plug had come out but, luckily, the fluid level was still above the low mark. After topping up the CSD fluid and reseating the plug, the engine run went as planned.

Williamtown Detachment

The Skyhawk squadron, VC724, was an interesting organisation to be a part of in the early 1970s. It was full of characters that were missing when I returned to the squadron in the early 1980s.

One was an unnamed naval airman who was fond of a drink or two, as were a number of others on the squadron. My first detachment was to RAAF Base Williamtown in 1971 and he was one of the support crew. It was in the days when the last of the RAAF Sabres were being handed over to the Indonesians. It was also when the Army parachute school was at Williamtown. Where is this going you may well ask?

Well, it seems his fondness for drink managed to get him in to the same on-base bar as some of the soldiers undergoing parachute training. The next day, and still in an alcoholic haze, he fronted up to the flight-line hut looking like he had been in a cat fight, i.e., scratches all over him. It seemed that the previous night, after numerous drinks, he had 'won' his parachute wings (half a dozen jumps from a serviceable aircraft). 'But you didn't jump from an aircraft,' we chorused. 'No,' he said, 'It was from the second storey of an accommodation block.' 'And where did all the blood and scratches come from?' we asked. 'Well,' he said, 'I kept landing in the rose bushes in the garden below the jump window.'

And you, Fatty

In the early 1970s, a number of Royal Navy (RN) chief petty officers (CPO) from all RN Fleet Air Arm branches came out to Australia to supplement the lack of Australian Fleet Air Arm chiefs. The RN CPOs, unlike Royal Australian Navy (RAN) chiefs, didn't wear any badge showing rank or trade on their shirts but just wore the three buttons of a CPO on the sleeves of their black jackets. Their blue working dress was also different to Australian grey working dress.

One day, an RN CPO, Pat Nolan, without his jacket and therefore without his rank showing, went down to the

724 Squadron flight-line hut to see how things were done RAN style. He was sitting down near some of the young blokes when the flight-line PO, 'Nipper' Vandenberg, needed an aircraft pushed back from the refuelling point at the front of the line to the back of the flight line in anticipation of the aircraft's next flight.

Nipper pointed to the sailors sitting down and said to them, 'All you lot go out to the aircraft and push it back to the rear of the flight line. Oh, and you, Fatty, can give them a hand.' Of course, 'Fatty' was the RN CPO sitting and watching the goings on. He soon sorted out the PO as to who should be pushing the aircraft and who shouldn't. It was most interesting watching the flustered PO apologising and trying to dig himself out of the hole he had dug himself into.

WORKING ON THE FLIGHT LINE

It was 'fun' on the flight line of a nighttime around August–October when the winds from the Snowy Mountains would come through unabated and cool you down a tad. I would wear a brown roll-neck jumper under my overalls; it came in very handy on those cold nights. The Navy issued jumpers, made of a combination of sheep's wool on the outside and steel wool on the inside, itchy if worn near the skin and annoying to wear.

The dew of a nighttime made clambering around the aircraft interesting. The soles of our boots were always a little greasy from walking on the tarmac which had years of fuel spilt on it and which the dew would bring to the surface. On a couple of occasions, I found myself sliding backwards on the upper surface of a wing hoping my fingers would catch on a panel gap so I didn't slide off and fall onto the concrete hardstand.

Of course, summer could be hot and humid, so we were lucky enough to get all the four seasons when on flight-line duties. We had wet weather gear that was odd sized, didn't fit and was unsuitable for the job we were doing. But who was complaining? That's all we had. The good stuff that fitted seemed to be worn by the stores people; I wonder how that happened?

David Prest

A YEAR AT SEA

It was time for our year at sea for those of us following the 'Professional' stream.[1] Once again, we were divided into two halves. The first half of the alphabet went to HMAS *Melbourne*, and the second to HMAS *Sydney*. The latter half did three trips to South Vietnam, but we in the first half were destined for better times.

On the first night on board, the training officer, Lieutenant Commander Blue, gathered us around and assigned us to Ship's Departments, and issued us our Task Books. These had all sorts of things that we had to achieve in our six months aboard ship. To my joy, I was assigned to the Air Department. We were told the carrier air group personnel had arrived that afternoon, that the ship was moving to a buoy to ammunition ship the next morning and would sail the next day for the aircraft to embark.

The next morning, newly kitted out with a blue handler's jacket, earmuffs and goggles, the three of us stepped out of the island to meet the Flight Deck Chief. He gave us a safety brief, of which all I can remember is 'this deck is dangerous, stick to your Yellow Shirt like glue, do whatever he says without question.' He then said 'Follow me' and led us down to the round down. There he indicated two deep, newly painted gouges in the flight deck. Those he told us, were made by the wheels of a Skyhawk that had a ramp strike two nights ago. The pilot had a lucky escape and took it to the '*tross* where he landed it into the wire. 'Gentlemen, you do not want to be pilots!' I kept my mouth shut, but I really wanted to be one now.

I cannot remember what we did for the rest of the day, but there was lots to do. Probably painting; it was a never-ending task. The next morning, we sailed and, after about an hour, the ship turned into wind, the Broadcast made some unintelligible noises, and my Yellow Shirt kept me way back from a line, which I later learnt was the Foul Line. He explained that soon the aircraft would arrive, first the Skyhawks, then the Trackers and finally the Wessex.

Then, overhead, four Skyhawks whistled down the starboard side and turned in sequence ahead of the ship. As they turned downwind, their gear extended, and they clearly slowed down and adopted a nose-up attitude. The

---

[1]   Prior to pilot training officers had to spend a year at sea, which would educate them in the full scope of naval operations and procedures.

first turned abeam the ship and gently closed across the centreline before rolling wings level. Before you knew it, it hit the deck, the arrestor gear screamed, and this tiny jet pitched heavily to a stop. A Yellow Shirt stepped out holding his arms up, two hookmen (I was told) rushed out, but before they got there the wire fell out of the hook as the aircraft gently rolled back, the hook came up, the speed brakes retracted, and the flaps came up as the Yellow Shirt waved at the aircraft. I was hooked, and bedazzled, by the flight-deck dance. Before the week was out, I had learnt the proper names for the jobs people were doing (and the colour of their jackets), the roles and responsibilities, and felt I was contributing as I helped push aeroplanes into spots and onto lifts.

My time in the Air Department was short and it culminated in a ride in a Tracker, when a small formation was launched for a south coast navex. The TACCO [Tactical Coordinator] was a young Sub-Lieutenant Al 'Nobby' Clark, with whom I would fly many years later. The cat shot was really something, but not startling. The arrest was the startling thing, because I had no idea of a 'cut pass' where the pilot closes the throttles at the cut call and then wire catches the aircraft.

I resolved to go goofing [watching flight-deck action from up on the carrier's island] whenever I could.

My time on board continued and, whenever the opportunity came, I hung around the aircrew in the wardroom. I listened to the likes of Gary Northern, John Hamilton, Peter Cox and Phil Thompson as they waved beers around and told flying stories. I was not stupid enough to stand on the 805 drinking mat, but I willingly went to the bar to get another round. I knew I wasn't part of the team, but I desperately wanted to join it.

Peter Greenfield

A CLOSE CALL

An excerpt from an HMAS *Melbourne* ROP (reports on proceedings) for September 1971:

> On Wednesday 1st MELBOURNE was off Jervis Bay conducting intensive night flying training. During night flying that night a Skyhawk piloted by SBLT P.J. Thompson hit the roundown [*sic*] heavily, damaging the undercarriage and necessitating its return to Nowra for an emergency landing.

It was nighttime already, the 'daylights were already out of me' after the first night deck landing (DL). While this first one, as I found out later, was not perfect, it didn't look so bad after my second night DL – the ramp strike.

I was thereafter the pilot the sailors could approach to say 'Jeezus, sir, you scared the bejeezus out of me' and these guys were in the front (as the 'birdies' [FAA] liked to call the bow) or wherever. The admiral (Rear Admiral WJ Dovers, known as 'Ming the Merciless') was in his cabin directly under the ramp. It had just been refurbished. He invited me up there to congratulate me on surviving and to show me (with good humour) the absolute chaos it had caused in his cabin, as the ceiling (made of painted cork for soundproofing) had fallen in on him. By the way, above the cork ceiling were many inches of specially strengthened steel. HMAS *Melbourne*'s deck (generally) was remade (before this to be able to operate A-4s) and in this area was supported by extra footings to enable it to take the A-4 bumps in the landing zone.

I guess I had better days and nights, but it was scary just to go out there for the first time not really knowing the drill, having a CCA (carrier-controlled approach) at low level to the 'slot' or 'groove', where we would start to look ahead to see the ball and start the approach, monitored then by the LSO (Landing Safety Officer). So, I guess the unknown is worse if it is poorly anticipated. However, I knew that to be the reverse – complacent – was not an option. Jet pilots probably get addicted to the adrenaline rush. I'm sure most of the young pilots were just 'powered by adrenaline' most of the time.

At this point, the aim was to have about 20 day catapults (and about twice as many deck landings – touch and goes and arrests) and, as getting the ship time was not always easy, to then move on to night DLs. An RAN pilot did not have his wings confirmed officially until his first day DL, so it is a big deal for lots of reasons. My first DLs were on board HMS *Eagle* on its farewell tour before being decommissioned. However, being a 'sprog newbie', I was only allowed to do four (hook up) touch and goes (they still counted as day DLs). That was 2 August 1971. At that point, I had done the required 100 day/night DDLs (dummy deck landings).

Just before my first DLs on HMAS *Melbourne*, I did a further nine night DDLs on 12 August and, on 20 August, eight more by day, before doing two hook-up DLs on *Melbourne* for the first time on 23 August; then I trapped for the first time on 24 August with six DLs and two catapults (so two out of the six were traps, just wanted to make the point there is no distinction between a hook-up or hook-down DL, if the latter is a good one).

My ramp strike did not count as a DL.

At this time of the year, the westerlies (winds) are howling and it is freezing at Nowra. Not a good time for a swim. By 1 September, I had 38 day DLs and 22 cats by day, the minimum experience (later changed to a larger requirement) to go out at night. As I say, the first hook-up touch and go was good enough, so I guess the second (also hook up) was fortunate in that, had the hook been down, I may not have been here to tell you all this. The hook would have tried to rip off some deck plates and then it would have been good night. It is probably obvious lots of good things occurred to help me survive that night, apart from being silly enough to hit the ramp in the first place. Believe me, it was not my intention to do so. Rather than go into details which require lots of explanation, I'll just tell the story as it comes.

My memory of this approach as it started to go bad is pretty much burnt into my brain.

So, if you think this is 'having the daylights frightened out of me', then you are correct.

As the ball (orange ball between line of green datum lights) started to drop rapidly as I was very close to touch down, I could see with my mind's eye that a series of bad events were unfolding. I had started high so had reduced power to get back to the glideslope. This is a pretty average start for a night DL from a carrier-controlled approach (ground-controlled approach from the ship) but, being inexperienced, the juggling then required to get back to the glideslope, etc., is the key.

Meanwhile the deck is moving, which is not always dampened at every point by the gyro-stabilised mirror. The LSO (a fellow A-4 pilot especially trained and experienced) watches the movement of the deck and how it is synchronising with the aircraft's approach. The LSO's judgement overrides all others when the aircraft is in the groove. He grades and debriefs us after our DLs.

On this night, another LSO from the S-2 Tracker squadron was being trained on the A-4 approach. He was very experienced on S-2s and A-4s in the States but had little night experience (with A-4s) here. Not that this is an issue, but I make the point that any one accident is a combination of factors. In this case, I take responsibility 'fully' for not making a better approach, or whatever it would take to keep me away from the ramp, so please don't misconstrue this remark. I also make the point that, most likely, the weather/sea state was marginal for my experience (as a subsequent report stated), but one has to fly to the conditions and make one's own judgements; this is the nature of military flying.

As the ball started to really accelerate down, I was already powering up to a lot of RPM, as I had decided that it was 'a ball of wax' and I was 'out of here'. Usually, on a reasonable approach that requires a bit of power, the LSO will smoothly say 'Power'. Sometimes, when it is urgent, he will start rapidly shouting 'Power, Power, POWER' followed rapidly by 'Wave Off, Wave Off, WAVE OFF' (if necessary), which we have to obey, even it if just a drill (practice wave off) on an otherwise good approach.

I didn't get the 'Power', but I got the 'Wave Off'; this was how desperate my situation had become. Meanwhile, I'm advancing the throttle to full power a microsecond earlier as I have decided for myself that the crap is in the fan. It takes an eternity for the A-4 engine to develop full power (I'm joking), but it depends on the circumstances. Luckily, the engine was accelerating already. Literally as the ball started to drop, (from the deck moon lighting) I could see I was going to go below the level of the deck (this surprised me tremendously). I was determined to make the best wave off I could, to get the maximum out of the optimum angle of attack (this is how we land, at the OAOA) to maximise my survival. This is SOP (standard operating procedure) anyway. But I was not 'spotting the deck' and I was not seeing the deck or the mirror at this stage, after the nose rotated up.

The A-4 had gone slightly below the deck (just my impression, mostly because the deck gave an out of sync pitch up, which happens) but it compounded my problem. If you ever saw or imagine the round down, then it is possible to be climbing out of the hole, so to speak, and be going up before striking the ramp. This is more or less what happened, but the only real witnesses, the LSOs, were not enjoying the show. Quite rightly, they had both hit the safety net off the LSO's station. This was a big loss of face for them and they never let me forget it. Can you imagine jumping off the deck into the black void hoping there was a net below? They knew their safety net was there, but they were unable to see it or the water at night (I was safe and warm in my A-4). Subsequently, the ship's Safety Equipment sailor on deck that night confirmed the out-of-sync pitch up.

Of course, there was an almighty bump as the wheels hit the deck and the undercarriage flexed so much the inner brakes gouged the steel deck before the undercarriage broke. I was going up at the time, if I had still been going down it would have been all over. Thank goodness for relative motion, etc.

The cockpit lit up with just about every warning light except the fire warning light, otherwise I would have ejected. Anyway, I was concentrating on doing my best optimum angle of attack climb out and checking things out. The ship was frazzled enough to direct me 'east' to Nowra from 'Mother', but I was heading west no matter what anyone said. The air controller had just been in the west off Perth, so it was their habit to go east to land there.

I had minimum fuel, but there was enough to fly at slow speed to Nowra. Another A-4 was airborne to take my slot for his own DLs. It was our Senior Pilot, Lieutenant Barrie Daly, who had a look at the dangling undercarriage and suggested I keep it down. This is SOP, along with carrying the empty drop tanks to use as an emergency undercarriage in such damaged landings. I had thought about this and read about similar landings in our flight safety literature, so catching the wire just past the threshold on Runway 26 back at Nowra was not a problem. There was no time for foaming the runway and, as I arrested (with a much longer pull out of the wire, as that is the nature of the wire at a Naval Air Station), the scariest moment for me occurred. The drop tanks still had fuel vapour in them, which, from the outside, caused a spectacular 'WHOOSH' of ignition and a brief tail of flames (remember this is night, fireworks time) which I saw as a bloody catastrophe in the mirrors and the bright reflections around me. The throttle was put to 'OFF' and I was out of that cockpit (without needing the customary A-4 ladder because I was on the ground already) running to the edge of the runway. Phew. Spectators said they had never seen anyone run so fast. I agree.

Later, I heard what this event looked like from those on the ship. They said the shower of sparks was amazing, as steel met steel. I was lucky also that the undercarriage leg stubs did not catch a wire; that would have been catastrophic. So, I was airborne again before reaching the No 1 wire. You can see on the photo (see page 57) how the black tyre marks start/stop and the gouges of the brake mechanism (inside the wheel) on the steel deck begin (before everything broke). I was told that paint marks from the drop tank fins were on the deck but painted over quickly, so I never saw them myself.

Phil Thompson

Skyhawk 885 in the wire at Nowra after Phil Thompson made a night short-field arrest on 1 September 1971. (Phil Thompson)

The tyre and scrape marks the next morning on the 'round down' edge of Melbourne's deck after it was struck by Phil Thompson on the night of 1 September 1971. By that afternoon, the marks were painted over. The Admiral's cabin is directly under the impact point. (Phil Thompson)

Another gear problem

There was another A-4G incident while the ship was in Hawaii, also involving one of the sprogs.

On arrival in the Hawaii Operational Area on 24 October, Sub-Lieutenant John Hamilton and his aircraft were among four A-4s to disembark to Naval Air Station Barbers Point. On 27 October, during an air-to-ground sortie on the Kaho'olawe Range, John's aircraft (887) suffered a malfunction, forcing him to carry out an emergency wheels-up landing at Barbers Point. The aircraft suffered minor damage and was subsequently made airworthy before rejoining the carrier on 17 November.

The malfunction was a worn latch on the undercarriage lever which allowed the undercarriage to extend during the weapon release recovery. Strong as it was, the undercarriage was not stressed to 450 knots and broke, necessitating a slow transit from the range and then a short-

John Hamilton's aircraft after a short-field arrest on its tanks at NAS Barbers Point, Hawaii, on 27 October 1971. The officer in short summer whites is the AEO. (FAAAoA)

field arrest. The foam path was de rigeur at the time, but later experience showed it was not necessary.

John was later awarded an Air Force Cross, partly for his actions in this event, probably helped by the opinion of the air traffic controller who described him as very calm and collected throughout. It is not known if John was required to fly the aircraft when it returned to the ship just prior to leaving the Honolulu area. He remained with VF805 until the air group disembarked in 1973 prior to the ship's refit. On arriving back in J Hangar, he walked across the floor to VC724 to begin a busy life of instructing.

In January 1971, VC724 commenced No 5 Operational Flying School (OFS) with four students. The ground school was held in January, with the flying phase beginning in February. Progress was initially slow due to poor weather, and niggling problems with serviceability, Fleet Requirement Unit demands, and instructor availability. By the end of the first quarter, these problems were mostly overcome and progress was improving, to the point that completion was estimated to be the end of June.

VF805 also suffered serviceability problems but noted the turnaround times from the Avionics Workshop were rapidly improving. Despite this, the squadron managed to conduct air-to-air firing exercises and three live-fire Sidewinder sorties. On 20 February, three EA-6A 'Electric Intruders' arrived from Marine Corps Air Station Iwakuni to conduct training off Jervis Bay. During their stay at Nowra, all their profiles were flown in company with aircraft from VF805, making it a worthwhile learning exercise.

In March, VF805 began armament training, which ran slightly behind schedule due to conflicting requirements. There was a continual effort to progress strike progression and instrument flying practice. Although VC724 reported good Skyhawk serviceability throughout the reporting period, VF805's availability was low. This was because of two hot-end inspections falling due,

This was the flypast as VF805 disembarked from the Melbourne after returning from Rimpac 71. (FAAAoA)

The Nowra flight line in the early 1970s, with Skyhawks in the foreground and Macchi trainers behind them. Skyhawks 872 and 871 were part of the second batch, so the photo was taken after their delivery in August 1971. (Seapower Centre)

and one aircraft grounded for two months with an unserviceable stabiliser trim actuator. On 1 September, there was Thompson's ramp strike. Interestingly, this was in HMAS *Melbourne's* ROP, but not that of HMAS *Albatross*. By 11 September, the air group had completed its workup satisfactorily and embarked prior to sailing for Hawaii.

HMAS *Sydney* had delivered the second purchase of Skyhawks to Jervis Bay in mid-August and, by the end of the month, VC724 had started receiving its new aircraft. As a result, No 6 OFS commenced on 6 July, with the first flying scheduled in early August. The new buy Skyhawks were being processed in the Aircraft Servicing Unit (ASU) and the first aircraft, a TA-4, was issued to VC724, with two A-4s in progress. The rest were maintained in suspended servicing until called forward. After its ramp strike, 885 was under repair with the ASU.

1971 snapshot

The air group embarked on 11 September and disembarked on 7 December.

CO VF805 was Lieutenant Commander Colin Paterson from 20 July 1970 to 5 June 1972. On that date, Lieutenant Commander Bill Callan assumed command.

The pilots were Lieutenants Barrie Daly (Senior Pilot), George Heron (Air Warfare Instructor), Keith Johnson (LSO), Gary Northern (LSO), and Sub-Lieutenants Peter Cox, John Hamilton and Phil Thompson. Lieutenant Dave Gillies was the Aircraft Engineering Officer.

CO VC724 was Lieutenant Commander Grahame King from 21 July 1970 to 21 July 1972. Lieutenant Commander John Park USN was Senior Pilot.

The fleet now stood at 20 aircraft: four TA-4Gs and 16 A-4Gs.

Chapter 7

1972: A VERY BUSY YEAR

The air group and HMAS *Melbourne* had another busy year in 1972. It began with a cruise 'up top' and a return home for a mid-cycle docking. The ship's programme then called for participation in Exercise *Rimpac 72*. It was a year with a lot of sea miles covered, and the very important test of air group composition as the ship closed Darwin on its return to Australia. Flying two extra Skyhawks to Darwin involved three long legs: Nowra to RAAF Edinburgh, then Alice Springs, then Alice Springs to Darwin. It could not be done in one day and relied on Fleet Air Arm self-help in both places. The deployment chronicle that follows is based on *Melbourne's* reports of proceedings (ROP) and a little between-the-lines interpretation.

The carrier was in drydock over the Christmas and New Year period. The dock was flooded on 6 January and, the following morning, the ship made a cold move to the Fitting Out Wharf. The Bailey Bridge was extended to the flight deck and re-storing progressed. After Basin trials were completed on the 13th, the Bailey Bridge and the donkey boiler were removed. On the 17th, the ship moved cold to the No 2 Buoy and AVGAS embarked in a very short period of two hours. At 1630 hours, the carrier slipped its mooring and proceeded to sea.

The fixed-wing component of the carrier air group (CAG) was required to requalify, so a considerable amount of flying was carried out while the ship manoeuvred inside Jervis Bay by day and night. On the Friday, the ship returned to Sydney for the weekend. Monday morning, it proceeded to sea and, during the transit south to Jervis Bay, the CAG – four A-4s, six S-2s and eight Wessex – embarked. Once anchored in Jervis Bay, CAG stores and personnel were transferred by boats from HMAS *Creswell*. Night flying was conducted inside Jervis Bay and, on completion, *Melbourne* sailed for Sydney, securing to No 3 Buoy at 0730 on 25 January.

Ammunitioning began immediately and author Peter Greenfield was detailed to stand in the rain as the barge safety officer.

> My shoes filled with water, my Burberry was sodden and, on completion at 1100, I had to have a long, hot shower to warm up. I did not feel guilty.

The carrier moved cold to the Fitting Out Wharf, to complete last minute storing, before a short overnight. At 1005 the next day, the ship proceeded to sea and turned north.

The speed of advance was only 13 knots and the task force exercised in accordance with the operations order. Two days later, *Melbourne* passed Frederick Reef and the weather changed for the better as the fleet crossed the Coral Sea. The ship was steaming on only the port shaft as the starboard shaft was declutched and trailed to make urgent repairs to B1 and B2 boiler air-supply trunking and a forward machinery space feedwater-pipe leak.

Elsewhere, the stores party spent a week unpacking crates and re-storing to properly locate and restow stores. There was also a serious defect found in the No 2 arrestor unit when a defective wire was found during pre-flight checks. The wire was removed, but the tail was found to be jammed in the below-deck sheaves. The ROP noted 'the requirement for scrupulous execution of pre-flight checks has again been demonstrated.'

HMAS *Melbourne* spent three days alongside at Cubi Point, Subic Bay, The Philippines. During this time, preparations were made for the upcoming Exercise *Sea Hawk* planned for the Subic operations areas. On Sunday 13 February, *Melbourne* proceeded to sea in company with HMAS *Duchess*. With Cubi Point available as a diversion airfield, flight operations were conducted into the night until 0540 the next morning when the ships entered Manila Bay. *Melbourne* anchored off the South Breakwater light at 0800, firing a 21-gun national salute to the Philippines in the process.

After two days of exercise briefings, *Melbourne* and escorts sailed on Wednesday the 16th for the Subic ops areas. This was the exercise workup period during which small evolutions gradually progressed to larger and more complex ones. Flying was conducted routinely, together with gunnery, air defence and anti-submarine exercises. At the completion of the workup period, the ships anchored off Corregidor Island.

After a night at anchor, *Melbourne* waited off Corregidor for the escorts and the high-value ships to exit the bay via the swept channel (mines remaining from the Second World War were still an issue in the region). *Melbourne* provided the aircraft in support of this exit and, for the next three days, Trackers and Wessex conducted 24-hour operations in support of the convoy. A-4s provided continuous combat air patrols in daylight hours and conducted a strike on a surface operations group attempting to attack the convoy. On the morning of the 17th, *Melbourne* entered Manila Bay, anchoring again off the South Breakwater light. This was to facilitate the post-exercise debrief and washup. On the 28th, the carrier weighed anchor and proceeded to Subic Bay where the AVCAT and AVGAS tanks were replenished while berthed at the POL (petrol, oil and lubricants) wharf. On completion, the ship proceeded to sea to transit to Hong Kong.

During the exercise, *Melbourne*'s air group, notes the ROP, 'conducted the most intensive periods of flying since the ship commissioned.' Of note, was the detachment of two Wessex to the destroyer tender HMAS *Stalwart* for close-escort anti-submarine flying. Full use was made of *Stalwart*'s hangar facilities and flight deck.

A pleasant ten days followed in Hong Kong, with a fleet reception and local shore leave for shopping expeditions. It was the largest fleet visit since the UK had reduced its forces east of Suez; the residents of Hong Kong welcomed the visitors with open arms.

A TRANSITEX was conducted on the passage from Hong Kong to Singapore from 10 to 27 March. Flying was conducted with Trackers patrolling ahead and detecting the opposing surface action group. A-4s were launched to strike the ships; it was judged the opposition was defeated. The submarine threat was provided by HMAS *Ovens*, which unfortunately went unserviceable. The proposed Ikara firing was cancelled due to the presence of Soviet AGIs (auxiliary, general intelligence, i.e., a 'spy' ship) and so the transit was continued to the waters of the Malaysian Peninsula.

The threat was provided by Royal Australian Air Force (RAAF) Mirages flying from Singapore, and fast patrol boats of the Royal Malaysian Navy. This was regarded as a workup to Exercise *Genesis*, the inaugural ANZUK exercise to be held after a short stay in Singapore. This exercise was conducted within the Singapore operation areas and deemed to be successful. Royal Air Force Nimrods flew as distant support to the fleet and both they and the S-2s detected the surface threats, which were dealt with by either surface action or a strike by A-4s. The submarine did what all submarines do, conducting several attacks, allegedly, but was never detected. The Mirages, however, managed to strike the fleet on several occasions by use of low-level approaches from overland. The attacks allowed little time for detection and air defence by the Skyhawks.

From Singapore, HMAS *Melbourne* shaped course for Jakarta for the first visit since the Confrontation had ceased. A 'Shopwindow' was organised to precede the visit and the guests were impressed by the firing of HMAS *Duchess*'s main armament, and the flying display conducted by the air group. After a short stay, the fleet departed for a west about transit to Australia through the Indian Ocean.

En route, S-2s flew off to deliver and pick up mail and, as the ship rounded North West Cape, three sorties of A-4s were launched for Army Co-operation exercises. The S-2s proved efficient mailmen, and the A-4s work with the Army was considered beneficial. A 'Shopwindow' was planned for Perth and rehearsed prior to arrival. On the day, 40 guests were embarked by helicopter while the ships lay in Gage Roads. The exercise was conducted to the north-west of Rottnest Island and suitably impressed the guests.

Perth was deemed a very hospitable port; sailors native to Perth were given seasonal long leave, to rejoin the ship in Sydney. On the Open Day, over 9,500 visitors came down to Fremantle to tour the ship. The transit to Melbourne was expected to be rough, but unexpectedly fine weather prevailed. As a result, two days of flight operations were conducted to ensure the aircraft and crews were ready for a planned display in Melbourne.

The meteorologist predicted bad weather for the arrival to Melbourne and so, with great reluctance, the display was cancelled. The ship berthed at Station Pier. The city's lord mayor presented a replica of the city's Armorial Arms to HMAS *Melbourne*; they were to be displayed on the quarterdeck alongside the battle honours. The ship was open to visitors on Sunday 23 April and over 4,900 people took the opportunity to visit their ship.

HMAS *Melbourne* sailed from its namesake city on the 26th and, after rounding Gabo Island in the early morning of the 27th, the air group was flown off to Nowra. At 1330 on that day,

Skyhawks 882 and 888 on the deck of HMAS Melbourne during the visit to the port of Melbourne in April 1972. (John Hopton collection)

the ship came to anchor in Jervis Bay and the CAG stores and personnel were disembarked for Nowra. Sailing at 1730, a quiet night at sea was had before the carrier entered Sydney to berth at the Fitting Out Wharf at 0900. A planned seven-week mid-cycle docking period was commenced.

During the docking period, the port shaft had to be replaced together with associated bearings and bushes. This had an effect on the scheduled assisted-maintenance period, which slipped by approximately a week. Nevertheless, the ship commenced its workup towards a Joint Underwater Control exercise. This, too, was going to be affected by industrial unrest. Three times, AVGAS replenishments were scheduled, but cancelled due to the unavailability of supply. Weather in the East Australian Exercise Area also forced the cancellation of flying planned to re-qualify the air group pilots and caused the ship to return to Sydney early. Advantage of this was taken to progress storing ship.

August began with the ship completing the Joint Underwater Control exercise, operating up to 200 miles out to sea and involving various serials. This included an AVCAT replenishment from HMAS *Supply*. On 3 August, the ship entered Sydney to berth at the Fitting Out Wharf and commence a ten-day self-maintenance period. This was to prepare the ship for a three-and-half-month deployment.

On Tuesday, 15 August, the carrier proceeded to sea to embark six A-4Gs, six S-2Es, and eight Wessex. The ship returned to No 3 Buoy and received a full AVGAS replenishment. On the 16th, ammunition was embarked and then the ship was cold moved to the Fitting Out Wharf. At 1000 on the 17th, the ship and its escorts sailed for Fiji en route to Hawaii and *Rimpac 72*.

En route, flying and operational exercises were carried out east and north of Fiji while waiting for HMAS *Supply* to make the rendezvous.

Of note in the ROP, Captain NE McDonald reported the ship had departed with no 'important' defects remaining. Particular attention had been paid to the cleanliness of the air-conditioning systems; living and working spaces were reported as being very habitable. The air conditioning also benefitted the operation of the ship's radar and displays in the Air Direction Room.

Unfortunately, the boiler-uptake trunking was not repaired successfully and there was still evidence of gas leaks and smoke contamination in the boiler rooms. The most significant defect was a hydraulic pump failure on the catapult that took three hours to repair. Approaching Pearl Harbor, aircraft were flown off to Naval Air Station Barbers Point and the ships were alongside by the end of the month.

Rimpac appeared to go well with reasonable weather allowing plenty of flying. Integrated into the exercise was an Ikara-proving firing for the guided-missile destroyers *Perth* and *Brisbane* with helicopter and fixed-wing support provided by *Melbourne* from just outside the missile range facility's operational area. The final phase was an opposed transit to an opposed entry, with *Melbourne*'s track planned down the east side of Oahu and along the coast to the entry point. A short period of relaxation in Pearl Harbor was allowed as the exercise debrief and washup followed for the command teams.

At 0900 on Thursday 21 September, *Melbourne* and her escorts set sail for Japan. As usual, there were passage exercises, flying, and the required replenishments. Emphasis was placed on lessons learned from the recent *Rimpac*, with shadowing and strike missions flown. Two typhoons were observed in the south-west Pacific during the days of *Rimpac* and, in the early days of the passage, a third was observed to be forming. Fortunately, the fleet was able to revise its passage plan to avoid it.

The only significant defect affecting flight operations was a hydraulic leak from the catapult jigger accumulator block. Hydraulic fluid at 3,000 psi leaked through a welded join; the fire risk necessitated an immediate shutdown of operations. Repairs were completed by ship's staff with great difficulty. The quarterly full-power trial demonstrated that sulphurous funnel gases leaked into both machinery spaces and the 4 Deck area around the fan flats; the gas leak was regarded as 'quite severe'. The carrier-controlled approach radar defect was unable to be diagnosed by ship's staff. However, assistance was provided by USS *Ticonderoga* with better test equipment.

The ship berthed in Yokosuka, Japan, at No 12 Berth at 1030 on 3 October. The task group was under the nominal command of the United Nations, represented by Rear Admiral JH Dick USN. A great deal of planning had gone into the visit and several expeditions were mounted to Yokohama, Tokyo and Hakone. Two groups climbed Mount Fuji and, with proximity to the Post Exchange and sporting facilities, a successful and entertaining visit was enjoyed.

Careful planning was required for the ships to avoid a threatening typhoon on departure for

Okinawa. After a replenishment from HMAS *Supply*, the ships pushed south and arrived off the north-east coast of Luzon in promising fine weather. The opportunity was taken to give flying practice to the pilots, but unfortunately a catapult defect caused the cancellation of night flying.

At 1000 on 15 October, the RAN participants in Exercise *Sea Scorpion* rendezvoused to the west of Corregidor Island. Just as the formation closed up, *Melbourne* suffered a fire in the K1 AC switchboard which affected the main gyro and conning intercoms in particular. The formation was disbanded and *Melbourne* continued to its assigned berth in the Port of Manila.

After the exercise briefing, the ships sailed for the exercise area in the South China Sea and the necessary flying training, combined anti-submarine exercises, air-defence exercises and other planned serials were performed prior to a replenishment from *Supply*. The exercise phase concluded on the 24th with a mini-war progressed towards Manila. During this period, many logistic flights were performed for mail, with an unusually high number of medevacs for appendicitis.

After the delayed formation photograph, the RAN ships proceeded to their assigned berths for the night. The next phase was the transit phase where *Melbourne* followed the minesweeper HMAS *Snipe* down a swept channel to clear Manila Bay. For the next three days until 28 October, the task group followed the transit plan until *Melbourne* detached to replenish AVCAT and AVGAS in Subic Bay. On the 29th, all ships proceeded to assigned berths for the exercise debrief and washup.

At 1700, task group ships weighed and proceeded in company for Singapore, and the ANZUK Exercise *Groundwork* en route. The exercise involved strikes by Republic of Singapore Air Force Hunters and Malaysian and Singaporean fast patrol boats. The task force ships were 'Blue Force' with organic air defence supplied by *Melbourne*.

The exercise completed as the task force approached Horsburgh Light and the Johore Shoals. The opportunity to rest and relax in Singapore was welcome after many miles of steaming and exercising.

Ten days after arrival, HMAS *Melbourne*, in company with *Perth*, sailed for Australia. Shortly after departure, a feedwater problem required the ship to steam on one shaft for three hours, then limited power on both shafts for a further 12 hours. Passing Surabaya, a Tracker was flown off to collect the Command Staff Officer Technical to bring back to the ship for technical liaison. Three days later, with the ship 140 miles from Darwin, four Trackers and two Skyhawks were flown off to Darwin. The aircraft returned with very welcome mail, and two additional Skyhawks. During this time, the ship was subject to strikes from the RAAF Mirage squadron based in Darwin.

The additional A-4s brought the aircraft complement to eight A-4s, six S-2s and eight Wessex. The mix was an operational trial and found to be quite successful. It demonstrated yet again the ability to transit Skyhawks across the continent to join the carrier at sea. The ship continued east across the Gulf of Carpentaria to transit the Barrier Reef down the east coast of Australia. Off Cairns, *Melbourne* transferred northern Queensland natives by helicopter to HMAS *Perth*, and brought southern Queensland natives on board by the same means. *Perth* was detached to land the northern Queenslanders in Townsville and refuel. Unfortunately, *Perth* was not able to rejoin, suffering an engine defect that necessitated a journey direct to Sydney. During the passage south, A-4s and S-2s were flown off to various airfields where they overflew the local cities and then remained overnight, returning to the ship in the morning. *Melbourne* rendezvoused with *Duchess*, anchoring off Mooloolaba to transfer liberty men to the destroyer. *Duchess* then proceeded to Brisbane while *Melbourne* continued south to Sydney.

Customs officers were flown on board from Coffs Harbour and the ship then made passage some 150 miles off the coast while the AVGAS tanks were flushed and cleaned. VF805 and VS816 were flown off to Nowra during the forenoon of the 24th and, at 0800 on the 25th, HS817 (the helicopters) was flown off. The ship entered Sydney at 0900 on 25 November, berthing alongside the Fitting Out Wharf at 1000.

The arrival in Sydney in November brought to a close an exceptionally busy year in which the ship steamed 51,000 miles. The carrier and its company played a leading part in two major international exercises. The major defect was the leaking boiler gases which were personally witnessed by CSO(T).

Ashore, VC724 had progressed its training task. No 6 Operational Flying School graduated on 27 March 1972.

How did those two A-4s get to the carrier off Darwin? Well, it took some help from VC724 and VC851 (the Tracker squadron which also flew a couple of C-47 Dakota transports). Here is how it happened from the maintainers' perspective.

To Darwin

In November 1972, I was part of a small party that went to Darwin from Nowra. Our job was to accompany a couple of Skyhawks on their journey to Darwin where they would fly to the aircraft carrier HMAS *Melbourne* and join it for an exercise. At the end of the exercise, *Melbourne* would then sail to Sydney and the aircraft would fly off to Nowra. We flew in the 'long-nose' C-47, which was a C-47 that had been converted into a flying classroom/navigation trainer for Sea Venom observers and which previously had a Sea Venom radar fitted in its vastly extended nose.

We flew out of Nowra loaded with a big and heavy gas-turbine-powered air-start machine, a GTC-85, which supplied electrical power and air pressure to start Skyhawks. The Skyhawk, being a carrier-borne aircraft with all the services it needed being supplied by the ship, didn't possess a self-start capability. The GTC-85 was fork-lifted in and stowed just inside the cargo door, so the aircraft may have been a bit tail heavy as we had to move about to keep the centre of gravity within limits until enough fuel was burnt off. On Day 1, we flew from Nowra to Broken Hill and overnighted there in a motel.

Day 2 saw us flying on to Alice Springs where, again, we spent the night in a motel. A riotous night was spent eating at 'The Steakhouse', enjoying ourselves as only sailors can.

Day 3 and, after seeing the Skyhawks off, we left for Darwin at an altitude that, temperature wise, you didn't know whether to put on or take off your jumper. When we arrived in Darwin it was 60 degrees C of reflected

VC851's long-nose C-47 Dakota. Originally a trainer for Sea Venom observers, it was also used on communication duties. (David Prest)

heat as we stepped down the couple of steps from the aircraft to the tarmac; we became instant grease balls due to the heat and humidity. We stayed in the RAAF accommodation near a railway line which had a crossing at the end of the hut. At 0300 and 1500 each day, a very long train would clunk/rattle over the joints in the crossing; that clunk/rattle seemed to go on forever. It was also my first experience in a car with air conditioning. One night we caught a taxi into town and, when we arrived and got out into the humidity, we realised we were far cooler in the taxi than out of it.

The trip back to *Albatross* was eventful. We had a bit of engine trouble before leaving Darwin. When we left, we flew to Normanton to refuel before landing at RAAF Base Townsville for the night. After leaving Townsville, we stopped at RAAF Base Amberley near Ipswich (Brisbane) to drop something off and the pilots shut the engines down. During pre-take-off power checks, we had a magneto (distributor) problem preventing the engines from developing full power, so we stayed at Amberley for two days before setting out again. We had to drop something off at RAAF Base Williamtown near Newcastle but didn't stop the engines this time. The aircraft then took us home to Nowra safely. It was a long but interesting detachment.

David Prest

So, we know two Skyhawks went to Darwin to join 'Mother'. We also know the effort involving VS851 and the maintainers to get them there. Now the story from Graham 'Vondo' Winterflood, one of the pilots.

Michael Daveson and David Prest in 1973, and yes, the negative was reversed! (David Prest)

In late 1972, VF805 was working up for a cruise on HMAS *Melbourne* to Far Eastern ports. For some reason known only to the chiefs in Canberra, two Skyhawks and three pilots from the squadron were left behind in Nowra, known as B Flight. The aircraft were 883 and 885, the pilots were Senior Pilot Lieutenant Commander Tom LaMay USN, Jack Mayfield and me.

In November, we received a signal from 'Mother' directing the two A-4s to rejoin the squadron in Darwin. Tom decided that, as his time in Australia was drawing to a close, it would be a good opportunity to see Ayers Rock, even if it was only from the air. Apart from an automatic direction finder, the A-4 was not equipped with any civilian navigation aids [and even that was not much use; there were only two UHF non-directional beacons in Australia, one at Nowra and the other on *Melbourne*], so it was decided to find Alice Springs first, before proceeding to the Rock. With this in mind, the amount of fuel became a problem. The solution was to fly to RAAF Base Edinburgh in Adelaide, refuel, then fly overhead Alice Springs, descend to low level around the Rock and return to Alice Springs.

Logistics that had to be considered included getting an air-start unit to landing fields. Thus, other squadrons such as VC724 and VS851 joined the party as a training exercise. Mike Nordeen, another USN pilot on exchange, flew a Macchi to Alice Springs a week before to organise a restaurant for the influx of Navy personnel. Tom asked me to fly as wingman in the second A-4; Jack had to passenger up in a 'Gooney Bird' (C-47).

B Flight departed HMAS *Albatross* on 14 November 1972 and flew to RAAF Edinburgh. Once refuelled, we set off high level, found Alice Springs, turned south-west, then descended and flew around the Rock for a few laps. Tom always carried a camera in the cockpit, so this is when he took the photo of 883 over the Rock. Tom had flown A-4s in Vietnam and he showed me a photo he took over North Vietnam. He heard an audio warning that a surface-to-air missile radar had locked onto him, so he grabbed his camera, took a photo of the missile coming straight up at him, then carried out a missile break. I was very impressed by his unflappable nature.

Tom briefed all hands that departure would be 0900 next morning, and a good night was had at 'The Steakhouse'. However, Tom quietly whispered to me that we were leaving at 0700. Our ground crew were briefed and we manned the aircraft early next morning. The duty runway was 12 and, as soon as we were airborne, I heard Tom's request in his very American drawl, 'Hey Tower, is it okay if we fly through The Gap?'

I cannot recall the exact response from the tower, but it was a positive one. One can only imagine the shock that woke everyone in town as we passed through the gap from south to north at 400 knots at 7am.

On arrival in Darwin, we stayed at the Koala Motel on the Esplanade. Tom was relaxing by the pool and I went back to the room to get another beer from the minibar when I heard on the radio there had been a hijacking in Alice Springs!

The next morning, I bought a copy of the *Centralian Advocate* newspaper as we had been told a photo of Skyhawks flying over Ayers Rock would be on the front page. It was not to be, however, as the hijack filled the front page with a large portrait of the policeman who had been shot, Constable Paul Sandeman. The Skyhawk photo was on page three.

Skyhawk 883 flying over Ayers Rock on 14 November 1972. (Graham Winterflood)

The following day, when HMAS *Melbourne* was at sea, Tom and I embarked our aircraft after a couple of touch and goes. We were advised there would be no further flying as the ship was making haste back to Sydney. We were surprised on 22 November when, at a morning briefing in the crew room, the Carrier Air Group Commander said to launch all the ship's aircraft for one-hour general flying. When the map of our location was displayed, we were just off Fraser Island, with the flying instructions 'Remain inland of the coast'. I could not believe my luck, as my home was at Maryborough, just inland from Fraser Island! So, within six minutes of being catapulted, I was flying over my home. Our house was a high-set Queenslander and I could see my parents running down the back steps waving a broom. I did not stay in the area for too long, however, as I knew airline traffic used the local aerodrome and we did not have VHF radios.

About an hour after arresting back on board, my name was piped to report to the Communications Radio Room (CRR). I had a dreadful thought I might be in trouble. On reporting to the CRR, I was handed a telegram. It had just two words: 'Tremendous, Dad.'

Postscript: I left the Navy in August 1974 to search for a civilian flying job. The timing was not good, as the price of oil had recently soared. The only position advertised in months was with a charter company, SAATAS in Alice Springs. By this time, I was married and we were expecting a baby. We took the job and, after the baby was born, decided to buy our first house. When the contracts were signed and settlement took place, we discovered the vendor was Paul Sandeman! He survived having been shot with five Winchester 22 bullets but was medically discharged from the force. In a later career move, I flew with Compass Airlines. My captain on one flight was Wally Gowans who had been the first officer of the F27 that was hijacked in Alice Springs. Small world!

Graham Winterflood

1972 snapshot

The air group embarked on 24 January 1972 and disembarked on 24 April. It was back on board on 27 July, but only briefly as it disembarked on August 3, only to return on the 15th. It disembarked again on 24 November.

CO VF805 was Lieutenant Commander Colin Paterson until 5 June, then Lieutenant Commander Bill Callan assumed command until 22 January 1974.

Pilots flying the A-4s were Lieutenants Keith Johnson (Landing Safety Officer, until 30 April 1972), Barrie Daly (Senior Pilot, until 30 April), Peter Cox (until 10 April), John Hamilton (until 30 April), Phil Thompson (until 30 April), George Heron (Air Warfare Instructor, until 30 April), Tom LaMay USN, Chris Olsson (SP), Gary Northern (LSO), Ralph McMillan (AWI), Charlie Rex, Rick Symons, Tom Supple, Graham Winterflood, Jack Mayfield, Tony DerKinderen, Graham Donovan and John Siebert. Lieutenant Dave Gillies was Aircraft Engineering Officer and Lieutenant Ted Wills was Aircraft Electrical Officer.

CO VC724 became Lieutenant Commander Brian Dutch from 21 July 1972.

The Skyhawk fleet remained at 20 aircraft.

Chapter 8

1973: THE FIRST LOSSES

With the rate of flying and the harsh conditions the aircraft operated in while at sea, it was perhaps inevitable, despite the expertise of pilots and maintainers alike, that incidents involving airframe loss would eventually occur. When skill and training averted apparent disaster, reflection was key.

Forty-three years after the event, John 'Boots' Siebert related this story from when he was a student with the Operational Flying School prior to joining VF805. He has offered a good analysis and 'lessons learned' from an event which was no doubt seared into his memory.

HIGH JINKS AND LESSONS LEARNED

Operational Flying Training (OFT) on the A-4G Skyhawk at 724 Squadron saw me, then an acting sub-lieutenant, being introduced to the special 'pleasures' of night high-angle dive bombing. Towards the end of the OFT I was teamed up with two very experienced ex-helicopter pilots, Lieutenants Jack 'Yak Yak' Mayfield and Graham 'Vondo' Winterflood, for our first night-bombing sortie on Beecroft Range.

During the course, we had done quite a few day sorties of 30-degree bombing, and rocketry sorties, as well as low-angle 10-degree strafing and high-drag bombing. As such, joining the weaponry circuit at Beecroft was very familiar to us – running in on the Line of Attack (LOA) of 055 Magnetic at release altitude, about 2,400 feet, and breaking up into the downwind leg, levelling off at the roll-in altitude of 5,200 feet. The circuit was made easy by the geography of Jervis Bay, and the Point Perpendicular lighthouse gave us a very handy cue to achieve the correct roll-in point from base to commence the weaponry dive. The delivery pass required the pilot to set 85% power (to achieve an acceleration that resulted in 450 knots at release), manoeuvre the aircraft to achieve a precise dive angle and aim it into wind such that the gunsight drifted to the precalculated 'sight picture' at the release point. Immediately after release, a 4g wings-level recovery to 20-degrees nose up was the standard drill. The Range Safety Officer (RSO) radioed the 'fall of shot' as we would roll out on the downwind leg.

For debriefing purposes, we had to make some notes on our kneeboard card about the release conditions and the fall of shot, e.g., '11 @ 50 ft … shallow'. It was all a bit basic in the days of fixed gunsights and lack of head-up-display videos! Despite all of this, we gradually gained in accuracy and achieved the required 50-foot criteria to graduate.

During the course, the conflict in Indochina was at its height and we had several US Navy exchange instructors who had served in Vietnam. These instructors flew mainly in the light-attack role. The tactics in Vietnam saw the development of high-angle (45 and 60 degrees) dive attacks in order to avoid ground fire. Exposure to these tactics was incorporated into our training syllabus. The high-angle delivery involved a roll-in altitude of 8,500 feet and a 'pickling' (bomb release) at 4,500 feet. For each dive angle, there was a pre-computed gun-sight depression angle. This Mili-radian (Mils) setting was dialled in manually to the unlit gunsight.

The aim of the OFT was to train a pilot to lead a division of four aircraft in the air defence and attack roles. After the general night-flying brief, Jack (the designated leader) briefed the night 30- and 45-degree night-bombing sortie. I was the deputy leader at number three, and Vondo plus a staff instructor flew the number two and four slots. Six passes at 30 degrees and another six passes at 45 degrees were planned with Mk.76 Practice Bombs from the outboard wing stations. The briefing covered the familiar NATOPS [Naval Air Training and Operating Procedures Standardization] format and the sortie was authorised by our instructor. As we were nearing the end of our course, we all felt quite comfortable with the planned mission.

The weather was quite good as we departed Nowra. We joined up and flew the short distance to Beecroft Range. There was 8/8ths high cloud around 10,000 feet, with generally good visibility below this layer apart from a few rain showers in the distance to the east and south. No moonlight meant it was very black from the north through east to the south-west. The lights of Nowra and Bomaderry, plus the Point Perpendicular light, gave us fairly good visual references to maintain circuit orientation and spacing by wingmen.

Joining the range was uneventful and the first six passes went quite well. As we transitioned to the high-angle pattern, as number three I was just entering downwind at 8,500 feet and 250 knots, tracking south-west. Lead was nearing the roll-in point and transmitted 'Three, confirm Mils … is it x or y?' (my memory fails me on the depression settings.) As the 45-degree setting wasn't generally used, I didn't have it in my immediate memory.

This question from the division leader caused me to do several things. Firstly, as we didn't have kneeboard lights, I turned on the issue 'gooseneck' torch, which was clipped to my chest, so it shone onto the primary instruments. I then detached the torch and focused on the kneepad card and then transmitted the Mil setting to the leader. This all took a few seconds. I switched off the torch and re-clipped it to my survival gear.

Looking at the instrument panel, I was bewildered by the AJB3A 'abba-jabba' all attitude/direction indicator. The top was black instead of the usual sky-blue colour! The Vertical Speed Indicator, airspeed and altitude were indicating normally. Instinctively, I pulled back on the control column and my world changed rapidly! The airspeed increased alarmingly and the altitude indicator started unwinding as the aircraft headed for the ocean somewhere near the Drum and Drum Sticks. My training in Unusual Attitude (UA) recovery immediately kicked in and I rolled rapidly to wings level and pulled about 3g to recover from the dive. To say I was scared would be a big understatement.

The problem with my recovery technique was that my inner 'gyros' were 'toppled' and my sense of balance was totally scrambled. As a consequence, my recovery turned into another UA with a very nose-high decaying airspeed situation. Again, the primary instrument training kicked in and I rolled to 90 degrees of bank and let the nose ease back to the horizon and then I rolled wings level. I was in cloud and heading east at 200 knots with the aircraft finally under proper control. My body was definitely suffering from a severe case of the 'leans' and my mental state was such that there was no way I could return to the bombing exercise. I called up the leader and told him I had a case of vertigo and that I would return to base. I called up Nowra Approach and got radar vectors from Shoalhaven Bight for a ground-controlled approach (GCA) to Nowra. My instrument scan rate during the approach was certainly much faster than usual and I think that was probably the most accurate GCA I had ever flown!

I am now approaching retirement after 43 years in uniform, but this incident has remained quite vivid in my memory. It certainly reinforced the importance of the old adage 'Aviate, Navigate, Communicate' in that order. With the benefit of hindsight, there are a few other learning points from this incident:

- Managing Risk – When the call came from the lead about the Mil settings, I should have taken a moment to think about the ergonomics of taking the torch to the kneeboard, illuminating the knee card followed by stowing the torch. A simple mitigation of the risk to aircraft control would have been increased attitude scan.

- Environment – The mixture of a very dark sky in the eastern sector and some ground feature lighting to the west lured me into a mode of relying more on visual flight cues. The false horizon effect of the conditions that night should have forced me into a more focused instrument scan.

- Task Saturation – The repetitive day weaponry circuit training at Beecroft Range built what I believe to be a false sense of confidence in my ability to conduct the night-bombing serial. The responsibility as deputy leader put unnecessary pressure on me to transmit the Mil setting. With hindsight, we were working very close to the limit in combined visual and instrument conditions in a new, somewhat stressful, high-angle bombing exercise. Youthful overconfidence got the better of me.

- Equipment – The cockpit lighting in the A-4G was woeful by modern standards. The lack of a kneeboard light (or a dedicated aircraft light focused on the kneeboard, like in airliners) was certainly a factor in my failure to maintain wings level downwind. Afterwards, I obtained a lighted kneeboard from a civilian pilot shop; I still use it.

- Training – The instrument flying training I received during pilot training at No 2 Flying Training School, RAAF Pearce, was, in my opinion, of the highest standard. The UA recovery techniques instilled into us definitely saved me that night in March 1972! The nose-down recovery involved a very rapid roll to wings level (the large ailerons on the A-4 can deliver a 720-degree-per-second roll rate) which probably further scrambled my inner-ear balance mechanism. But the recovery got me away from the ocean and the next UA recovery, by comparison, was a much more controlled affair. The training on the pilot's course was, in hindsight, invaluable.

In conclusion, the lessons learned on that night reinforced the 'Aviate, Navigate, Communicate' priority. The importance of including the aircraft attitude in the scan, even when flying in visual conditions, was certainly highlighted with this incident. Distraction can be a killer.

John Siebert

The first and second losses

It was mid-winter 1973 and VF805 was busy working up for its next cruise. Lieutenant Commander 'Sailor' Bill Callan was in charge and had a challenging programme: a series of opposed strikes deep into Royal Australian Air Force (RAAF) airspace, attacking a towed target sled provided by RAAF Williamtown's Marine Section. Opposition was enthusiastically provided by Mirages.

The VF805 Squadron Diary recorded this:

05/06/73, 20 nautical miles east of RAAF Williamtown, New South Wales.

Tuesday was to be a sad day for VF 805. The second in the series of strikes in R550 briefed and took to the air. Shortly after take-off, the escort leader developed undercarriage problems and returned to NAS Nowra. The remainder of the flight – 4 strike and 1 escort – proceeded up the coast to wreak havoc on the 'hard to find' splash target. All went well until the first encounter with the Mirage aircraft.

Strike 2 was detached to act as Escort 2. The ensuing engagement proved a little too much for 873. After breaking off the fight and accelerating, 873 developed loud engine noises. SBLT DERKINDEREN, the pilot, climbed, headed for RAAF Williamtown, transmitted a MAYDAY call, and endeavoured to trouble shoot and remedy the situation. NATOPS emergency procedures failed to rectify the problem. After being advised of flames emitting from his jet pipe by Escort 2, flown by SBLT SIEBERT, SBLT DERKINDEREN decided to eject. The ejection sequence worked as advertised and a wet and cold SBLT was recovered by a RAAF helicopter approximately twenty minutes later.

The end results were:

a.   The RAN one A-4G down on its P.L.

b.   SBLT DERKINDEREN listed as the first pilot to have ejected from an RAN A-4.

c.   The RAAF justly proud of its efficient SAR team.

d.   Both aircrew and maintenance personnel more than happy that all survival equipment worked as advertised.

e.   VF 805 down one bent probe aircraft.

f.   SBLT SIEBERT wishing he had taken along his camera.

In the evening, when the intrepid birdman was returned to Nowra by an HT723 Iroquois and declared fit to sleep in his own bed, a social gathering in the wardroom ensured his early retirement for the evening. All that remained was for the Board of Inquiry to convene and the paper war to start. According to a reliable source, as soon as the weight of paper exceeds the weight of the aircraft lost, the war stops.

Tony DerKinderen's wingman for the day was John Siebert. He provided some additional comments:

> The Hi-Lo-Hi profile was designed to simulate launching from a carrier off the coast of a target country and letting down to low level to avoid radar detection. A coast-in feature with a readily identifiable shape could be seen on the lead's radar. On this one, Port Stephens/The Rocks was that coast-in point.
>
> The route was from NAS Nowra, tracking high level in controlled airspace then let down about 100 miles off Sydney if my memory serves me correctly. We then tracked north and ran in on a westerly track to The Rocks. The strike was a four-ship Navex with bounce from Mirages … utilising the so-called strike progression manoeuvres.
>
> I was next to him when he ejected and I did the briefed NATOPS LoCap procedures, i.e., keep a visual on the survivor and communicate with the team in the HiCap who had longer range comms. The CO ordered me to climb and join the guys at altitude. The Boss went low but DK wondered why an A-4 was circling some miles away from him. We diverted to Nowra when it was clear that SAR was underway.
>
> John Siebert

And some 50 years later, former maintainer Chief Petty Officer ATA Ian Scott commented:

> DK stepped out of 873 off Newcastle due to turbine failure, it apparently shot out through the side of the fuselage. His wingman, SBLT Siebert, warned him of fire, told him to bolt. RAAF picked him up.
>
> Brief Aircraft History
>
> • Delivered to RAN August 1971. Unloaded from HMAS *Sydney* onto RAN Lighter *AWL 304* at Jervis Bay on 11 August, then transported by road to Nowra.
>
> • With VF805 1 June 1972.
>
> • Crashed 5 June 1973, 20-nm east of RAAF Williamtown, NSW, after turbine shroud failure, SBLT Tony DerKinderen ejected over water and was recovered by RAAF helicopter (first ejection from A-4G).
>
> From memory, the root cause of the turbine loss was traced to the oil scavenge or return line at the rear of #6 bearing. For their protection, the three lines were encased in crinkle formed flexible titanium outer tubing, with a filling of what was probably asbestos. Due to vibration, the asbestos wore away allowing the titanium to contact and chafe the stainless-steel oil pipes.
>
> Alert SB (Alert Service Bulletin) for the fleet was to wriggle/slide up the tailpipe, remove the exhaust inner cone (may have also been a cover plate?) and inspect the titanium crinkle formed outer tubing for movement. Any movement found resulted in engine removal and oil piping and protective covering replacement. We did find a few.
>
> Ian Scott

This loss has an uncanny similarity to that of 870 six years later. In discussion with Ian Scott, he pointed out that, although the wreckage was never recovered at the time, SAMR (Superintendent of Aircraft Maintenance and Repair) would have had access to US Navy data and been made aware of the probable reason, and even the Maintenance Alert.

The final say is the following from the VF805 Linebook:

> How 873 bit the dust
> The third of June was a very sad day,
> When up to Willy we went to play,
> 805 were fighting well …
> Till there came a terrible yell,
> "Mayday mayday mayday" Tony cried,

"There is no noise, my engine's died."

Our attack on the Crabs just had to wait,

'Cause we wanted to help our mate,

Then at last he made up his mind,

And I can't think of a word to rhyme,

But Tony used his Escapac rocket,

So 873 went to Davy Jones' locker.

It's a costly way to get a thrill,

And what's worse the Crabs claimed a kill,

Twas a very sad day when 73 died,

But at least D-K is alive.

THE END

Not quite, For D-K

Skyhawk 873 taxiing for the catapult during its relatively brief RAN career between delivery in August 1971 and its loss on 5 June 1973. (FAAAoA)

Throughout the life of VF805, the pilots attempted to provide a formation display team, the *Checkmates*. At first the team consisted of just three pilots but, in 1973, and thereafter, four pilots flew together.

FORMATION CHANGE ON THE RUNWAY!

In 1973, a four-plane A-4G formation team called the *Checkmates* was reconstituted under the leadership of the Commanding Officer of VF805, Lieutenant Commander Bill Callan. The pilots were: Bill Callan (No 1), leader; Peter Cox (No 2), left echelon; Graham Winterflood (No 3), right echelon; and Chris Olsson (No 4), box.

Bill Callan was quite a character, highly respected but in some respects always won an argument or, more correctly, always wanted to win!

The pre-flight briefing included a diamond formation take-off, climb to altitude, loops, barrel rolls and bomb bursts, and a diamond formation approach and landing. From memory, the formation landing was to be the first for the group, with emphasis being on who had control if a landing was to be aborted. For example, if the formation was too low on approach, the man in the box (Olsson) was to call 'Go Round'.

All exercises at altitude were completed successfully, and the flight returned to HMAS *Albatross* for the landing. During the approach to Runway 26, which was noted for downdrafts due to the gully before the threshold, we appeared to be too high. I could sense that power was being reduced by the leader, and in my peripheral vision saw that Chris Olsson's aircraft was getting very close to the tailpipe of the lead.

Suddenly over the radio came the call from Chris, 'GO ROUND!'

The immediate response from the lead was 'TOO LATE' and he continued with the landing. A second or two later, Chris's aircraft touched the ground, and it looked as though Bill's aircraft was going to come down on top of his nose. My A-4 was on the ground by this time, so to avoid the impending collision I applied a quick burst of power and shot ahead of No 1. The CO, on seeing my aircraft dash past him, thought I had a brake failure, and applied some brakes himself. Chris, about to crash into Bill, jammed on right brake which blew a tyre, and he swerved into the space left by my aircraft. Chris, who by then was rapidly gaining on me, swerved to the left and ended up in the leader's position prior to all of us coming to a halt. Number 3, Peter Cox, had managed to retain his position on the left echelon, and Bill was then in the box! I think we all realised we had nearly destroyed four Skyhawks in one go. Hardly anything was said in the subsequent debrief. We knew what had gone wrong.

Graham Winterflood

By November 1973, VF805 was back at sea on a trip up top. Lieutenant Commander Callan was still the CO for a few more weeks. Lieutenant Olsson was Senior Pilot (SP). Barry 'Baz' Evans remembered a day he has never forgotten. It left the Skyhawk fleet at 18 aircraft.

SINK OR SWIM

On 8 November 1973, at 1559 local, an event happened that changed my life forever.

I was embarked on HMAS *Melbourne* and we had been to Hawaii for *Rimpac 73*, transited back to Sydney and then on to Singapore. We were involved in various ADEX sorties involving the RAAF Mirages based in Tengah and it was the third sortie for the day. My aircraft and Murray Smythe's were ranged in Fly 3 differently than was briefed and I ended up taxiing before him instead of after him. As it turned out, this was very significant (Authors: the previous year, on 6 December 1972, Murray Smythe had taken Barry's Macchi for a flypast at HMAS *Creswell*. That Macchi had a Barometric Fuel Control Unit failure downwind at Nowra and Murray ejected). I was loaded on to the cat and all pre-take off checks were performed normally. The Cat Officer gave me the windup, I checked my engine and gave him the salute.

It became apparent IMMEDIATELY that it was a cold shot. From what I was told later, the first 10–12 feet of the cat shot was normal with enough steam pressure to break the hold back (more of what caused the cold shot later). I immediately went for the top [ejection] handle with my right hand – my left hand never left the thrust lever – training in those days taught us that the top handle was the primary handle and I was quite surprised there was no drag and the blind was quite long. I felt the canopy go and then nothing (it has been suggested that, had the seat fired, I would have been out of the envelope, but I would argue otherwise). The aircraft's nose dropped very rapidly and I hit the water not far off the vertical. I was braced for this impact and, while it knocked the wind out of me, it didn't hurt. My head went forward and hit the canopy rail, breaking my helmet and dislodging my oxygen mask. The cockpit filled with water instantaneously and I confess I didn't have the presence of mind to try to find my mask to give me something to breathe.

Having hit the water and survived, I relaxed a little, forgetting there was 20,000+ tons of ship bearing down on me. The impact surprised me A LOT and I confess to panicking for a second or two. The aircraft tumbled what felt like end over end and it went immediately dark. I found myself grabbing for the harness-release handle without success so I told myself to stop panicking, count to ten and then slowly find the handle (Authors: to this day Barry has scars on his left thigh where he clawed his way through his G-suit and flight suit trying to reach the release handle). Counting to ten involved the count of 'one, ten'; I found the back of the seat, ran my hand down it, found the handle and pulled like hell. Now being free from the seat, and rapidly running out of breath, I tried to force myself out of the cockpit. To my horror I found myself stuck with probably the parachute caught somewhere and my knees hitting the canopy bow. I managed to work my way back into the cockpit and remembered the correct way to vacate the cockpit (put your chin on the canopy and then roll forward). As I was doing all this, the unmistakeable sound of the ship's propellers (very loud) went over my head.

I was concerned about ascending too fast (the things you think of when your brain is functioning faster than it ever has in your life) and getting the bends. I later learnt this was not possible, but it is something I thought about. As I was now completely out of air (having held my breath for approximately 90 seconds), I decided I wanted to make sure I surfaced so I inflated my LP2. I recall the water becoming lighter, but I do not remember breaking the surface. I must have come to quite quickly because I immediately looked up and Pedro was hovering right above me (they had positioned themselves over a drop tank that had been dislodged when the ship hit the aircraft).

For reasons never explained to me, the diver never entered the water. The strop was lowered, but not dipped into the water as I expected. It passed over my head three times and I wasn't prepared for it to pass over one more time, so I grabbed it (there is a reason why they dip the thing in the water – believe me, I know). I was winched up to the Wessex where the crewmen and I had a small disagreement. I stress they were only doing their job and I should have known better but the adrenaline was flowing, both mine and theirs. I had a small cut above my right eye and another on my right thumb. I didn't realise this; the blood mixed with saltwater was making it look like I had sustained some serious damage. We put down on spot 6, I was placed into a wire litter and, with the assistance of many, carried to the forward lift. Such was the enthusiasm of the people carrying the litter, I was dropped a number of times before reaching the lift. Many instructions were being passed to me as we reached the lift (mainly DON'T MOVE); as I mentioned, with the mixture of blood and salt water it looked far worse than it appeared. After several 'Down Lift' calls were made, the lift operator made his way over to me and said very apologetically, 'Sorry, Sir, the lift's fucked – you're going to have to walk down.'

Bearing in mind I was soaking wet and still dressed in my flying gear with parachute and seat pack still attached, an effort was made (don't recall by who) to release my gear. When that didn't work, someone produced a knife and was preparing to cut it off me when my saviour in the form of Graham Donovan appeared, removed the guy with the knife, undid the buckle on my harness (can't remember what the harness was called) and said, 'Follow me, Baz.'

I found myself lying on the operating table in the sick bay in just my jocks with about 20 people in the room when the admiral and his entourage walked in. He asked me how I was, suggested I had been incredibly lucky and asked if there was anything I wanted. You could have heard a pin drop when I said that there was – could he arrange a phone patch to my wife back in Brisbane so I could tell her I was okay before she got any conflicting information from the news. He agreed, turned and walked out.

The actual message my wife received from Navy Office and my HF phone patch is the subject of another story.

Epilogue:

I volunteered to be the first cat shot once it was fixed but they decided to launch a Tracker before me – don't know why – but I was the first A-4 to be launched.

The reason for the cold shot was determined to be the failure of an electrical interlock that prevented the cat from being cancelled once the fire button had been pushed. FLYCO had pushed the cancel button moments after the fire button had been pressed when he saw a drop in wind over the deck (we were operating at very low-end speeds and every knot was critical), but this should have had no effect, and the launch should have proceeded as normal albeit with a lower-end speed.

The reason for the seat failure was that part of the seat mechanism, namely a striker plate that was struck by a pin when the handle was pulled, failed to rotate because it was seized. The plate was the interface between the seat and the airframe and when rotated it pulled a sear pin and initiated the rocket motor. The armourers always believed the airframe guys were responsible for servicing it, and vice versa. There were no servicing instructions in any of the manuals. Four of the remaining seven aircraft on board had the same problem.

Barry Evans

1973 snapshot

The air group embarked on 20 August 1973, disembarking on 7 December.

CO VF805 was Bill Callan from 5 June 1972 to 23 January 1974. Lieutenant Commander Grahame King succeeded him.

The squadron's pilots during the year were Lieutenant Commander Tom LaMay USN (SP, posted off on return to Nowra), Lieutenants Ralph McMillan (posted off 13 October), Charlie Rex (posted off 23 October), Rick Symons, Tom Supple (posted off January), Graham Winterflood (posted off October), Jack Mayfield (posted off May), John Siebert, the fortunate Tony DerKinderen (posted off June), Graham Donovan, Murray Smythe, Chris Olsson (SP, posted off January 1974), Peter Cox (Landing Safety Officer, posted off June 1974), and Sub-Lieutenants Jerry Clark, John McCauley and the incredibly lucky Barry Evans.

CO VC724 was Lieutenant Commander Brian Dutch until 22 October. Lieutenant Commander Alan Hickling was SP.

Ten per cent of the fleet was lost in 1973. At the start of 1974, it stood at 18 aircraft: four TA-4Gs and 14 A-4Gs.

Skyhawk 889 which was lost on 8 November 1973 after a failed catapult launch. The shuttle is just behind the nosewheel, with the bridle being the two taut wires leading from it to the catapult hooks in the mainwheel wells. The holdback is the taut wire under the flaps at left, with the holdback restraint the two loose cables under it. The Flight Deck Officer is waving his green flag in his right hand. (FAAAoA)

Skyhawks 888 and 889 in flight, seen with a red and white chequered pattern decorating the rudder, the first appearance of which probably coincided with the (re)establishment of the Checkmates display team in 1973. Both the Checkmates team and the red and white chequered marking originated from the VF805 Sea Venom era in the early 1960s. (Seapower Centre)

Chapter 9

1974: TRAGEDY

The first few months of 1974 passed relatively pleasantly for the crew of *Melbourne*, with a trip across the Pacific. However, it would prove a bad year for both squadrons, with industrial unrest affecting fuel supplies, a tragic accident, more industrial unrest affecting the dockyard, and, lastly, a major catapult failure while the air group was embarked, disrupting the flying plan. Budget cuts also affected flying and, to cap it all off, a national disaster required the implementation of Operation *Navy Help Darwin* in December.

HMAS *Melbourne* came out of refit in late January 1974 and spent February and March conveying freight and 120 Army personnel to Pearl Harbor. The ship sailed on to San Diego to deliver historic relics from the Second World War to the Admiral Nimitz Museum. Passage was then made to San Francisco where the carrier embarked new CH-47 Chinook and Iroquois helicopters for the Royal Australian Air Force (RAAF). The ship returned to Australia via Pearl Harbor where the Army personnel were re-embarked for the passage home. The ship berthed at Bretts Wharf in Brisbane at 1200 on 17 March. The aircraft, stores and personnel were disembarked over the next two days.

The ship sailed at 1630 on 1 April and, at 0900 the next day, two A-4Gs arrived from RAAF Amberley to conduct ELWO-2 VCD checks.[1] On completion, the aircraft departed for Nowra. The ship continued to Sydney, arriving on 3 April to enter a scheduled maintenance period. Army vehicles freighted from America (M113 APCs) were offloaded and aviation fuels, in particular AVCAT, were offloaded into fuel bowsers from HMAS *Albatross* to alleviate critical fuel shortages at the naval air station. The ship sailed again on Monday 22 April to begin a workup period.

Meanwhile, at *Albatross*, work focused on second-line squadron training and preparing the carrier air group squadrons to embark in May. The flying programme was hampered by industrial action which kept fuel supplies very short. In the East Australia Exercise Area, two exercises were to be held, both requiring air support. The first of these was *Southern Cross*, held in late January, where ships of the TNI-AL (Indonesian Navy) exercised with units of the Australian fleet. The second was *JUC 92* from 18 February. Additionally, the Army requested aviation support for its annual Firepower Demonstration at Puckapunyal, gun-layer training for anti-aircraft units, and Special Air Service Regiment training activities. Flying tasks were prioritised due to the shortage of AVCAT; VC724 aircraft based in RAAF East Sale were to carry out tasking and training supported by an A-4G fitted with a Buddy Store for aerial refuelling (ARF).

---

[1] ELWO-2 was the big air-surveillance radar antenna that was on the top of *Melbourne's* island. It was Dutch so the acronym is in Dutch as well. The VCD was the vertical coverage lobe diagram. It was resurveyed every time the ship came out of refit.

Administratively, VC724's aircraft establishment was increased to seven Macchis, three TA-4Gs and four A-4Gs, with one of each type considered to be in maintenance. VF805's establishment was increased from six to eight aircraft although, with one aircraft in deep maintenance with Qantas and another in squadron-level maintenance, it was not fully affected. ARF sorties from RAAF East Sale were used to assist in essential flying training for the workup and, towards the end of the period, five aircraft were detached to RAAF Amberley to achieve some degree of operational training. The prediction was that the squadron would not achieve full use of its annual flight hours allowance, nor its practice weapons allowance.

In February, David Prest was posted to *Melbourne*'s Aircraft Engineering Department (AED). He wrote this piece about what was actually a hard ship to live on.

My Life at Sea

Living

I drafted on board *Melbourne* shortly before Christmas 1973 and remained aboard until just before Christmas 1974. On 11 February, we sailed to the USA to pick up Chinook helicopters from San Francisco for No 12 Squadron RAAF. On the way there, we dropped off a company of Australian Army soldiers in Hawaii. Our trip to the USA and back took us until 3 April.

We, the newly arrived, were indoctrinated by our 'sea daddy' who told us what to do and what not to do, i.e., don't arrive back on board drunk, don't wake people up, don't present people with cold pizzas bought up the street, don't offer booze smuggled on board to freshly woken up people, don't create havoc, etc., etc. Within a few days of us being in the mess, he ably demonstrated what he had told us not to do.

The fold up bunks of a typical mess deck. (David Prest)

The mess was reasonably quiet and cohesive and in 12 months I only saw one very brief blow up between two blokes; I can't even remember what it was for. The ship had plenty of places where you could get away to find a bit of peace and quiet.

Going to Action Stations meant, if you were heading up to your station, you went up on one side of the ship and, if going down to your station, you went down on the other side to prevent clashing on the ladders when travelling between the decks.

Home sweet home. I was three high and three back, near where the sailor with the white shirt is in the photo above. This photo is not of my bunk but very similar to it. We had about this much space between the nine of us. In one of the other messes, they were 'lucky' enough to have the catapult track running through their mess so, every time an aircraft was fired off, not only was it noisy, but down came the asbestos dust from the asbestos insulation. We all breathed in, and lived in, asbestos dust on the ship. An admiral (Rear Admiral Sir David Martin) ended up dying from the asbestos he breathed in while on *Melbourne*.

Going to the heads presented some problems if we were at sea in a bit of a blow. The heads drained straight overboard with the overboard drain having a flapper valve on its end. In a bit of a sea, the flapper valve was always slow to shut so you had to keep your knees together because, when the ship bit into the wave, a blast of wet air would come back up the tube and up between your legs; not very nice.

We weren't allowed to eat meals in the cafeteria on 2 Deck in overalls, so I used to sit outside in the forecastle on a bollard eating my meal (usually in a breeze which cooled the gravy somewhat), watching the sun rise or set and the flying fish flying down the waves. Just magic as the ship gently rose and dipped.

Of course, the ship was never quiet, with people going about their duties all day and night. One night, the fire and flood sentry doing his rounds decided to have a punch at the speed ball, the basketball-size boxing ball hanging from the deckhead, and bounced around like Muhammad Ali, the boxer. The speed ball was one deck up, i.e., on 2 Deck, directly above our mess. That woke some of us up with one bloke getting up to sort him out. Lying in bed you could imagine the 'boxing supervisor' going about his duty, e.g., five seconds to the mess door, door opens, five seconds to the ladder between 3 and 2 Deck, climb ladder for ten seconds, turn corner and boxing practise stops.

A reading of the 'would be' boxer's horoscope takes a few seconds then the reverse happens, walk to the ladder, down the ladder, walk to the mess door and door opens. It's called situational awareness as you needed to know where you were, to get out of the ship if it all turned pear shaped.

We were allowed a beer issue of one can, per man, per day, 'perhaps'. The cans were the big Fosters or KB beers and were probably about the 500-ml size, with the standard beer can about 375 ml. Of course, the 'perhaps' was applicable if there was night flying, during which there would be no beer issue. The big cans cost 20 cents, based on a distant memory.

Dining

Dining at sea (not quite a silver service) in the petty officers' cafeteria, 2C Port, was always interesting, particularly when at Flying Stations. That meant lots of activity on the deck right above you as the deck head was also the flightdeck, or 1 Deck. You see, the cafeteria had the catapult running through it so, therefore, you were the next best thing to being on the flightdeck while flying was taking place.

As you are eating away, you can hear the activity as the aircraft is prepared for the launch and you can picture the flightdeck activities in your mind. The first thing is that the aircraft taxies up to the catapult; you can hear the engine roar. Then the noise drops as the aircraft now is up against the wheel chocks. About this time, you can hear the catapult shuttle come from its position up in the bow to just in front of the aircraft. All is relatively quiet as the flightdeck team hook the catapult bridle up to the aircraft and the shuttle – the ship and the aircraft are now one. All the while you are eating away with one ear cocked, waiting.

The next thing you hear is the jet engine or piston engines roaring. By this time, you have your fingers firmly jammed in your ears trying to drown out the sound directly above you. Once the noise subsides, you can then resume eating and listening for the next launch to happen.

While lunch and dinner usually were reasonable meals, breakfast could be a bit dodgy if you were only having cereal. You see, the milk would be brought out frozen and was placed in a container to defrost some hours before breakfast, while the container sat in the open air. By day 1, the first lot of milk was generally watery cream. The second day, it had defrosted enough to be milk and, by day three, there was just a little bit of scum on the top, but it was still okay. Day four, a bit too much scum on the top, with an off taste, so a hot breakfast was to be had.

Working

I worked down the aft end of the ship in 3R Port AED workshop. It was roughly above the ship's propellers so therefore reasonably stable in a blow. It was equipped to undertake small mechanical tasks and engine oil analysis to test for metal in aircraft engine oils. It had electrical and gas welding equipment, an anvil, a lathe, a metal grinder, etc., etc. The workshop was opposite the Officers' Galley and the chefs would give us their broken cooking equipment to fix. When finished, they would feed us cakes, etc.

One day, shortly after I came on board, a chef asked me to fix his trumpet. The joints were broken and required silver soldering to put it back together. I spent a day doing that and the chef was most grateful. His mess mates on the other hand were not exactly happy with that and appeared en masse at the door of my workshop the next morning. It appeared they had 'an agreement' with my predecessor ('Smiley' Lisle) not to fix it as the chef, with a beer or two under his belt, would play the trumpet in the mess, much to his mess mates' disgust. Of course, I didn't know about this agreement and, when I mentioned it to Smiley, he said, 'I knew that I had to mention something to you but forgot.'

VISITING

The exchange rate in 1974 was $100 Australian for $150 US, i.e., one Australian dollar was worth $1.50 US.

While in Long Beach, the good folk there invited the crew to their homes to provide us with some comforts of home and entertain us. Some of the crew were 'lucky enough' to sit and drink coffee while making small talk for hours. However, one of the mess members (the dental hygienist) and I were 'unlucky enough' to spend time at the home of a bloke who had had a really, really great time in Brisbane during the Second World War. We had to endure drinking copious quantities of beer and food and ended up having a riotous time before he drove us back to the ship. To this day I'm not sure if he made it back as he was 'a tad affected.'

I was on duty one day in San Diego and was witness to an interesting sight. A Second World War veteran, complete with the typical multi-badged forage cap, came up to the ship and wanted to talk to the captain. He was most insistent, so the officer of the watch, after talking to the boss, accompanied him in to see the captain. Some time passed and the captain appeared with the veteran, shook his hand after which the veteran saluted and left the ship. Apparently, the veteran, while in Australia during the war, had done something he was not proud of (nobody but the captain knew what it was) and needed to confess and get it off his chest.

We tied up at Alameda Naval Air Station on Tuesday morning and left on Saturday to go back to Hawaii. I wanted to have a look at Alameda but was only able to after secure/end of the day. I had a walk around and ended up having a beer with some US Navy sailors. At some stage, a black sailor walked past and one of the sailors let out a yell, and I'm sure the black sailor turned white. 'What was that he yelled out?', I asked. Came the reply: 'That's a Rebel Yell.' Colour discrimination was alive and well in the US Navy in 1974.

Standing on our flightdeck, we could look into the hangar deck of *Coral Sea*, such was the size difference [and *Ranger* was bigger again!]. We are all lined up on the flightdeck, called Procedure Alpha, which afforded you a great, but cool and windy view of passing under the Golden Gate Bridge, passing Alcatraz, along the harbour and into Alameda. A great view when entering or leaving a harbour for the first time.

RETURNING

We had a Melbourne Cup day on *Melbourne* with two dice being thrown; one for the horse and the second for the number of squares it moved forward. The sailors were running to place a bet.

HMAS Melbourne approaching her berth at NAS Alameda, across from San Francisco. The aircraft carrier on the left is USS Ranger, and on the right is USS Coral Sea. (David Prest)

Melbourne Cup Day 1974 on Melbourne, with RAAF Chinooks at the end of the flight deck. The rectangular thing under the tarpaulin is an aircraft tow motor derived from mining equipment. (David Prest)

A dozen RAAF Chinooks for 12 Squadron had been loaded in San Francisco. They were enclosed in their vinyl dry bags to keep the salt air off them to prevent external corrosion on the trip to Australia. They didn't work too well in the constant wind over the deck and in the heat. The aircraft were internally fitted with dehumidifiers to help keep the moisture out. The remainder of the Chinooks were in the hangar together with a large number of M113 Armoured Personnel Carriers for the Army.

Melbourne was no luxury liner and it burnt Furnace Fuel Oil (FFO), a heavy oil just short of tar consistency, to propel it. The FFO had to be heated to make it fluid enough to be burnt and, when it burnt, it produced a sulphur smell. While the ship was heading into the wind that was okay, but if there was no wind or a following wind, then the smoke hung around, made your eyes water and you could taste it in the air. Years later, due to the difficulty of getting FFO for ships, *Melbourne* was converted to burn ship's diesel (which is different to automotive diesel).

David Prest

The air group embarked on 13 May. VC724 aircraft and pilots reinforced VF805, with ten A-4Gs embarked for Exercise *Kangaroo 1*. The pilots were engaged in close air support, maritime strike, and air defence against F-111 strikes. They felt they had successfully achieved the air aims of the exercise. The report of proceedings (ROP) merely noted the A-4 strikes proved the flexibility, time on task and overall effectiveness of the aircraft in the close-support role.

However, there was a tragedy during the workup. On 19 May, a combined church service was held as an FAA Commemorative Service. The opportunity was taken to use it as a memorial service for Lieutenant Ralph McMillan who was killed in a flying accident on 16 May. Monsignor

F Lyons and the Venerable Archdeacon W Wheeldon officiated; the cinema was packed out for the occasion. VF805 pilots attended both the memorial service held on HMAS *Melbourne* and the service held at HMAS *Albatross*.

The Tragedy

At 1055 on 16 May, a Skyhawk was reported to have crashed into the sea during a strike on ships at sea. The aircraft, TA-4G 879 from VC724, was flown by Lieutenant Ralph McMillan. He was leading an A-4G (876) being flown by Lieutenant Jack Mayfield.

The aircraft were engaged in a fleet requirements sortie briefed and correctly authorised for a strike on HMAS *Melbourne* and escorts. They were opposed by two A-4Gs from *Melbourne* flown by Lieutenants David Ramsay and David Collingridge, assigned separate combat air patrol (CAP) stations, probably adjacent to, and either side of, the designated threat axis. At the time, Ramsay was vectored on the intercept, with Collingridge brought on scene to assist. Ramsay sighted the inbound strike aircraft and executed an attack in which he considered he had stabilised astern long enough to fire a missile, and, therefore, they were shot down, and pulled off high to return to CAP station.

When he looked back, he saw signs of an impact on the water, but could not sight either aircraft. Collingridge had also seen the strike but from further away and lost contact while manoeuvring. Mayfield came up on Guard asking where his playmate was and stating that he thought an aircraft was in the water. This was heard by Tracker 843 nearby. The crew asked if they could help locate the crash and asked the Skyhawks to stay above 5,000 feet. They reported they were on top of the crash site at 1055 and that they could see wreckage and an oil slick.

The accident investigation was extensive; the Accident Investigation Board wrote a long and detailed report (which can be found on the Fleet Air Arm Association of Australia website) that sparked much debate between concerned senior officers. From today's perspective, looking back to May 1974, all that can really be said is that 879 hit the water. How and why, with no real witnesses, are questions that can never be answered.

The impact on the Skyhawk community (both VC724 and VF805) was very real. Ralph had been a VF805 plank owner and he was well known and respected among the pilots and maintainers. He was a respected fighter pilot who was good at his job, with a level of knowledge and self-assuredness gained from experience. The fact his memorial services on HMAS *Melbourne* and HMAS *Albatross* were so well attended bears that out. Note: refer to Chapter 22 where Ralph's friend and fellow air warfare instructor (AWI) pays his respects.

TURANA FIRING AND OUR RESPONSE

At the time, HMAS *Melbourne* had put to sea with HMAS *Swan* in company. I was on the latter for watchkeeping duties. Although we closed up on *Melbourne* for RESDES [plane guard] duties each evening, during the day we were released to an area off the Jervis Bay Missile Range to conduct Turana [target drone] trials. On the 16th, I had the Forenoon watch as officer of the watch. It was an interesting morning as we had several senior officers from Navy Office, with foreign naval officers of equal standing, up on the 01 Deck aft of the boats, in a good position to watch the launch of a Turana.

We fired – the red-painted beast roared off the Ikara launcher and did its usual severe pitch up and equally severe pitch down into the sea. The scattering of pieces was spectacular as it crashed just yards off the ship's side, accompanied by the sound of the collision alarm. I stopped engines and the divers went into the sea to pick up as much as they could find.

The captain returned to the bridge and sat in his chair just as the yeoman at the tactical console yelled, 'Flash Message, Sir.' The captain promptly leapt out of his bridge chair. As the Tactical Operator wrote on his message pad, the yeoman read it aloud, and the captain crisply gave me orders: 'Full ahead, come right course 040.' I repeated them to the helmsman, and then the captain told us why; a Skyhawk had reportedly crashed during a ship attack on HMAS *Melbourne*.

We were 40 miles away and at 30 knots it would take us an hour and 20 minutes to reach the crash site. It was good to know this was a normal response from a fleet unit. As it happened, *Melbourne* was close by and its helicopters rapidly reached the scene. There was very little to recover and we were directed to return to our tasks.

Peter Greenfield

TA-4G 879, which was lost on 16 May 1974, suspended on a crane outside J Hangar. It is suspected that it is being reweighed. (FAAAoA)

The real reason for the crash has been established by research. Pilot reports indicated the angle of attack (attitude of the aircraft as it flies) in 879 was very different from other aircraft when flying at the same speed in formation. Since angle of attack is weight dependent, it was suspected the weight of the aircraft was incorrectly listed. In fact, it was found to be retaining seawater. The aircraft had ditched in its earlier life, been recovered, repaired, and then upgraded and sold to the RAN as a TA-4G, complete with water. It was heavier!

AILERONS MISMATCHED

From my first days on VC724, I was surprised to find most of the A-4s' ailerons having a mismatch with the wing flap profile. Line practice was to even both ailerons' deflection before dispatch. As a more senior petty officer, I approached the C Mech (Chief Mechanician) for permission to remove an aircraft from service for a couple of days to see if I could return the ailerons' rigging to the manual's standard. This was granted and achieved. The plan was then to address the remainder of the squadron's aircraft. One of the last worked on, and arguably one of the best from a rate of roll perspective, was TA-4 878, which sadly crashed shortly after [see Chapter 16].

Ian Scott

SKYHAWK SUPPORT AED

While on *Melbourne* as a member of the ship's AED in 1974, one night the AED Warrant Officer (WO), Doug Eastgate, came into the workshop dragging a very second hand-looking leg from a Skyhawk tow bar. It appeared the aircraft handlers had tried to move a Skyhawk in too tight a circle and had managed to bend one arm of the tow bar against the nose undercarriage. Doug led me down to the Engine Room Workshop where I proceeded to cut out the damaged area and machine a piece of aluminium bar to bridge the gap. My last metal machining effort had been on a lathe in *Nirimba* some eight years before, so I was a little rusty, but it was all coming back to me as I gingerly took small cuts into the bar. Doug, getting a little frustrated at my precise but slow machining of the aluminium bar, pushed me to one side and ripped into the bar, sending swarf all over the place as he machined it with great gusto. I hid behind his back as the metal flew off in all directions, expecting the bar to reach escape velocity, detach itself from the lathe chuck and fling itself into the workshop. After Doug finished the machining, I then bolted the machined piece into the tow bar and Doug went on his merry way back up to the flightdeck, taking the tow bar with him.

AED was also responsible for servicing the aircraft tugs, modified coal mine machinery tugs.

David Prest

This was the cover photo of the AED Directory. The pinup lads are Dave Prest ('What is the black stuff, PO?') and China Lee ('It's oil, Dave'). (David Prest)

Exercise *Kangaroo I* kept the pilots of VF805 very busy. Here is another contribution from Barry Evans.

BAZ THE MECHANIC, 10 JUNE 1974

I believe this event occurred during *Kangaroo I*. 'Dusty' King was the CO and Barry Diamond the Senior Pilot. We were embarked and exercising east of Townsend Island. I have no idea whether we were the Blue Force, the Orange Force or whatever other colour they thought up. The Yanks were involved but they didn't bring a carrier. Opposing us were mainly the RAAF and a couple of our patrol boats. Can't remember where the Kiwis fitted in, but they had a squadron deployed at Amberley.

The weather was far from ideal, so much so the patrol boats were sighted sheltering behind a small island; the sea state was so bad there was no possibility they would venture out to attack our force. Someone convinced the upper echelon that it would be a good idea to launch a flight of four Skyhawks to 'attack' the patrol boats. It was obvious to everyone, except those who thought up the idea, that the whole exercise was fraught with danger. The launch went okay but it was only with very good timing on the part of the cat officer that none of us were launched into the water. We never did find the patrol boats (too many white caps) and returned to the carrier after a brief search.

I was flying as number 3 in the formation so, after a standard break, we set ourselves up for an arrested landing. The weather at this point was about 300 feet solid overcast, the wind blowing in excess of 30 knots with rain, and the ship was pitching well outside our landing limits. It came as no surprise when I heard the first two aircraft get waved off and, as I got into the groove, I could understand why. I actually saw the ship's propellers as it pitched into a wave and then the view changed to a plan view of the ship. The Landing Safety Officer was working overtime and I gather his plan was to allow us to continue if it looked as though we could pass over the deck as it became level. After all of us had two attempts, it was decided we should divert to Amberley; none of us got anywhere near the deck.

As we were joining up to climb through the cloud, I had an electrical failure but even after I had deployed the RAT [ram air turbine, a small wind turbine used to power instruments, etc., if electrical power is lost], I still didn't have a radio. We climbed to around 15,000 feet and continued in loose formation toward Amberley. The lead, via hand signals, ordered me to land last so, when we closed up to descend through the cloud, I was positioned as number 4 in echelon right. The weather at Amberley was similar to the ship's with quite heavy rain and I confess I was surprised when we joined via initial and pitch under a 3–500-foot solid overcast.

From our previous detachments, I was aware the arrestor wire that was there for the F-111s was thicker than ours but there were no restrictions regarding trampling it. I touched down approximately two feet short of the wire (I confess to not actually seeing it in the rain) and, immediately, the righthand main tyre blew. The aircraft swerved uncontrollably to the right and, with full left rudder but without spoilers or nose-wheel steering, I had no way to prevent it from leaving the runway approximately 30 degrees off runway heading. I stop-cocked the engine as I left the runway but was unable to tell anyone of my predicament. I considered ejection, as I was still well within the ejection envelope, but elected not to (hey, it was raining and I didn't want to get wet). I maintained wings level as best I could until the left main gear dug into the mud, causing the aircraft to roll left before coming to an abrupt halt with the nose and the left external fuel tank in the mud.

I sat there for a second or two trying to regroup, put the pins in the ejection seat and decided to wait in the cockpit, out of the rain, for assistance to arrive. I had been sitting there for quite some time when I saw, through the fogged-up canopy, movement outside. I cracked open the canopy to see a firey running toward me, his silver suit half on and ready with his axe to 'rescue me'. He was very disappointed when I stopped him and said all was well.

A sling and the necessary parts soon arrived from the ship via helo, the aircraft lifted, the gear washed off, and then it was towed to the apron. My memory is a little fuzzy as to whether all of us stayed that night (I believe we did), but I was stunned when informed the next day I was to remain, replace the unserviceable generator myself and then rejoin the ship. I was to enlist the assistance of a New Zealand Flight Sergeant from the visiting A-4s.

I had only the flight suit I was wearing when I diverted, and no money. The RAAF were very understanding; I was permitted to go to the bar each night in my flight suit and was never short of a drink. The Flight Sergeant and I spent two very hot days in the forward hell hole and down the intake replacing the Green House, constant-speed drive and the generator, and, at the end of the day, we could account for all our borrowed tools and had no parts left over. I felt bad that I had no way to repay my helper, but he insisted he was happy because I was the one signing off all the work.

I did one quick engine run and, when all worked as advertised, I was advised the ship's position, filed for a low-level navigation trip, thanked everyone for their help and departed. When I raised the gear, I felt it lock up, but the indications still showed three down and locked. Rather than recycle the gear, I asked the tower for a slow flyby (of course they thought I wanted to do a beat up) to confirm the gear was up and locked. Their visual inspection confirmed the gear doors were closed so I elected to continue to the ship.

About 30 minutes out (the trip lasted just over an hour), the engine started hunting, which concerned me quite a lot. I eased up to around 1,500 feet to give me a chance to get out if it quit. The hunting stopped about five minutes prior to arriving at the ship so I kept that piece of information to myself. I then tried to explain that I needed a low flyby with the gear down to confirm it was in fact down. Flyco obviously couldn't put two and two together because they kept asking me what my indications were, I confirmed each time that I had three down and locked but that I had the same indication when it was up and locked. They wouldn't approve the flyby but fortunately Paddles ('Boots', I think) understood, gave me a late wave off and, as I was passing his position, confirmed the gear was down and locked.

Of course, I was ordered straight to the bridge to explain myself to the captain, who had been listening over the radio. He thought it quite humorous that Flyco hadn't grasped the obvious.

I was later informed by the Aircraft Engineering Officer that I had done a brilliant job replacing the generator and that they were still trying to establish why the gear indications were screwed up. He didn't appear a bit concerned when I told him about the engine 'hunting' and probably figured I was going to hear all sorts of noises from the aircraft since I was involved in the repair.

Barry Evans

As noted at the start of this chapter, VF805 had detached to RAAF Amberley due to the AVCAT shortage at home. Looks like the pilots acquired some useful information about the local conditions.

At Nowra, the disruption in the fuel supplies due to industrial unrest led to consideration of ways and means to overcome the issue. The problem was storage capacity, particularly for AVCAT. Only the Trackers consumed AVGAS and the limited tank storage for AVCAT meant daily deliveries of 12,000 gallons of the latter were required. As an interim solution, it was proposed the Army be approached to loan some rubber tanks to increase holdings to 100,000 gallons.

During the second quarter, the Navy introduced budget cuts due to Federal reductions in spending. This resulted in the hours allocation on squadrons being reduced by approximately 40%. On VC724, it meant the entire allocation was reduced to 1,200 hours per year, which would be nearly completely absorbed by fleet requirements tasking. After much thought, and as directed by higher authority, No 9 Operational Flying School was reduced from five students to two. One was already sidelined with a broken leg, so it meant the two most junior pilots were sent to sea for watchkeeping duties. One went to a patrol boat in Darwin and the other to HMAS *Anzac*.

The Skyhawk fleet ran into an engine problem in the third quarter. A problem had arisen in a second-stage turbine air seal of the J52 which resulted in extrusion of the seal. This resulted in urgent discussions between Qantas, Superintendent of Aircraft Maintenance and Repair, and *Albatross*, which resulted in Qantas Engineering being requested to locally design and manufacture special tools to implement modification 'PPC 215'. A reallocation of engines resulted in all aircraft on the squadrons having appropriately modified engines, plus one spare for hot-end inspections. Qantas embarked on a campaign to modify the spares holdings with a promise from the Contracts Branch for funds to regularise payment for the work required.

Additionally, a modification programme on the ejection seats was initiated. Further information arrived describing the availability of the Ballistic Spreader system for earlier opening of the parachutes. Early approval was being sought for incorporation of this modification to improve the function of the Escapac ejection seats.

On 24 October, personnel and stores were embarked on *Melbourne* at Garden Island, having been transported by road. The next day, the ship sailed at 1300 to embark the squadrons for the air group workup. On Saturday 2 November, while at anchor in Jervis Bay, a catapult defect was found, the urgency of which required the ship to return to Sydney on the Sunday. The Marine

Engineering Department worked around the clock on the catapult, while the ship's company paraded for Admiral's Divisions and then Rounds.

The nature of the problem is not revealed in the ROP, but it took until the morning of the 18th to rectify and required removal of large parts by the Fleet Maintenance Party (FMP) to HMAS *Nirimba* for machining. All this work was conducted by ship's staff with assistance in stages from the FMP. Two successful light shots proved the catapult system, but the ship was forced to wait until the dockyard workers returned on the 24th to conduct the required deadload trials. With a successful trial, *Melbourne* proceeded to sea at 1000 on the 25th to conduct flying operations. The squadrons were then flown off on the 27th, with personnel and stores being transported by road on return to Sydney.

The huge effort expended by the Engineering Department, on a job never done before by ship's staff, was given a 'Bravo Zulu' in a signal from Commander Australian Fleet, who was not then embarked. So, everybody could now proceed on much-needed seasonal leave but, unfortunately, Cyclone *Tracy* decided to visit Darwin on Christmas Day.

Operation *Navy Help Darwin* was launched in the afternoon of 25 December, but the huge effort did not involve the Skyhawks of VF805 and VC724.

Skyhawk 884 launching, showing the new VF805 chequered marking on the forward fin adopted circa 1975. (Seapower Centre)

1974 snapshot

The carrier air group embarked on 13 May 1974 and disembarked on 18 June. It returned to *Melbourne* on 25 October and, after the major issue with the catapult, disembarked on 27 November.

CO VF805 was Lieutenant Commander Grahame 'Dusty' King from 23 January 1974 to 22 January 1976.

The pilots flying the A-4s during the year were Lieutenant Commander Barry Diamond (Senior Pilot), Lieutenants David Collingridge (AWI, 22 April to 18 June), Peter Clark (posted 18 June), Peter Cox (Landing Safety Officer, posted 18 June), Tony DerKinderen, John Siebert (LSO), Jerry Clark, John McCauley, David Ramsay and Barry Evans. Lieutenant Commander John Jordan was Aircraft Electrical Officer from 7 January 1974 until 28 July 1975 and Lieutenant Jack Lutze was Aircraft Engineering Officer from 15 July until 10 February 1976.

CO VC724 was Lieutenant Commander Alan Hickling from 22 October 1973 until 17 January 1974 when Lieutenant Commander George Heron assumed command.

The Skyhawk fleet now stood at 17: three TA-4Gs and 14 A-4Gs.

Three Skyhawks, a Wessex and a Tracker on the deck of HMAS Melbourne in Jervis Bay, with the naval college, HMAS Creswell, in the background, circa mid-1973. (Seapower Centre)

Chapter 10

1975: *RIMPAC 75*

With January justifiably consumed by the response to Cyclone *Tracy*, the air group and *Melbourne* started working up in early February for their major deployment. Upon returning to Australia in mid-April, the Skyhawks were kept busy with further exercises, training and fleet-support activities. The lack of further seagoing deployments for the year, sadly, did not prevent the loss of another pilot and Skyhawk.

There was promise of a better year for the Skyhawks as 1975 dawned. Lieutenant Commander Grahame 'Dusty' King was still in charge of VF805 and manning had remained stable since his assumption of command.

And a new year

After returning from Operation *Navy Help Darwin*, HMAS *Melbourne* berthed alongside the Fitting Out Wharf at 0900 on 24 January. The ship's interrupted leave programme had to be restored, the interrupted maintenance period meant defects had to be re-prioritised, and the workup programme itself revised. The only fixed date was the commencement of *Rimpac 75*.

Melbourne, despite the worst efforts of the dock workers, managed to get to sea at 1800 on 4 February. The next day, the carrier air group embarked and the routine of the pre-deployment workup established. Flying progressed, with all qualifications being updated until, on the 10th, a Tracker was lost at night during a routine recovery. The aircraft 'boltered' (missed the arresting cable, so took off again at full power) and failed to climb, crashing into the sea off the port bow. The crew was recovered, shaken but unhurt, by the plane guard destroyer. The usual Board of Inquiry ensued.

A replacement aircraft was flown on from *Albatross* early the next morning and, at 1000, the ship secured to No 3 buoy to re-ammunition. On completion, the carrier returned to the Fitting Out Wharf, for a week of exercise briefings, meetings, re-storing, visits by naval staff and so on. It was a busy week alongside as the ship's company drew breath, caught up with the programme and prepared to sail for Exercise *Rimpac 75*.

Meanwhile, VC724 was having its own troubles.

GYRO SWAPPING

At J Hangar, we were having a lot of trouble with the A-4 main gyro units and resupply was quite a problem, so much so we soon learnt not to disturb any units that were working properly. Removing one for robbery action was fraught with danger as they almost always went unserviceable (U/S) when 'transplanted' in another aircraft. The flyboys had their problems too with their disrupted flying programme. The 724 Commanding Officer (CO) called me into his office and told me he wanted to remove a serviceable gyro from a U/S A-4 to service another aircraft. I told him I didn't want to authorise that for the reasons mentioned above; he essentially overrode my objections and directed me to do it. As you can guess, the gyro unit went U/S and we had another hard-down A-4. Judging by the CO's cool manner towards me in the next few days, I felt he believed I had something to do with this. By the time the CO and I parted company, things were reasonably okay to the extent I aero towed one of our Blanik metal trainer gliders with him on board, while my wife Roslyn was able to introduce him to a new experience on motorless flight. I know he enjoyed it immensely. I got on heaps better when the new CO took over prior to my going to 805 with Barry Diamond as CO.

'DONNY' JAMES AND THE UGLY WIFE

Don James was a lovable and funny Aircraft Engineering Officer. He was good for such quips as when a sailor came into his office complaining about no time to go for his evening meal. Don would offer to give him an 'excused meal' chit, which usually broke everyone up and relieved the tension. Don was also 'famous' for his quip to the same CO, who was a Pom/English and often lacking in humour. Anyway, during night flying he walked into the CO's office and said, 'You must have an ugly wife, sir!' The CO was absolutely startled until Don added, 'You are always here at work and your wife never sees you.' The CO saw the compliment and the humour in that. I can't imagine anyone other than Don getting away with that. He was very popular on the squadron and used to conduct a reasonably regular lunchtime jog around the airfield perimeter track. The CO, who used to participate when he could, always addressed Don as 'Donny'. They got on very well together, something that eluded me with that CO.

PEARCE AND THE CHEAP PHONE CALLS

Soon after arriving at Pearce in the C-130 Hercules for the A-4 deployment there, I was led by one of our troops to an airman's mess lobby where they had a green Telecom phone. Some enterprising wag had undone it from the wall in such a way as you could swing it out. Behind the unit was a single power cable with a clip attached. You could unclip the cable, place 20 cents in the machine and then ring STD [long distance] to anywhere in Australia. Even your money was refunded! Reconnect the wire and set the phone up properly and no one was the wiser. Naturally, the phone was very popular with the 805 Squadron maintainers.

John Crawley

FLIGHT LINE

On the Skyhawk flight line, a new fuel pipe was being laid; this involved a trench, about 1.5-metres deep and 0.5-metres wide, which traversed the area between the flight-line administration hut and the flight line. During night flying on 724 Squadron, a petty officer armourer, Barry Skaysbrook, and I were walking out to the line to check on the next dispatch. We were chatting and walking when he suddenly fell silent. I had walked across the narrow board pathway spanning the trench, but he had forgotten about it! I looked around in time to see him climbing out of the trench and muttering advice to himself! He didn't appreciate me having a laugh at his misfortune.

Ian Scott

The ship sailed in company with her escorts at 1000 on Tuesday 18 February for passage to Hawaii. The carrier refuelled in Suva on 24 February, the escorts having been replenished the evening before prior to detaching. At 1920, *Melbourne* departed Suva with the intent of using the Trackers to find the escorts and the A-4s to conduct a strike. However, deteriorating weather curtailed that plan and the escorts rejoined in the evening of the 25th. Passage was resumed to Pearl Harbor. The escorts were replenished during the forenoon of 1 March. *Parramatta* was detached to sail to Pearl Harbor while *Hobart* was retained as RESDES (rescue destroyer, or plane guard).

Two officials arrived via a carrier onboard delivery aircraft on the 2nd to provide an air-traffic-control briefing for the aircrew. On the 3rd, successful A-4 strikes were flown against Kaho'olawe in the forenoon, prior to a replenishment being conducted with USS *Ponchatoula*, in which 2,000 tons of fuel were transferred between 1400 and 1900. With *Parramatta* as RESDES, a final session of night deck-landing practice was flown for the Trackers and, at 0940 the next morning, the ship berthed at M1 and M2 piers in Pearl Harbor.

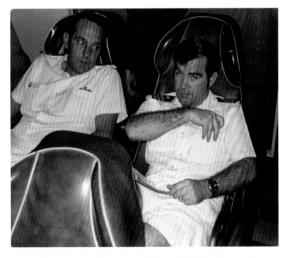

A ready room conference. At left is LCDR Grahame King, CO VF805, with LCDR Barry Diamond, SP VF805. (David Ramsay)

The carrier remained alongside in pre-exercise preparation for *Rimpac 75*. A fleet reception was held on the 7th, followed by a pre-sailing briefing on Monday the 10th. At 1400, *Melbourne* and *Parramatta* sailed for Barking Sands Underwater Range, being joined the next morning by *Hobart*. All Australian units, including the Wessex helicopters and Trackers, launched or dropped torpedoes on the range. All exercise units converged at 2359 to commence Phase Two of *Rimpac 75*. The exercise proceeded satisfactorily with generally good weather for flight operations. The task group returned to Pearl Harbor on the 21st for rest and recreation before sailing for the return passage to Sydney on the 27th.

The plans for the passage were disrupted by Cyclone *Betty*, which was forecast to pass close to the south of the main islands of Fiji. *Melbourne* and *Hobart* berthed in Suva at 0700 on 7 April and commenced refuelling immediately. Late in the forenoon, it became apparent *Betty* had changed course. *Parramatta* sailed from Lautoka while *Melbourne* and *Hobart* initiated a General Recall. *Melbourne* sailed at 1600, with *Hobart* remaining for a further hour to gather up as many as possible of the ships' companies. Both ships sheltered to the east of Viti Levu overnight. The ships returned to Suva Harbour the next morning to recover libertymen and, afterwards, *Hobart* was detached to act as a target for a planned shadowing exercise.

Weather conditions precluded an A-4 strike on *Hobart* on the 8th; it was postponed until the 9th. In the forenoon of the 10th, Customs officials embarked from Coffs Harbour by helicopter. In the afternoon, the fixed-wing aircraft were flown off to Nowra. At 0830 on 11 April, the Wessex of HS817 were flown off for the last time (prior to their replacement as anti-submarine helicopters by the Westland Sea King), and the task force entered Sydney at 0915, *Melbourne* berthing at the Fitting Out Wharf at 1000.

On the training side, four aircraft (a TA-4 and three A-4s) flew from Nowra to Perth in late February. They were supported by a twin-engine HS748 from VC851 and a Royal Australian

Air Force (RAAF) C-130 as four Trackers also deployed to Perth on their way to Broome. The aircraft were deployed to support the Festival of Perth. Personnel of No 9 Petroleum Platoon, 33 Supply Battalion, completed installation of a temporary AVCAT fuel facility.

Skyhawks from VC724 also provided a weapons display at Puckapunyal on 17 March for the Army Staff Course. On the day prior, two Skyhawks, supported by an HS748, deployed to Launceston for a static and aerial display. No 10 Operational Flying School (OFS), with an improved intake of four students, commenced during the first quarter, although the target completion date (mid-year) was most unlikely. Of some concern, three of the last four Skyhawks delivered from progressive aircraft rework at Qantas were found to have loose tools on board. Additionally, the last one delivered from Qantas was found to have defects in the tail area. Superintendent of Aircraft Maintenance and Repair was asked to liaise with Qantas to, firstly, provide maintainers to rectify the omissions on the last Skyhawk and, secondly, to devise a plan to implement some form of tool control.

Back from sea, VF805 supported the 1st Task Force in Exercise *Bounty Rider* at Tianjara from 20 May to 3 June. On the 17th, the squadron deployed to RAAF Amberley for Exercise *Spanish Dollar*. Personnel and equipment were flown to Amberley by C-130. Amazingly, No 10 OFS graduated three pilots on 1 July (see Chapter 19). VF805 was awarded the Collins Trophy (awarded for efficiency and distinction) during the second quarter. Of note, a contract was let to install a High Intensity Lighting System on Runway 21, thus designating it as the primary instrument runway.

Another tragic loss

Sadly, Sub-Lieutenant Malcolm McCoy was killed in a mid-air collision on 17 July between his own aircraft (872) and his leader, CO VF805 Lieutenant Commander Grahame King (870). McCoy was killed instantly and his aircraft reduced to pieces on impact on the Beecroft Range. King's Skyhawk was seriously damaged along its belly, suffering a major fuel leak. He nursed the aircraft back to a short-field arrest on Runway 26 at Nowra. A Board of Inquiry was convened. Subsequently, the damaged aircraft was conveyed on board HMAS *Betano* to Sydney for repair. Squadron aircrew attended a memorial service in Adelaide, and McCoy's parents attended the later funeral at the Base Chapel of St. Nicholas. Sub-Lieutenant McCoy's ashes were laid to rest in the Naval Memorial Cemetery in Nowra.

A quartet of Skyhawks landing in formation in April 1974. Skyhawk 872 on the far right was lost in a mid-air collision on 17 July the following year. (Seapower Centre)

VF805 participated in Exercise *Irish Hussar* over the period 2–8 August. Skyhawks from both VF805 and VC724 deployed to RAAF Pearce over 11–21 August to support Exercise *Wells Fargo*. In the closing remarks of the *Albatross* report on proceedings for the second quarter, there was a strong comment about the lack of spare displacement gyros for the Skyhawks. The overhaul process was variable and the Navy actually had no spares in stock. Concessions locally had been given to allow aircraft to fly with partially serviceable gyros, a situation CO *Albatross* did not like.

From 19 October to the 29th, VF805 deployed to RAAF Williamtown for Exercise *Iron Man*. This was a close air support exercise involving all three services. As *Melbourne* was in a sorely needed refit, VF805 deployed to RNZAF Ohakea to operate in support of Exercise *Tasmanex* from 17 to 29 November. This necessitated a 1,200-mile overwater flight 'across the ditch'. The necessary support for search and rescue, personnel and equipment transport was provided by the RAAF. VC724 also benefited by providing long-range strikes on fleet units and provided support by flying Delmar target sorties in Port Phillip Bay for HMAS *Stuart*. The sorties were flown from Nowra utilising in-flight refuelling.

The A-4s flew in support of Navy Week with flights over Sydney, Adelaide and West Maitland during the week. The West Maitland flypast was in support of the unveiling of a retired de Havilland Sea Venom, restored by the Newcastle Aero Club as a display aircraft. CO *Albatross* noted VC724 had suffered a pilot shortage during the last quarter which was expected to be alleviated by the posting in of recently graduated Macchi pilots from RAAF Pearce (Author Peter Greenfield: that is yours truly and company arriving). A general shortage of aircrew in the middle to senior lieutenant bracket had been noted. This was mainly due to resignations and, although not presenting insurmountable difficulties, some concern was felt at the resulting loss of experience available to the squadrons.

Of course, in a little note, No 2 Air Warfare Instructors Course was progressing satisfactorily. The students were Lieutenants David Ramsay and Barry Evans, posted from VF805 on 7 July, additional to VC724.

In a final note, Nowra's Commanding Officer, Commodore AJ Robertson, acknowledged the list of achievements for the naval air station, not just in the aviation-related facilities, but in on-base accommodation, maintenance facilities and health facilities, off-base housing and, importantly, the relations with the 'Navy' town of Nowra. He also noted, with some pleasure, the operational relationship with the other two Services.

WILLIAMTOWN DETACHMENT

The squadron had arrived at RAAF Williamtown and it struck a few of us that the RAAF Mirages had their radar noses beautifully lined up and that was too good of an opportunity to miss. Armed with a couple of VF805 stencils and red and white spray cans of paint, we adorned around 20 aircraft until we were met at the end of the line by the RAAF Senior Engineering Officer, RAAF Warrant Officer Engineer and a junior ENGO. They inquired as to whether we were finished, to which we responded in the affirmative. We were then invited to return to our flight line! Which we did!

Ian Scott

GUNNERY TARGET TOWING

I had a number of back-seat rides where target towing was the requirement, but one ride sticks in my mind. We flew out of Avalon airport near Geelong to fly in an 'aerial box'; we had to stay within that box. We carried the Delmar target system whose bright red body, with the radar reflective iron spheres inside, was the 'target' for the gunnery range near HMAS *Cerberus*. To fly within the 'aerial box' we had to fly in a tight, right-hand circle and could see the red target immediately off to our right. We could watch the shells bursting around the target and I remember thinking, 'I hope they don't lock onto us instead of the target.'
David Prest

LIQUID OXYGEN SPILL

Historically, the J Hangar LOX Bay had been built on top of an area that had seen lots of piston-engine activity in previous years. The LOX Bay's surface concrete blocks had gaps between them, leading down to the oil-contaminated dirt below. As part of a safety upgrade, the area was made into a bund, including a high simulated speed-bump entry built at the gate.

For the oxygen bay supervisor, replenishment of the LOX storage tank at J Hangar occurred about every 4–6 months. The next refill occurred on a weekend and, as the Duty Salvage Petty Officer was an ex-oxygen bay supervisor, he offered to supervise the Saturday refill. All went well until the CIG LOX truck arrived and drove into the bay. The truck had transfer plumbing that ran under the chassis to transfer connections. As it traversed the new bund provisions, the plumbing impacted the concrete, split, and dumped the LOX load onto the concrete. The attending firies were stumped for action, as were the remainder.

LOX and oil are an explosive combination and do not require an ignition source to cause an explosion. For some reason best known to God, nothing ignited and, in a great silence, the spill eventually stopped. Shortly after, the cracks between the concrete slabs were filled with silicone, and the CIG truck's plumbing repositioned to avoid a recurrence!
Ian Scott

CAN YOU DROWN MAINTAINING AIRCRAFT? PART 1

On 724 SQN, as an Able Seaman in 1975, I was getting into some more complex tasks and had great supervisors showing me the 'ropes'. One day, we had an aircraft in for a bunch of different maintenance tasks and it had parts out everywhere. The tailpipe was out, and my job was to replace an elevator servo assembly (a part of the Aircraft Flight Control System), which was located in the base of the fin and only accessible internally from within the rear fuselage. To get to it, I was lying on my back on blankets in the rear fuselage and working overhead to change the fittings. There was no room to sit upright in the rear fuselage. I had several hydraulic lines undone and they were hanging down just over my head.

At the front of the aircraft, there was a hydraulic power rig attached to the external hydraulic connections so we could pressurise and test the system once everything was connected back up. Some other maintainers were working on other systems up the front and the work progressed over the day.

Sometime after lunch, I was connecting up the elevator unit in the rear fuselage, working in the uncomfortable space with my arms aching from the overhead work. I could hear the usual hangar noises of work in the background and then something caught my attention. I heard the hydraulic power rig start and thought 'No, they wouldn't do that, they know I'm in here.' Soon after, I heard the distinctive noise of the rig valves being operated to supply pressure to the aircraft. I yelled out, 'NO … HEY … I'm in HERE!' as the noise changed and the hydraulic pressure came on. The disconnected hoses were still above my head and I was frantically trying to wrestle and wriggle myself out of the rear fuselage. Too late; the open hoses started spurting hydraulic oil (MIL-H-5606 Red for those interested!) all over me!

I wriggled out of the rear fuselage, now drenched in oil, and ran around the back of the aircraft to the front where an astonished crew were faced with the sight of me, completely soaked and dripping oil in front of them. They quickly shut the rig down and said they were focused on their job and had completely forgotten about me in the back of the aircraft!

After a few choice, NAVY-style words, I headed off to the showers.
Joe Hattley

Can you drown maintaining aircraft? Part 2

One day, in 1975, on 724 Squadron at HMAS *Albatross*, the aircraft had just returned from an early morning sortie; I was working on the flight line with my mate, Steve Hardisty. The aircraft taxied in and shut down, with no reported faults, and we were about to refuel them and get them prepped for the next sortie.

We were getting the fuel hose cart ready, rolling out the hoses to connect the aircraft to the in-ground fuelling point. Steve went to open the fuel valve where the fuel cart hose connected to the underground pipe from the storage tanks. The hose connected into the ground connection and a T-Handle was pulled to activate the valve and allow fuel to flow to the fuel cart and then into the aircraft. Previously, a fuel truck was used to refuel aircraft.

Steve was leaning over to operate the T-Handle and, as he did, the ground connection fitting failed and a geyser of fuel launched into the air like a fountain! Steve was knocked back onto the ground by the jet of fuel which hit him in the head and chest! I ran over and, between the two of us, and while working in a raging fuel storm, we managed to shut off the ground valve and stop the fuel flow. Steve couldn't see because he had fuel in his eyes; we were both soaked, but Steve had taken the brunt of it. We went to the hangar and showered, and Steve was sent to the sick bay for medical attention. I think he ended up with a few days off until his eyes recovered from the onslaught.

We both had red 'fuel tans' from our soaking and our overalls smelt like fuel for ages, even after repeated washing. We found out later the in-ground fitting had fractured. Steve was lucky the top part of the fitting missed him as it headed for orbit. We were both very careful around that ground fitting after that.

Joe Hattley

Bomb Release Trial

The Aircraft Maintenance and Flight Trials Unit needed some video of BDU-33 bombs leaving the multiple-ejector bomb rack, so an aircraft was positioned nose away from the hangar, next to the LOX *The blue BDU-33 practice bomb. (Ian Scott)* Bay fence. Rather than have the bombs fall on the concrete, a piece of foam was sourced and placed under the drop point. Sadly, the foam had been contaminated by jet fuel. On release of the first bomb, a combination of a spark from its steel casing and the fuel contamination in the foam resulted in a handsome fire, right next to the full port 300-gallon fuel tank. A flurry of activity followed and the fire was extinguished by a nearby Petty Officer ATA with a 50-lb CO2 bottle.

Liquid and gaseous oxygen

The Skyhawk pilot, while in flight, breathed pure gaseous oxygen from a LOX converter situated near the speed brakes on the starboard side. An emergency supply of gaseous oxygen, in a U-shaped tube, was in the seat pan under the seat cushion.

This emergency supply could be initiated by the pilot pulling a green loop, the 'green apple', or automatically through seat ejection. As a Petty Officer, I had spent 12 months in charge of the Liquid and Gaseous Oxygen Servicing Workshop. One of my tasks was to service and test the thin-walled emergency oxygen tube, mounted within the seat base, to 1,800 psi. This had to be done slowly as filling it quickly could overheat the thin tube and cause it to rupture/explode.

Once the task had been completed, the cushion top of the seat was installed onto the seat base and the 'green apple' firing lanyard connected to the tube. One day I had an apprentice with me doing work experience. As I manoeuvred the top over the base, the firing lanyard snagged on something and the bottle fired! A loud explosive noise followed by the shriek of escaping gas ensued.

My faithful apprentice did three very fast laps of our little hut and hid under the bench. Snap-decision time, I placed a hand on the bottle: hot and it was going to be thrown out onto the car park; cold and it got to stay! It was cold. After the dust and nerves had settled, I sent the apprentice out for a brew and didn't see him back again!

The orange circle is a hole in the seat base and enables the pressure in the emergency oxygen pressure gauge to be read. Within the base is a survival kit. The ring on the other side manually initiates the supply of oxygen to the pilot. During an ejection, the moving seat initiates the flow of oxygen to the pilot as there is a link between the seat and the aircraft floor.

Ian Scott

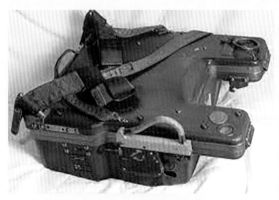

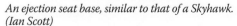

An ejection seat base, similar to that of a Skyhawk.
(Ian Scott)

The underside of the ejection seat base, showing the green u-shaped oxygen canister. (Ian Scott)

1975 snapshot

The air group embarked on HMAS *Melbourne* on 3 February, disembarking more than two months later on 11 April.

CO VF805 remained Lieutenant Commander Grahame 'Dusty' King. His Senior Pilot was Lieutenant Commander Barry Diamond.

Other pilots to fly the A-4s were Lieutenants Tony DerKinderen, John Siebert (Landing Safety Officer, posted 1 May), Dave Ramsay (posted 7 July), Jerry Clark (posted 10 August), John McCauley (posted 29 March 1976), Barry Evans (posted 7 July), Nev French (posted 24 April) and Malcolm McCoy.

CO VC724 was Lieutenant Commander George Heron until 7 July, then Lieutenant Commander Peter C Marshall assumed command. Lieutenant Commander Clive Blennerhassett was Senior Pilot.

The fleet was now 16 Skyhawks: three TA-4Gs and 13 A-4Gs.

Chapter 11

1976: OFS AND VC724

So far most of the writing has been about VF805. However, VC724 operated the TA-4Gs and about four A-4Gs; the number varied according to VF805's airframe requirements. Peter Greenfield's first real exposure to the Skyhawk was on VC724. It began with supporting the Air Warfare Instructor (AWI) course. It was in the trainees' interests to help the AWI students because the latter would probably instruct them in due course. It was 1976 and No 2 AWI course was almost complete. The two pilots for No 11 Operational Flying School (OFS) were marking time, waiting for a third to arrive on the squadron.

THE AWI COURSE REACHES ITS CONCLUSION

The AWI course had two people on it, Dave Ramsay and 'Baz' Evans. They had reached the Strike Progression phase where they had to lead a division of four to a waypoint, and then return to Beecroft Range. Strike Progression was taught on the OFS, but it was taught to a higher level on the AWI course. The OFS did not have to deal with a bounce aircraft except for the final mission, but the AWI course did more missions and had more bouncers.

It also demanded more aircraft and pilots: four A-4s for the strike and whatever aircraft could be found launched to be the bounce. The Senior Pilot (SP), Clive Blennerhassett, solved the problem by borrowing aircraft and pilots from 805 while the bounce was provided by 724 and included Macchis and A-4s. This particular day was a lovely one on the south coast of New South Wales. The strike was to fly south and turn around a hill near Bega before heading north again. The bounce was provided by Joe Hart (our US Navy exchange officer) in an A-4 and me in a Macchi. We taxied separately about five minutes after the strike departed. Joe disappeared south over the sea at low level; I decided the best way to spot the strike coming north was to climb as high as I could.

So, I headed south, climbing steadily and finally topped out at 43,000 feet, well above the condensation layer. I set up a lazy orbit and spotted Joe's aircraft off the coast about 20 miles south of me. On the second orbit, I saw the strike coming northbound and carefully turned so that I rolled out on their heading just behind them. I lowered the nose with a trickle of power on and began falling out of the sky and saw the four aircraft come out from under my nose, but they were not going much faster than I.

I decided to target the right rear aircraft and gently turned onto his tail. It had to be gentle because at my speed there was not enough control left to make it anything but gentle. As I got lower, I was able to introduce some power and keep my overtake, and then, finally, the left side saw me and called a break turn. That was more than I could cope with, so I pitched up and barrel rolled over to threaten the left side of the formation. The formation reacted by reversing so I barrel rolled over to the right side. As I went over the top, I saw Joe down low and going fast like an ambushing shark. At that point I was starting to run out of energy and decided to head for the hills. My last sight of Joe was of his aircraft pitching up through the formation. The debrief was, shall we say, interesting, and monitored by the SAWI (Station Air Warfare Instructor), Peter Clark.

AT LAST, THE OFS

And then this new guy arrived. Smiling, slow-talking Mick Maher, a Midshipman straight from pilots' course and posted to the A-4 OFS. Without delay we launched into the Skyhawk OFS and, just like the Air Force, it began with ground school. Senior maintainers somewhere at the 'tross (I cannot remember where) had a classroom full of training aids, projection screen and blackboards. Knowing the Navy, it was probably the same place where all the troops learnt about their aircraft. In any case, it was done the traditional way with chalk and talk, and question-and-answer sessions. It gave us the required grounding in how it all worked. This was all achieved in a month.

We were issued with the big blue sleeping pill, the NATOPs Part 1 [Naval Air Training and Operating Procedures Standardization], and we set to work. Fitted out with the new torso harness, survival vest, and new A-4 helmet, we were ready to go. In September 1976, the flying started with my first two rides under the calm control of Joe Hart. It took four rides to be ready for a solo, but my logbook tells me I flew in the back of a Macchi as the observer for two test flights for 861 in between those familiarisation flights. The SP, Lieutenant Commander Blennerhassett, took me up for the last fam trip and signed me out for a first solo on type. Everybody told me I would be at 8,000 feet before I caught up enough to raise the gear. Well, they were wrong. I realised I was heading west at 6,000 feet, and turned left and raised the gear, and then I had a fun-filled hour before it was time to land.

The rest of the month was busy with a formation hop, then lots of instrument flying practice, culminating with the instrument rating test with Peter Cox at the end of the month. There was one salutary lesson which stayed with me for the rest of my career. The SP took me on a night Delmar trip. Quite clever really because he killed two birds with one flight. The T-bird had a Delmar pod on the centreline and the SP had a Delmar sortie to complete for the fleet. I sat in the back and got to fly on instruments under 'the bag'. It was a two-hour trip in the dark and on return I flew a TACAN [tactical air navigation system] approach to Runway 03. As we crossed the final approach fix, I set up a rate of descent and smartly arrived at the minima. At that point, the SP took control and told me to come out of the bag. He had the landing light on, and it illuminated the trees flashing past very close beneath us. So, he went around, I closed up the bag, and flew another TACAN. This time I set up a gentle sink rate to arrive at the minima for a visual approach. The SP showed me a constant descent approach long before people talked about it in the commercial world.

(And I hope he reads this. The SP was an excellent trainer, somebody I modelled myself on when I ultimately began training pilots myself. Let somebody make a mistake, do not rant at them, just quietly explain the error, its consequences and suggest a better way; then reinforce it with immediate practice. Thanks, BH!)

Somewhere in this time, the Boss decided to make me the Squadron Staff Officer and the Junior Sailors Divisional Officer. He must have looked at my personnel file and seen I had completed the Small Ships Correspondence and Confidential Books Courses. I was lucky because I had an excellent Regulating Chief who helped me a lot, especially when it came to managing the Permanent Loan List.

The flights continued: formation trips; air refuelling with Joe Hart; a first radar navex; more navexs; a night radar mission, which was spooky because it included terrain avoidance over the Snowy Mountains; and then endless air-to-ground, which I found quite hard despite having already done it in the Macchi. I had a ride with the Boss, who just quietly observed my yanking and banking and honking the airplane around, and then demonstrated a smooth-as-silk circuit from the back, and at the end said, 'It is not aggression you need, Peter, it is assertiveness. You fly the airplane to where you want it.' I understood.

There was one introductory session of FCLP (Field Carrier Landing Practice) and then more armament sorties. On one of those there was another lesson to be learnt. It was low-

A TA-4 about to plug into an A-4 tanker. (FAAAoA)

angle strafing and the danger of target fixation. The delivery pass was at 10 degrees, firing on a target banner strung between two poles. In the back seat was the AWI, fortunately. I set up the pass but fired a little late and kept the dive going wanting to get hits on the banner. I suddenly realised it was closing fast and started pulling, there was an oath from the back, and another pull, and we registered about 6g on the g-meter. The range officer said there was quite a rooster tail of dust as we rotated.

The flights continued but we began to integrate the skills. So, there was night FCLP, night air refuelling, night weaponry including flare dropping, and a series of Strike Progression exercises culminating in a graduation exercise dropping live bombs on a rock in Bass Strait. We voted the youngest member to lead, so he could display his brilliance. The Boss flew the tanker, and the AWI flew as No 4. Peter Cox departed before us and was the range safety officer at the target, and then the bounce on the way home. We met up with the tanker somewhere near Bega. Lead plugged in and took his planned fuel. No 2 had some trouble getting into the drogue and, after several attempts, lead sent him home. No 4 and I had no problem taking our fuel, so the Boss peeled off and we went on to the target. The lead found the northern tip of Flinders Island, our initial point and we hurtled off at 480 knots on our run in to the target. Cox gave us a clearance and we popped and delivered our three Mk.82s each on target. Funnily enough, there was no bounce on the way home.

The next day was our NATOPS Evaluation in which I flew a single and was chased by the AWI. The other two guys had a T-bird each with an evaluator in the back seat. My evaluation ended with a hydraulic disconnect and a manual flight control approach. The instructor made me execute a late go-around, which actually wasn't that hard, but it scared him when I let the aircraft pitch up. The circuit and landing was smooth and it was all over. The OFS took from 1 August 1976 to 27 May 1977. We all repaired to the bar and proceeded to get happily sozzled. It was a joyous occasion and I had achieved my ambition.

I have strayed somewhat into the next year because our OFS actually ran to May the following year, but it was a great time to write about the new pilots learning to use a warplane.

Peter Greenfield

The year progressed relatively normally, revealing the mature regimen that had formed within and around the Skyhawk force. VF805 took part in the multi-national air defence Exercise *Summer Rain* during a three-week detachment to Williamtown from 16 February. VC724 continued a busy period of aircrew training and fleet requirement tasking. Unfortunately, the

TA-4G 881 with two other VC724 Skyhawks showing the yellow and blue chequered squadron marking used in the mid-1970s. (John Hopton collection)

No 2 AWI Course had only completed two-thirds of the syllabus prior to the course's departure to the USA. The four pilots ex-Pearce were undergoing tactical training on Macchis. This would continue until the OFS commenced mid-year.

VC724 provided considerable support to the Army throughout the quarter. A-4s took reconnaissance film in the Mildura area; unfortunately, as the continuous negative processor had not been delivered to the Photographic Section, the reconnaissance value was effectively lost. Macchi aircraft provided support to Redeye operator training in the Tianjara area from 17 May to the 20th. The month before, on 6 April, VF805 provided flares for No 77 Squadron Mirages engaged in night bombing at Beecroft Range, which resulted in some bushfires on the range. VC724 provided flare support at Singleton Range the following week and this was judged most successful.

In late May, No 2 AWI Course returned from the USA and immediately began flying. The course completed at the end of June and No 11 OFS commenced its Ground School phase. During June, both VF805 and VC724 conducted extensive FCLP in preparation for embarkation on *Melbourne*. It was intended to supplement VF805 with four VC724 aircraft and five deck-qualified pilots for the strike phase of *Kangaroo II*.

HMAS *Albatross* had brought forward its winter leave to assist the workup programme of HMAS *Melbourne*. When the programme slipped, the carrier took to warmer climes north of Brisbane to complete its workup. This involved exercises with F-111s from Amberley to coordinate strike operations.

Melbourne sailed for *Kangaroo II* on 11 October. The exercise planning was for a transit phase to a forces integration with USS *Enterprise*'s task force. At that point, the Trackers would be

An armourer's dream. Wall to wall 5-inch Zunis, with BDU-33 bombs in the foreground.
(RNZAF)

flown off to Nowra and VF805 reinforced with four A-4Gs direct from the naval air station. The exercise then took the flavour of close air support of troops ashore, concluding on the 25th with a 'hot washup' completed at anchor off the Keppel Islands. On completion, the ships weighed anchor and proceeded south for Sydney. On the 27th, the four VC724 A-4s were flown off to Nowra, and the S-2Es returned. The ship continued south for a visit to the City of Melbourne, where several dignitaries and prominent businessmen were hosted for a presentation on naval power and then a formal luncheon.

H Hangar fire

The other excitement for the year's activity was the disastrous fire in H Hangar on the night of 4 December. Twelve aircraft were stored in the hangar. Of these, six were totally destroyed, three damaged beyond repair, and three deemed salvageable for further use. It was the last week before the seasonal leave period and all aircraft had been put away for 'safekeeping'. The Wardroom was having its summer party, themed as Hawaiian, with the Senior Sailors Mess having a similar celebration.

Being a geographical bachelor, I had offered to swap duties with the rostered Duty Air Officer so he could take his wife to the party. The Duty Executive Officer (DXO) was a very senior lieutenant who had not a clue about aircraft. When the fire alarm sounded at around 2045, we both went down to the main gate where the Duty Watch was mustering. The Duty Air Petty Officer (DAPO) was also from VC724 and told me the fire was in H Hangar, so I told the DXO I would investigate and telephone him at the Guardhouse.

The DAPO, Petty Officer Toby Edwards, and I proceeded to H Hangar where clearly there was an internal fire. As we got out of the car, there was an almighty explosion, a tongue of flame shot into the air, and large sections of the roof sailed away in showers of sparks. Both of us got such a fright we leapt involuntarily over the fence. Inside that, I told Toby I needed a phone, to which he responded by kicking in the nearest door. There was a phone and I rang the Guardhouse, connected with the DXO, and told him we needed outside fire brigade assistance, and that I would stay by the hangar to direct firefighting.

The two of us went to the south end of the hangar where the doors were really hot. A lone sailor was unrolling a fire hose and connecting it to a fire hydrant. I told Toby to check the doors of J Hangar, and then to empty it of aircraft, using squadron sailors as they came to hand. I then proceeded to enter the hangar via the Judas gate and lift all the locking pins so the doors could be moved. Once I opened the doors about a foot, I could see sailors appearing around the corner, and then cars and gaily dressed officers and senior sailors.

Suffice to say that people started organising themselves as they had been trained, into fire-fighting teams and handling parties. The doors were opened and the first three aircraft moved out. At the same time, J Hangar was rapidly being emptied of aircraft, with them all being parked on the flight line, fortunately upwind of the fire. The Air Operations Officer was manning a tractor and 'the sailor in a brown corduroy jacket' brought up a Tracker tow bar. In what seemed like a short space of time, the first two rows of aircraft were moved clear.

Authors: 'The sailor in the brown corduroy jacket' was subsequently identified as Leading Seaman ATA Ian Carroll and properly awarded a Bravery Medal. He retired many years later as a Warrant Officer with the RAAF.

The XO, Commander Wally Rothwell, had brought his brand-new car down and used it to illuminate the scene. Something exploded and shrapnel went straight through the windscreen and out the back window without harming him. In fact, the only casualty of the night was the sailor who had lit the fire, who, it transpired later, was the one I had seen unrolling the firehose.

The Air Operations Officer and I were called away to the Operations Room about an hour later to handle communications. And somewhere in that, we wrote statements and witnessed each other's aide-memoires. It was a terrible night and a real tragedy, one I cannot forget, but, in true Navy fashion, we just got on with it, and got the job done.

Peter Greenfield

THE TRACKER HANGAR FIRE

On 4 December, while on the way out to *Albatross* to pick up a friend, I noticed a lot of smoke above the base. When I reached the base, climbing a water tower to get a better view, I found out that H Hangar, the Tracker hangar, was on fire. In disbelief, I saw smoke rising from a hole in the hangar roof followed by a white spot on the roof and then an explosion. I drove down towards the fire and, after parking my car, ran up the taxiway in my fire-fighting gear of thongs, jeans and an old Army jacket.

Upon reaching the far end of the burning hangar I started to use a fire hose on the fire, all the time wondering why the hangar sprinklers weren't working. After a short time, the keys sailor for J Hangar, the Skyhawk hangar (beside the burning hangar), arrived to open up. With J Hangar now open, we emptied it of its 24 aircraft in one of the fastest aircraft moves I've seen. Only one aircraft was slightly damaged by the radiant heat from the burning hangar.

At some point, the Nowra Fire Brigade arrived and proceeded to wash off the dry powder from the burning aircraft's magnesium wheels, causing them to burst back into flames (Authors: and they also drove over a hydrant, cutting off the water to the hangar, a tiffy had to isolate it). As the fire subsided, I towed those burnt aircraft, that were capable of being towed, down to the flight line, leaving one gutted wreck inside the hangar. This gutted wreck would occasionally burst back into flames, requiring it to be extinguished yet again.

In spite of getting home about 0430, I was required to be back at the base at 0800 to be fingerprinted as part of the arson investigation. All those employed on the base were fingerprinted as were any visitors who had been to the base in the days preceding the fire.

Ian Scott

This was the last Tracker pulled out. As it crossed the door tracks, it blew up. It kept erupting into flames all night. (Ian Scott)

1976 snapshot

The air group embarked on 4 August and remained on board the carrier until 4 November.

CO VF805 was Lieutenant Commander Barry Diamond from 23 January.

Active pilots for the year were Lieutenant Commander Barrie Daly (SP), and Lieutenants Gerry Pike USN (posted January 1978), Jack Mayfield (AWI, posted 21 October 1977), Tony DerKinderen (posted 26 August), Ian Shepherd (posted 21 October 1977), Andy Sinclair (posted 21 October 1977), Kim Baddams (posted 7 February 1977) and Nev French (Landing Safety Officer).

CO VC724 remained Lieutenant Commander Peter C Marshall, with Lieutenant Commander Clive Blennerhassett as his SP.

Happily, the Skyhawk fleet remained at 16: three TA-4Gs and 13 A-4Gs.

VF805 Skyhawk 874 in the mid-1970s with a drop tank and Sidewinder missile visible under the port wing. (Seapower Centre)

Chapter 12

SUPPORT PEOPLE

The pilots on the two jet squadrons, VF805 and VC724, and all the other squadrons not mentioned in this volume, were supported by a large number of people of wide-ranging specialisations, both as officers and naval airmen. From pilots to air traffic controllers, medical and dental officers and meteorologists, to the chefs and stewards, the stokers driving various vehicles, the aircraft handlers in the fire party, yeomen and communicators working in the comcentre, the met office, and air operations, the writers and storemen in the Supply Department and Base Administration (the latter properly known as the Captain's Office), the armourers working in the bomb dump, the maintainers working in Air Support Unit, and even the range party. All were linked by the Station Broadcast, operated from the air traffic control tower.

For those on the jet squadrons, the most celebrated character was probably the 'Sawbones', 'Doc' Flynn. Peter Greenfield first met him in 1973 while a passenger in a Macchi flown by the doc on a fleet-requirements sortie over Port Phillip Bay. After arrival at Nowra at the end of 1975, he had his first medical with him as an FAA pilot. After much humming and ah-ing as he flicked through the file, Doc said, 'You are chronically underweight' (Author Peter Greenfield: I was 68 kilograms at the time and had been since joining up in 1968). 'I prescribe a steak and a pint at least once a day. Hopefully, when I see you next year, you will have put on some weight.' The next year Peter was 78 kilograms, his collar had gone up three sizes, and the doc was much happier. Mick Flynn contributed the following:

THE FLYING DOCTOR

It has been an instructive exercise, going through my one and only (Navy) logbook. It basically summarises my whole military life, including tropical surgery in Papua New Guinea (Manus Is), Tiananmen Square (1989), Gulf War I, Persian Gulf, East Timor, and the Banda Aceh tsunami (2004). Interspersed with all of these events was my increasing access to aviation assets as a pilot in command, or co-pilot – DC-3s (with Farmer Talbot over the mountains in PNG), Russian helos in Timor, and even Caribous at Pearce. I eventually managed to get 250-plus hours in Hueys, which was a story in itself. During Operation *Morris Dance* (the Fiji coups), I found myself as the only Huey pilot left at Nowra. With an aircrewman course going through, I managed to get 30 hours recorded in one month – not bad seeing I was also the Senior Medical Officer (SMO), seeing outpatients at both ''tross and *Creswell*, while either giving anaesthetics or undertaking surgery. You cannot make this stuff up, and most up and coming medical students and young doctors simply do not believe it; however, my logbook does not lie.

When I first applied for pilot training, it was approved on the basis of me getting my wings (if I could), and then settling back to be a 'good, understanding' flight surgeon who had a feeling about what flying was all about. At the time, there was a glut of Navy aviators (post–Vietnam), and the Navy wanted to keep the training pipeline open, hence I got a tick in the box. I managed to finish second on the course (behind Dave Ramsay), much to the chagrin of the RAAF, as it was their prestigious 'academy' group that went through with us (we recently had our 50-year reunion at Point Cook; most of us have survived, and we are still on friendly terms).

On my return to Nowra, first as JMO, then SMO, my flying credentials became increasingly in demand, as the aviator excess had somehow disappeared. I then sought, and gained approval for, a 'limited' A-4 conversion: enough to go solo and one short-field arrest.

When I did my Flight Surgeons' course in Pensacola (VT10), Florida, my A-4 qualifications were noted and, unlike the others, who were sent solo in the T-28, I was sent to the TA-4J. I was then posted to the experimental fighter squadron, VX4, Point Mugu, as Assistant Flight Surgeon. Apart from six F-14s and ten F-4s, they had two TA-4Js and two S-2A/Bs (basically gutted anti-submarine platforms), used as transports ('gash haulers') up and down the West Coast. I fairly rapidly got NATOPs [Naval Air Training and Operating Procedures Standardization] certified in both. The A-4s were used as 'aggressors' (think *TOP GUN*), and I was able to score many rides in both the front and back seats (also one memorable ride in the back seat of an F-4N (no controls, rather scary).

On return to Nowra, CO 724 looked at my logbook and decided he could use me as a spare pilot in both Macchis and A-4s, particularly at night, or at weekends, when the RAAF chappies were disinclined to fly or, in the case of Army support out to the west of Cobar, were in danger of running out of fuel in their Mirages (I had one back-seat ride in a Mirage and was somewhat alarmed to see how rapidly the fuel gauge was winding down). I later had the satisfaction of barrel rolling an A-4 around a Mirage as he was coming off the range at Beecroft; he was not watching his six.

Without having undertaken a formal Operational Flying School course, I felt somewhat of an outsider; however, as my tasking and performance in the air increased, I somehow 'morphed' into the A-4 community. I never did get to do a night deck landing on the carrier (later, I did this in an F-18 simulator) or fire a Sidewinder. However, I did manage just about everything else. Naturally, it included many memorable occasions, and in-flight 'incidents' that, in hindsight, should have warranted at least a PAN call. However, I had trust in the A-4 and heeded as much advice as I could from senior pilots such as Ralph McMillan, Tony DerKinderen, Peter Marshall, Al Hickling, George Heron and Errol Kavanagh. I was programmed not to reduce the throttle to idle in flight (not <70%), even in air combat manoeuvre (ACM) evolutions, after someone (I do not remember who) had a flameout downwind in the circuit at 26 and had to bang out.

I recall a 2-v-1 mission against an A-4 from either 805, or *Melbourne*, flown, from what I remember, by Jack Mayfield. I was able to vector my No 2 into a perfect 'Fox-1' firing solution. At the debrief, I was questioned about this, as I had never been formally instructed in the art of ACM (horizontal, rolling and vertical scissors), but I had read the theory and it seemed to come to me instinctively.

My most memorable flight was in a TA-4 (881, 23 June 1976), at night on a fleet-requirements 'feet wet' somewhere out over the Tasman. The weather was foul on take-off, IMC [instrument meteorological conditions] at 200 feet and then breakout on top at FL 200 [20,000 feet]. I was then able to sit back and enjoy doing benign race-track circuits under the guidance of an Air Warfare Officer on either *Melbourne* or one of the DDGs, while admiring the spectacular light show in the clouds below. It was a serious storm. I was then advised Nowra was about to close because of the deteriorating weather, and it was suggested I 'come home' (I am paraphrasing this somewhat).

As I was still heavy on fuel (16,000-lbs all-up weight), and reluctant to dump, I elected to do a high TACAN [tactical air navigation system], followed by a ground-controlled approach and then a short-field arrest (SFA) on Runway 21. Again, IMC at FL 200 and not getting visual until a little above minima (200 feet). The runway was seriously wet with blinding rain, and I was 'heavy'. I had not declared any emergency, just that I needed to do an SFA without really explaining the reason to Approach control. The hook and the wire worked perfectly and the fire crew soon disentangled me. On taxiing back to the lines, I was able to appreciate the ferocity of the downpour and was drenched getting back to the crew rooms. My post-flight entry was fairly innocuous, 'mission shortened due wx'. I never did expand on any of this to Caroline at home, just that I had been 'night flying'.

My last flight in an A-4 was in the back seat of an ex-RAN T-bird with the RNZAF (NZ6254) on 31 May 1995 (by now I was an O6 [captain]). The flight out of Nowra was a fleet-requirements support mission and the squadron leader up front clearly knew his stuff. However, being in the back seat, flying at full throttle at 50 feet above sea level (ASL) was scary. I then realised I had undertaken exactly the same mission several years earlier. The brief was to fly under the wing of an S-2E (or G) at FL 120 (they did not have oxygen) and, when directed, drop to 50 feet ASL (not 48 or 52 ft) on RADALT [radar altimeter] at max throttle, following vectors to somewhere over the horizon and a DDG [guided-missile destroyer], while simulating a Russian *Styx* [anti-ship missile]. I remember glancing at the Doppler and seeing 660 knots – somewhat greater than what was in the flight manual – but I then realised we had a 20-knot tail wind, and the bird was probably 'clean'. Pulling up to 200 feet ASL, after passing ahead of the DDG below masthead height, was a relief. Having been the medical officer on board several DEs [destroyer escort/frigate] and DDGs, I was very much aware

LCDR Mike 'Doc' Mike Flynn. (Mike Flynn Collection)

of the usual flock of fairly large birds that would gather at the stern to pick up scraps from the ship, and also of an RNZAF TA-4 driver who lost his eye after a bird hit his canopy. I once again reported home with the usual story of 'just another night fleet support flight'.

You will probably have gathered by now I have somehow been privileged to have experienced many aspects of naval aviation both as a fixed-wing pilot, a rotary wing pilot, a flight surgeon, doing medevacs and, somewhat regrettably, autopsies. Possibly unique.

I ended up with nearly 300 hours in the A-4 (actually 272.2) and I enjoyed every minute.

Commodore Mike Flynn

(Author Peter Greenfield: I can say I always felt comfortable with Doc when it came to medical time. I remember him and BH (Clive Blennerhassett) having a long conversation about weapons profiles, which resulted in Doc riding front seat in a T-bird while an Air Warfare Instructor talked him through the various delivery profiles. Those flights were a win-win because we got Doc to see the profiles and he did not deliver (or ever carry, I believe, any weapons). And then there was his expert testimony at various Boards of Inquiry which has not been mentioned.)

Mark Radisich was the junior Air Traffic Controller (ATCO) at *Albatross* from mid-1976, outranked by the only other midshipman ATCO who was slightly more senior because his name started with a D. Nevertheless, Mark made his impact, becoming fully rated by the end of 1977 and going to sea as a Carrier Control Approach operator with the air group in 1978.

Skyhawk pilots had considerable interface with the ATCOs, especially with Mark. They had to file flight plans with him; the bane of their lives were the Low Jet Routes (LJR).

DAWN STRIKE

I think the year was 1977. There I was sitting in the blacked-out Approach Radar room in the Air Traffic Control Tower at *Albatross*. The cry 'Watch out for the ship!' from an A-4 Skyhawk pilot on the strike safety frequency still features large in my memory. 805 Squadron had taken on an adversary role against approximately 20 Mirages doing a multi-wave dawn strike out of RAAF Base Williamtown. The Mirages had been tasked to bomb Beecroft Range as part of the 2OCU [Operational Conversion Unit] training of Fighter Combat Instructors. After a period of intense 'fighting', 805 Squadron, flying combat air patrol, had successfully driven off the aggressors with few, if any, bombs being successfully delivered on target at Beecroft. Employed primarily in ground attack and air defence, the Skyhawks and pilots of 805 Squadron had displayed the Fleet Air Arm's lethal fixed-wing fighter capability to the RAAF.

PRE-EMBARKATION WORKUP

The following events occurred sometime between the mid- to late-1970s. Pre-embarkation workups by all carrier air group (CAG) squadrons were intense periods. HMAS *Albatross* could see as many as 1,000 aircraft movements in a day. Everybody would fly: 723, 724, 805, 816, 817 and 851 Squadrons. So, we would have a mix of Bell 206, Wessex, Iroquois, and Sea King helicopters, and Macchi, Skyhawk, Tracker and HS748 fixed-wing aircraft flying. Add to the mix visiting and transiting RAAF and civilian aircraft and, yes, it was busy.

It was a challenge for all to get the mission done and to do it safely without injury or loss. The air traffic controllers in the thick of it earned their pay, and a beer or two at the Mess when they came off watch.

Skyhawk pilots did their deck-landing practice on HMAS *Melbourne* somewhere off the coast out in the East Australia Exercise Area. This was essential training, so each pilot would do as many landings on the ship as their fuel allowed. Usually, the Skyhawks would return to *Albatross* (Nowra) from the *Melbourne* very close to minimum fuel.

Now, add a dash of rain and bad weather to a lot of aircraft movements and you have a recipe for adventure. On one day, it was raining very heavily at the airfield. Visibility was very poor, and the cloud base was below 200 feet above ground level. We were intermittently below the authorised minima for a landing, even for a ground-controlled approach (GCA) which, at the time, was our best instrument approach option. For accuracy, the GCA was the equivalent to a modern-day instrument landing system (ILS). The GCA controller used a precision-approach radar (the AN-FPN 36 Quad Radar that was used by the RAAF and RAN in the 1970s–80s) to talk pilots down by giving them essential glidepath and centreline information, and their distance to touchdown. The controller would make very fine-tuned adjustments of the radar's azimuth and elevation antennas so he could track the aircraft through the rain, which ironically tended to swamp the radar picture with unwanted clutter just when a clear picture was needed the most.

On one occasion, a single Skyhawk returned to Nowra with only enough fuel to do ONE approach. If unsuccessful in landing, he was looking at having to climb out on the overshoot and find a safe place to eject. He didn't have enough fuel to divert to another airfield.

(Author Peter Greenfield: that was me! Not quite as dramatic as it sounds, but it was at GCA minima, a wet runway and I had insufficient fuel for a diversion. The ship was CAVOK [ceiling/clouds and visibility okay] and nobody looked out the window to see the front rolling up the South Coast. And I think that I did a short-field arrest on 21.)

Nevertheless, because we were now looking at an emergency with a possible ejection, it was decided to provide a talk down to touchdown. As you would expect, the 'pucker' factor and tensions were high during the approach. Fortunately, the aircraft landed safely thanks to the skill of both the pilot and the controller doing the GCA talkdown.

On another day involving a lot of rain, four Skyhawks returned to *Albatross* from *Melbourne*. The bad weather, their high tyre pressures and the wet runways meant they would all need to do a GCA recovery, and to use the arrestor cable on landing – one on each runway 21, 26, 03 and 08 in turn. The challenge was to sequence the landing times for each Skyhawk so the 'Salvage' crew could check and rig each arrestor cable, get the aircraft unhooked from the cable and then drive their truck as fast as possible to do the same for the next arrest on another runway. Obviously, to avoid a collision, the preceding taxiing Skyhawks also had to have vacated the active runway as they returned to the squadron lines.

LOW JET ROUTES

The Flight Planning Office at HMAS *Albatross* was located on the ground floor of the control tower, near the Met Office. As a midshipman junior ATCO, I spent a lot of time there processing flight plans and NOTAMS [notice to airmen]. Skyhawk pilots would often come through there to submit flight plans. Many of these involved them flying on LJRs below 500 feet above ground level. LJRs were published, usually with standard route profiles. When LJRs were activated, civilian pilots could take this into account for traffic-avoidance purposes.

I recall two low-level Skyhawk flights I believe were non-standard LJRs. The first involved a flight through the Moss Vale area that triggered complaints from a horse stud owner who claimed his horses had been spooked by a low, loud and fast Skyhawk. Unfortunately, a horse had bolted, galloped into a fence and injured itself. Subsequently, sensitive areas were established around the area to avoid a repetition. There was no suggestion of any irresponsibility on the pilot's part.

The second flight involved a rightfully proud pilot keen to celebrate and share with family and friends his achievement in becoming a Skyhawk pilot. He flew a non-standard LJR over his hometown of Yea, Victoria. Somebody in town complained about his 'display' and I believe a sheepish young pilot was admonished by his CO and possibly Commander Air.

(Author Peter Greenfield: we had standard LJRs in our syllabus, but the originals published by the Department of Civil Aviation only covered RAAF Mirage and Macchi routes from Williamtown. Nobody bothered to find out what the Navy did. So, as we filed a standard low-level NAVEX 24 hours prior, I think ATC submitted it twice, once for promulgation and the second for publication.)

SKYHAWK CRASH – 1980

April 28 1980 was to be a calamitous day for one Skyhawk pilot at HMAS *Albatross*, resulting in the loss of an aircraft. I was on duty as the Surface Movement Controller (SMC) in the tower. Only a week earlier I had returned after my first cruise as a member of the CAG on HMAS *Melbourne*. Three ATCOs were assigned to Carrier Air Group 21 on board *Melbourne* at any one time. They provided flight planning, airspace management, aircrew briefing, flight following, and aircraft separation and recovery services to 805 Squadron's Skyhawks as well as to the other embarked squadrons.

We had been to Hawaii for *Rimpac 78*. The Navy had performed well in simulated combat against the Americans; as I recall it, our A-4 Skyhawks in 805 Squadron had managed to average a 6:1 notional kill ratio against our opposition. I think one A-4 had even claimed a 'guns' kill on a submarine.

(Author Peter Greenfield: again, that was me!)[1]

Meanwhile, back at *Albatross*, 805 Squadron Skyhawks had been practicing for an air display. A copy of my statement for the Board of Inquiry into the crash shows that, after completing their display practice, the three Skyhawks comprising Checkmate Division had rejoined the circuit. When in the mid-downwind position, Checkmate Leader, side number 878, flamed out and the pilot ejected. The aircraft crashed about two miles south of the airfield.

In those days, aircraft emergencies were sufficiently frequent at HMAS *Albatross* for the base response to be prompt and professional. I contacted the hospital, Search-and-Rescue (SAR) Flight and Salvage Section via the tower's direct line. The Tower Controller notified the Duty Fire Crew, and an emergency pipe was made notifying the base of the crash. The SAR helo, callsign 894, was ready for take-off within four minutes of the crash. It recovered the pilot of 878 and returned him to 723 Squadron dispersal within minutes of landing at the crash site. Ambulance Two transported the pilot to hospital shortly after that.

Skyhawk 878 was a two-seater. So, when the pilot ejected, both seat rockets fired, ejecting the front and rear seats. This was a design feature intended to protect any person in the rear seat from injury when the front seat ejected. The fact that both seats were seen to leave the aircraft created some initial confusion as to how many people were on board 878 but this was quickly resolved. There was only one.

Unfortunately, our radios and communications equipment was ageing and difficult to maintain. As Murphy's Law would have it, the Tower Controller's radio box failed shortly after the crash, and the SMC's radio box chose the same moment to act up. I can still vividly recall the extremely painful sound that blasted my ears through my

---

[1]   Note according to Chapter 14, this submarine 'kill' occurred during *Tasmanex* in 1978, shortly before *Rimpac 78* which might explain the confusion.

headset. Many transmissions received on SMC frequency were badly distorted and sometimes unreadable. This added to the difficulty of coordinating our emergency response. We had so many unserviceabilities with our radios, communications and radars in those days. If the tower had been an aircraft it would have been a 'hangar queen'!

Mark Radisich

The Navy is an Australian leader in equality for women. To that end, it recruited Women's Royal Australian Naval Service officer cadets to be trained as ATCOs. In 1976, the first two young ladies arrived as brand-new sub-lieutenants, fresh from the School of Air Traffic Control at RAAF East Sale. Naturally, the squadrons were keen to help the ATCO Training Officer by providing guest appearances in the back of various aircraft. This contribution is a series of memories from Margaret Maher (nee Dennis):

A GIRL'S MEMORIES

Doing a run down Martin Place in Sydney around October 1977 for some special naval occasion [Authors: it was Navy Week], there were A-4s and Macchis. 'Purps' (Peter Greenfield) was flying in a Macchi with an ATCO, Margaret Dennis, in the back seat. Prior to take-off, the briefing had covered everything and went into the minutiae of the route through the city, the turn onto Martin Place, the height and the meet up once through the city. All cranes had been told and re-told to turn away from overhanging Martin Place between something like 1030–1100, and all had confirmed they had done it. Flight up was great as expected, descended to around a few hundred feet, seemingly below the height of existing buildings at that time. Turned into Martin Place and all of a sudden there came an exclamation from Purps, followed by a hard right bank/jink turning the aircraft almost 90-degrees sideways, done under very trying circumstances in a tiny bit of airspace surrounded by other RAN jets. One of the cranes had suddenly swung out, above the aircraft with a great piece of stuff hanging below. Had Purps not carried out that manoeuvre, the aircraft's wing would have been sliced off and, at that height, the ejection seats may not have worked. Took him until about Kiama on the return trip to calm down enough from wanting to sort out the crane driver.

A-4 conversion course in late 1976/early 1977 had three students on it, Peter Greenfield, Colin Tomlinson and Michael Maher. On the second last day of the course, there was a Dining-in night in the Wardroom. In true FAA tradition, there was no flying the next morning or day. Only the SAR chopper guys were on duty, and they were not allowed to attend the Dining-in. The A-4 guys had to finish up the course, and then the CO, Lieutenant Commander David Collingridge would announce to the squadron who had passed or not.

Fast forward to after the toast to The Queen, by which time copious amounts of alcohol had been consumed by almost every person there. The Mess President, Commander B St-John Moore, suddenly announces he has something to say, and announces that Michael has come top of his A-4 course, so drinks all around. So much for the announcement that David Collingridge was supposed to make the next day. So much for Purps and Tommo finding out in a more private session.

(Author Peter Greenfield: I don't remember this but that is probably because we were doing our NATOPS check the next morning and were forbidden to attend.)

One day I asked Peter Cox if there was anything that had scared him when he was flying and he said yes! He and Jerry Clark were doing some stuff with the ships and, at the end of it, *Sydney* (the retired aircraft carrier) asked if they could do a flypast at about deck height. So, Jerry and 'Coxy' line up and start the flypast when Coxy realises he is below deck height, and on the INSIDE of the radio antennas that hung down from the deck. He can't jink out of the way, and they go down too low for him to have a go at getting out by going lower. When you consider it would have all been over in a couple of seconds, the actual going past *Sydney*, it must have made a very deep and lasting impression on him at the time.

(Author Peter Greenfield: Pete Cox had a reputation for low passes over or around anything. If he remembered this one, then it must have been really something.)

Michael Maher had a 100% passenger illness rate when taking people on jet rides. He maintained this record when he took Margaret Dennis up on her A-4 ride a couple of days after she arrived on base to start her ATC training. Ensuring they would not be hungry upon return he had generously organised an early lunch at the Flight Line Cafeteria. He demonstrated his A-4 circling technique, Margaret thinking it would be in a large, gentle, circular motion going around the clouds from the top to the bottom. Instead he demonstrated the A-4's 720-degree-per-second rate of roll. He also demonstrated the diving ability of the A-4, the climb rate, the flying upside-down ability and all other parameters of the operating envelope. Upon return, she exited the aircraft with three completely full sick bags. Photographic proof exists in the photographers' filing cabinets.

There was an old lady who lived somewhere down south of Nowra, maybe near Ulladulla. She constantly complained about the aircraft noise and rang the Commodore each time to tell him. The Commodore kept carpeting the pilots who had flown that morning, despite their protestations they had not gone near her place, had not overflown it, etc. In the end, a no-fly zone was issued overhead her home. One Friday morning, following a Dining-in night the previous night, there was only one person flying and that was the Commodore in a Macchi [Authors: he had not been in attendance at the Dining-in]. Upon his return, the little old lady telephoned to tell him about the terribly noisy aircraft that had overflown her place – again. The Commodore realised all his pilots had been telling the truth, as he had also not flown overhead at a low height or at great speed. So, he told the jet boys the story, forgave them and lifted the no-fly zone. On the Monday morning, apparently, there were a couple of A-4s who happened to do a really fast, really, really low flight overhead her house. Apparently, she never complained again.

A-4 drivers had to do lots of different types of flying practice: high, low, down in the weeds, zero feet above the water. While on an exercise in outback Queensland, one A-4 driver (Johnny someone?), after completing his mission, happened to fly over his hometown, somewhere really deserted in the absolute outback. He flew down the main drag, at about nought feet to get everyone to come out into the main street (it was that small a town). Then he put on a flying display for the whole town, including his family. Then he returned to the base he was exercising from in Queensland. Two weeks later, he returned to Nowra with the A-4 squadron on completion of the exercise. The Commodore greeted all of them and asked Johnny to see him when he had unpacked. Johnny goes to the Commodore's office and the Commodore asked Johnny how the exercise had gone, had he enjoyed it, had he gone off course anywhere and had he done anything unauthorised? Johnny replied that of course he hadn't done any of those things. Then the Commodore handed Johnny a letter, written to the Commodore, thanking him for letting Johnny put on such a lovely flying display and how the whole town loved all that he did. And it was signed by Johnny's mum. Shopped by your own mum!

Margaret Maher

David 'Gravy' Staines was a senior ATCO in charge of ATCO training at the 'tross. He sent this little gem from his early days as a trainee running the Ops Desk:

THE OLD AND THE BOLD

The A-4 guys did regular instrument flying practice sorties in T-birds in the early days. The instructor in the front seat was an Instrument Rating Examiner and liked to surprise them with a diversion to RAAF Richmond. To do this, he would file a diversion flight plan before the flight. One of the students asked me how the flight plans were transmitted; I explained I approved them and passed them to the teletype operator in the room next door.

So, these smart guys found his telephone extension and would ring him up before the flight to see if the instructor had filed a plan for RAAF Richmond!

David Staines

(Authors: as an AWI once said, 'A fighter pilot always cheats to win.')

THE FLIGHT LINE CAFETERIA

The Flight Line Cafeteria was a standard hut very close to the VC724 Operations Hut. The quick way there was to walk through the Safety Equipment section and out the back door and then dodge slightly left and into the side door of the Flight Line Kitchen. Really, it should have been called the Flight Line Galley in Navy style, but the occupants, two leading chefs and a petty officer (PO) chef, always referred to it as the Flight Line Cafeteria.

The Wardroom and Sailors' messes were a long way and up hill from the squadrons, which were all located along the main taxiway. It was at least a ten-minute drive with limited parking, and walking was out of the question. The respective Mess Committees did not allow flight suits or overalls to be worn to eat lunch so the Flight Line Cafeteria was introduced on 26 October 1970 to provide flight crews lunch and, on those days when night flying was planned, a night flying supper.

VC724 had the hut closest to the Flight Line Cafeteria and we seemed to use it the most frequently. The next most frequent were probably HC723, the Huey guys. They were always busy and really needed the feeder to keep their energy up!

The cuisine was excellent, with almost personal service and at least three choices. I never heard anything like 'Sorry, Sir, that's off.' If it was on the board, you could have it. As we were the most frequent users, we 724 pilots received excellent service. Lunch hours were 1130–1330, with supper 1730–1930. On not so rare occasions, we would have an early launch before sunrise for a strike exercise or a weaponry display at Puckapunyal. If we asked nicely when the Flypro came out, the PO chef would organise an early 'Combat Breakfast' for the pilots, four or five of us. Those breakfasts always seemed special and it was nice to launch with a full tummy.

So, to all those chefs who served in the Flight Line Cafeteria, a big 'thank you' for wonderful service from me, my tummy and my compatriots.

Peter Greenfield

The Nowra control tower built in 1958 and replaced, finally, in 2004. (RAN)

Chapter 13

1977: SPITHEAD REVIEW

The new year of 1977 began with the graduation of the students of No 11 Operational Flying School (OFS). Barry Diamond remained at the head of the VF805, the highlight for the squadron, and the air group in general, being the long cruise to the UK for the Spithead Review, part of the celebrations for Her Majesty's Silver Jubilee. Lieutenant Commander Dave Collingridge led VC724 with Lieutenant Commander Charlie Rex as his Senior Pilot (SP).

THE END OF THE OFS

On 31 May, I made myself a switch pig and dropped a rocket pod on the range. I returned shamefacedly and admitted my error to the Boss, who did not make a big fuss. And the next morning, the armourers had the pod sitting on a trolley in the hangar where everybody could see it.

The next day was my second as a staff pilot and I sat in the front seat of a T-bird monitoring the SP, Charlie Rex, while he did his thing on an instrument flying practice sortie. His final approach was a radar/ground-controlled approach and, as he put the gear down, there was a huge bang and the aircraft yawed. He asked me what happened and I squirmed around in my seat. I could see the starboard drop tank was skewed about ten degrees to the right. I told Charlie this and he promptly gave me control and pulled the hood back. From his viewpoint, he could just see a witness mark on the inboard side of the tank, so he told me to land the airplane gently with no heavy braking.[1]

As a staff pilot, I was rapidly refamiliarised on the Macchi and, for the next four months, regularly swapped from one type to another. At the end of August, the squadron did a detachment to RAAF Amberley for *Misty Point*. This came about because the RAAF refused to invite the Navy to the IADS (International Air Defence System) Exercise, so the SP, the Boss and Major Feakes (the Carrier-Borne Ground Liaison Officer), organised an invitation from the Army to operate out of Amberley to support a big Army exercise, *Misty Point*, at Tin Can Bay. The Air Force higher ups objected and claimed there were insufficient resources to support the Navy, but the Army general must have been more senior as he won. We took three A-4s and a T-bird to Amberley, made the point of having to jettison fuel to make landing weight, and then flew touch and goes in front of all the Mirages lined up on the northern apron. The troops lived in tent city and our ramp was the short cross runway. All maintenance was done in the open, but we had no major problems the troops needed to fix, and, in time honoured fashion, the SP led a three-ship flypast down the runway at Brisbane and then over the city, en route to Amberley. We all had a good time, especially watching the Mirages attempting to cope with strikes by A-4s from New Zealand and Singapore, and the F-111s who had been moved to Williamtown for the exercise.

Peter Greenfield

But there were some unusual problems as well.

LOW POWER ENGINE

VC724 Maintenance was having difficulty achieving required figures on a new engine undergoing trim. I was asked by the Chief Mech to double check the figures. We did a run and confirmed the engine couldn't make military power per the maintenance manual. Qantas engineering visited, confirmed our figures and announced they would apply for a concession to allow the engine to operate at lower than military power. I

---

[1] A witness mark is an engineering term. When one piece of metal strikes another piece of metal with great violence it imprints an outline on the static piece.

became unpopular when I advised them I would refuse the engine unless it made power in accordance with the manual. I mentioned the different operations to civilian aircraft operations, like catapult launches and military capability, to the Qantas personnel. My position was supported by Superintendent of Aircraft Maintenance and Repair (SAMR) and, with bad grace, Qantas took the engine back to workshops for a revised overhaul. NB: in civil aviation, it is a common practice to apply for a concession for a marginal engine.

Ian Scott

J52 ENGINE SUPPORT

After my 12 months on HMAS *Melbourne*, I was posted, at the end of 1974, to SAMR in North Sydney. After working on the Iroquois engine for about 36 months, I moved over to the Skyhawk engine, the J52, and worked for Bill Butler. Bill was an interesting character who joined the Fleet Air Arm in 1948 after working as a tool maker during the Second World War. I learnt a lot from him. Part of the job meant travelling down to Nowra to find out what was going on and liaising with the Navy at *Albatross*. I didn't mind the travel, but others thought it meant too long a day for them.

J52 SUPPORT AND QANTAS

Qantas was the engine overhaul contractor for the J52-P8B. While at SAMR, I heard about a Skyhawk engine that wasn't producing enough power even after hours on the engine test bed. It was taken back into the workshop to be disassembled to find that one of the compressor rotors had been installed upside down/back to front. Once reversed to the correct configuration, it ran perfectly.

David Prest

The Carrier-Borne Ground Liaison Officer

The purpose of the Carrier-Borne Ground Liaison Officer (CBGLO or 'CeeBalls') was to provide an interface between the carrier air group (CAG) and the Army units requiring close air support. The position was created in the British Pacific Fleet during the Second World War. Its function was similar to that of the forward air controller invented for the Tactical Air Forces as they landed in Normandy.

In the Navy, the CBGLO was usually a major with an artillery background, and he had a sergeant and a private as staff. He was embedded in the CAG Staff and thus went to sea, and ashore was found in an office near the CAG Staff. Being an expert in map reading, and nasty things that went bang, he and his staff were very good to know. They also communicated with their Army brethren using Navy channels. Ashore, they worked with both VF805 and VC724.

The Amberley detachment was done to annoy the Royal Australian Air Force (RAAF). That year, the RAAF had the IADS exercise at Amberley, with oodles of Mirages defending. The F-111s and the Singaporean A-4s were deployed to Williamtown as the offensive force, with maybe a few token Kiwis as well. We were excluded because the RAAF thought the Navy did not play by the rules (and, no, we did not, quite).

The CBGLO, Major Feakes, colluded with the Boss to organise an invitation to provide support for two simultaneous Army exercises – one at Tin Can Bay and another out near Roma. The Air Force declined the invitation to perform because they had the big show-and-tell of their own. The SP was Charlie Rex, and he organised the arrival for the end of the Air Force Day. The Skyhawks jettisoned fuel in formation above 6,000 feet on their way to initial for Runway

18 at Amberley. They then did two bounces and a full stop, before taxiing in as a formation. It was funny watching the RAAF doing their imitation of the bounces the next day as they arrived back from their warm-up navex, a simple triangle completed in 40 minutes.

The Air Force tried to stipulate the Skyhawks' departure and arrival times, but the General in charge went over the Air Commander's head. He won and the A-4s taxied whenever they had to. The RAAF Air Ops cell had the OpOrder and delivered excellent support throughout. All arrivals were via the safe lane because the Airfield Defence Guards had exercise missile batteries at the initial points. However, the Skyhawks launched with full tanks and about four hours' endurance, spending a lot of time with the Army.

Jerry Clark and Pete Cox were the delivery pilots for the photo-recon product delivered twice daily. The photo product was delivered in a red vinyl pouch whipped up by the safety equipment section. It had a long orange streamer attached and the pouch and streamer were lodged carefully in the port speedbrake well. When the speedbrake opened, the streamer dragged the pouch out. Simple, but it only worked if the speedbrakes were not used before 'delivery'. The rest of the pilots had fun beating up armoured personnel carriers, chasing trucks through the bush, and cruising up and down the beaches in between serials.

When the air group went to sea, the CBGLO and his staff were to be found in the Air Intelligence Office in 5P. They worked very closely with whoever was the ship's Intelligence Officer. Major Feakes was possibly a little bored with the transit phase once the continental shelf was left behind. He invented all these little cardboard computers to work out the orientation of the Delta pattern from the Mean Line of Advance.[2] They were also handy if having to recover through the inevitable cumulonimbus the ship managed to find.

Upon arrival in Hawaii and entering the Amphibious Phase of a *Rimpac*, Ceeballs had something to do. He would appear with a target briefing in the Aircrew Briefing Room and either the Air Intelligence Officer or Ceeballs would brief the four-ship strikes.

CEEBALLS'S DRIVER'S AMOROUS ADVENTURES

The CBGLO had a driver, a lowly private. One day, his new driver appeared at the door of the 724 Squadron Aircraft Maintenance Control Office and, bewildered by the number of white uniforms and unfamiliar ranks, stamped to attention, threw a big Army salute, shouted 'Sir' and stood waiting for a response. After finding out who he was and what he wanted, we sent him over to the admin block where the CBGLO was located.

I'm not sure if he was the one who borrowed the CBGLO's utility to go to the Wollongong drive-in one Saturday night. His car had broken down so borrowing the CBGLO's utility to take his girlfriend to the drive-in was a no-brainer. The CBGLO would be none the wiser if it was sitting there for him to use on Monday morning, so what could possibly go wrong? Well, the private was sitting in traffic and was rear-ended on his way to Wollongong. He not only missed out on seeing the movie but probably ended up on a significant charge as well.

Anonymous

---

2   The Mean Line of Advance was the fleet's average track, while the Delta pattern was a racetrack circuit flown 3,000 feet above the carrier while the aircraft were waiting for Charlie time (the commencement of landing operations).

LET THERE BE LIGHT

In October, I became the Glow-worm king! I had three two-hour sorties dropping flares at Singleton to help out the RAAF Mirage Fighter Combat Instructor course. They were doing night bombing and requested flare support from us. The sortie began with a nearly maximum weight take-off at dusk, loaded with five pods of flares and full of fuel. At the end of the serial, I had two tubes of flares to get rid of so it was great fun to fly over the range 'chonking' out the flares in a long string. Then a longish trip back home via overhead Williamtown, then Sydney, to land on 26 at the 'tross, and no, I was told not to drop the remaining flares overhead Sydney.

In November, the three of us walked across the hangar to join VF805 and started earning our pay. We knew the SP, Barrie Daly, from No 2 Flying Training School, but the CO, Barry Diamond, was new to us. The flying we began to do was also very different. Multi-role in one sortie and visiting different ranges. Right at the end of the month, my logbook tells me I flew an AIM-9 firing profile, and then the next day flew the real thing. I fired a Sidewinder at the Jindivik, but it survived. In December, we ended each of our sorties with a field carrier landing practice period, and there was a new stamp put in my logbook. For the first time, it was signed off by CAG, the Carrier Air Group commander, beside the stamp signed by our new CO, Lieutenant Commander Collingridge, who had come across from VC724 after us.

VC724 was always a busy squadron. It had eight Macchis, three TA-4Gs, and nominally all the A-4Gs not required by VF805, on strength. Of course, some of these were always in the tender care of the maintainers, or at Qantas who were contracted to perform the Progressive Aircraft Rework. The Macchis were for fleet requirements, currency for staff pilots and new joiners holding for an OFS, and they were flown hard. The TA-4s were also for currency and instrument rating tests and, together with the A-4s, were flown for currency, fleet requirements tasking, the OFS or Air Warfare Instructor (AWI) courses, and passenger flights.

Skyhawk 882 in company with a Macchi trainer, both from VC724. This photo shows the new squadron logo adopted in 1977, a yellow speedwing on a blue background. This was adopted as it matched the overall blue of the Macchis. Also visible are matching yellow and blue speedlines painted on the A-4's droptanks. (Seapower Centre)

Flyaways and the RAAF Warrant Officer Disciplinary

Annual flyaways were done by 724 Squadron [Authors: 'detachments' is the official word, but sailors are sailors] to RAAF Williamtown to familiarise our aircrew with RAAF ground radio control, tactics and procedures, and to familiarise RAAF control and reporting units, i.e., radar and communications, with fleet training procedures.

Preparation for one of these events usually saw a couple of tiffy Petty Officers head up there during the week before the fun started, so the workspaces and accommodation could be sorted out before the squadron arrived. One year, they had everything sorted and ready, and were invited to attend an RAAF Senior Non-Commissioned Officers' (SNCO) Mess family picnic day, which was to be held at Lemon Tree Passage on the Saturday afternoon.

Things were going along socially until the Deputy Mess President came up to one of the Petty Officers and asked if he knew where the other one was. With the reply in the negative, it was suggested he make his way to the other Petty Officer's car, where he was last seen showing it off and explaining its niceties to a young lady. Why was this a concern? The young lady was the daughter of the Base WO Disciplinary (WOD), which was grounds for caution, and she was 14 years old. The two Petty Officers had a very quick discussion about the young lady's 'shortage of years on this planet' and how that might impact legally, as well as their ability to remain on the flyaway should things get out of hand. Crisis averted!

They were invited to a social gathering in the SNCO's Mess later that week and both set about to make sure the WOD wasn't displeased with them. Sometime into the function, probably about 8pm, or four hours after the function started, the WOD announced he'd better head home for his dinner and left the mess to ride his bike home to the 'Married Patch'. Probably about 45 minutes later, he staggered back into the mess, in a very dishevelled state with uniform torn, grazes on his arms and face and so on. The immediate thought of anyone who saw him at this point was that he'd been beaten up or hit by a car. While he was being cleaned up, one of the Petty Officers went outside to inspect the push bike, in case it could shed light on what had happened. He climbed on the bike and rode it up and down the street, then declared it was serviceable. The WOD saw this and declared, 'If I could have ridden the bloody thing as far as the bloody PO had, I would have been home by now'. Everyone present realised the WOD had had more to drink than he could handle and had fallen off his bike a number of times in his attempt to ride it home. At least the POs' part in plying him with drinks didn't get mentioned!

Two years later saw 805 Squadron fly to RAAF Butterworth to take part in a Five Power Defence Arrangement exercise. This agreement had been set up to deal with Communist insurgents entering Malaysia from Thailand and creating mayhem in the civilian community. The squadron's participation in the exercise was not an insignificant event, and HMAS *Melbourne* was having maintenance carried out in Sydney, so the squadron (a number of A-4s accompanied by the maintainers and the ground equipment which were crammed in the back of two RAAF Hercules) flew from Nowra to Rockhampton, refuelled and continued on to overnight in Darwin. The next day saw the armada head to Bali to refuel and then head to Penang, arriving there at about 9 or 10pm. Everyone was pleased to leave the Hercules until they saw their mate, the WOD from Williamtown, waiting at the foot of the front stairs. He was there to make sure everyone, i.e., those Petty Officers, understood there would be no shenanigans on his base this time!

Rob Hall

Handling on Landing

The A-4 had a difficult geometry with respect to self-aligning forces of the undercarriage and the aerodynamic keel centre of effort. The aerodynamic centre of effect of the total keel area was in front of the centre of effort of the undercarriage. The analogy is sailing a dinghy where it carries too much weather helm – if you stop pushing, it abruptly falls off the wind, you gybe and capsize. Basically, this means the Skyhawk was difficult in a crosswind and even worse with a wet runway too. The crosswind limit was 15 knots, if recalled correctly.

The standard arrival of the Skyhawk was a constant descent rate onto the runway with no flare. This meant the aircraft positively touched down on all three wheels, the high-pressure tyres punched through any film of water on the runway surface and the spoilers deployed instantly. The recommended technique in a crosswind was to then immediately apply considerable forward pressure on the nose wheel and fight the aircraft straight with up to full rudder (or take the short-field arrest).

The problem was the A-4 wanted to weathercock the nose downwind contrary to nearly all other tricycle undercarriage aircraft. If you lost control, it would dynamically rollover, as the Kiwis found out. The NATOPs [Naval Air Training and Operating Procedures Standardization] manual forbade aerodynamic braking (holding the nosewheel off) for specifically this reason. Of course, the pilots had to try it and it worked as long as the wind was down the runway. Somebody had a minor problem one day and scared himself in full view of all the armchair Landing Safety Officers (LSO), and then compounded it by talking about it within hearing of the Boss. Result, a NATOPS brief by the SP the next morning; nobody repeated it.

The Kiwis, of course, being Air Force, did it their own way. They added a brake 'chute (which slowed the aeroplane spectacularly), but they also added ten knots and always flared the aeroplane. You just never did that with any Navy aeroplane, especially the A-4. The brake 'chute would never straighten out the aircraft because it was not meant to be used until the nosewheel was on the ground.

RNZAF A-4 NZ6218 flipped on its back at Townsville on 3 August 1984. The flaps and speedbrakes are deployed, the spoilers are retracted. Note the main tyres are undamaged. (RAAF)

NZ6218 was the former 877 in RAN service. It was accepted into RNZAF service on 3 August 1984 and, apart from line servicing, little was done to fit it out as an A-4K. It was still in its RAN 'patches' camouflage, with only the roundel repainted with a red Kiwi. The accident occurred on 3 June 1985 at RAAF Garbutt, otherwise known as Townsville airport.

While landing in torrential rain, the pilot subsequently reported (incorrectly) that the main tyres had blown. The runway was 01/19, 8,000 feet long with an asphalt surface. With bad weather of the sort that produces torrential rain, it was always a strong direct crosswind from the south-east.

The aircraft finished resting on its back, facing north. The spoilers were not deployed, and the starboard wing struck the ground hard. It can be deduced the aircraft was landing on 19 (sensibly), with a crosswind from the left, veered right (downwind) and then rolled over.

It was very badly damaged, but the tyres remained intact. The authors of the informative *Skyhawks: the History of the RNZAF Skyhawks* describe the aircraft as not having a straight panel in it. The pilot was, understandably, trapped in the cockpit. The book reports the fire service broke the canopy and made a hole large enough for him to crawl out. The aircraft was disassembled and returned to New Zealand by C-130. The rebuild effort took five years. Ex-RNZAF Skyhawk pilots blamed the accident on the lack of a drag 'chute, not the crosswind issue as deduced above.

Carrying On

When No 12 OFS completed and three students became staff pilots, VC724 Squadron began accumulating the next candidates. The long-range plan was to start No 12 OFS at a time that would allow the students to have progressed to holding an instrument rating and be at a stage where they could take advantage of deck time made available during the workup to carrier qualifications.

By December 1976, they were all on strength with VC724, their OFS beginning in July after No 11 completed in May.

VF805 embarked on 20 January 1977 for what became known as the 'Spithead Cruise'. It was a very long cruise involving two transits through the Suez Canal and the Mediterranean Sea, an exercise period in UK waters for familiarisation, and then a North Sea exercise providing fixed-wing naval aviation assets to the RN. The squadron finally disembarked to Nowra on 5 October.

This tale is told by a maintainer about the CO, Lieutenant Commander Barry Diamond. It is told with his approval and shows the trust and respect between the 'fixers' and the 'flyers':

LAUNCH THE TANKER!

During the 1977 Silver Jubilee trip on HMAS *Melbourne*, 805 Squadron Skyhawks were embarked and flew most days. One day, during Exercise *Highwood* in the middle of the North Sea, our aircraft were off the deck for a day's flying and the tanker aircraft was positioned just behind the ship's island. The tanker was fitted with the 'buddy store' in-flight refuelling pod and the aircraft was looked after by my 805 Squadron mate, Able Seaman ATA Steve 'Hector' Crawford. The tanker would be launched if any of the returning squadron aircraft had any difficulties landing and needed a 'top up' so they could safely remain airborne.

Steve kept this aircraft in great shape, but the rest of us squadron guys teased him as it never actually went anywhere. It was always prepped and fuelled and ready to fly, but for days and days just sat there, looking like a princess!

Hector shrugged off all the jibes and mindfully kept his aircraft in tip-top shape. After the sortie aircraft started returning, a call came through that one of our aircraft was in trouble. The aircraft (874) was being flown by the CO and he reported problems with all his electronic systems, particularly the navigation systems, and he could not navigate back to the ship. He was also getting low on fuel.

The ship's radar picked him up and, at this stage, he was over 30 nm from the ship and heading in the wrong direction!

The squadron SP raced to the flight deck and the call went out to 'Launch the tanker!' Hector scuttled around and removed all the blanks and covers, got the SP strapped in, the aircraft started, and all flight controls checked in record time. Within a few minutes, the tanker was on the ship's catapult and launched into the air.

Hector was exhausted from the frantic activity and I cheerily called out 'This better work, Hector!' in a very supportive tone!

Then we waited and waited …

After what seemed like an interminable time, a report came through: 'Two A-4s approaching the ship.' We searched the sky and saw two tiny dots heading our way. A huge cheer went up as they grew into the familiar shape of our Skyhawks, and they did a low and fast flypast down the ship's side. Sweeping into the landing circuit, both the CO and SP made perfect deck landings.

The CO and SP told the story of the CO being almost out of juice, not sure of his position and looking at the uninviting sea below, when he saw the SP's aircraft overtake him above with the buddy store hose streaming out, ready to start in-flight refuelling. After plugging in and topping up, the SP guided the CO back to the ship.

An eventful day indeed. Thanks to the excellent piloting skills of both the CO and SP, and to Hector Crawford and his 'princess' tanker, for saving the day.

Joe Hattley

Postscript

Following this event, 874 went into the ship's hangar for extensive work by the electrical and avionic crews. Some wiring issues led to the faulty systems. Once repaired, the aircraft returned to service and flew the rest of the deployment without any issues.

Neither the CO nor the SP, Barrie Daly, chose to make a contribution. However, Hattley contacted Barry Diamond with the text and asked for his approval. The approval came back as follows:

I will always be grateful for Hector's diligence with his work on the buddy store and Barrie's skill in getting to me in time! I was not confident I would have got back to the ship without 'tanking'!

Barry Diamond

DAVID RAMSAY AND THE COURTEOUS BOW

On the Jubilee trip in 1977, 805 Squadron Skyhawks were flying regularly and four A-4s had been out on a sortie. As they returned to the ship, I was stationed up in front of the ship's island to receive the incoming jets. David Ramsay ('Ramsdog') was in one of the aircraft and made his approach to a pin-point landing. As the jet slowed under the drag of the wire, David said he started to complete his after-landing checks, getting the 'all clear' to retract the deck hook, 'clean up' the aircraft and taxi forward to clear the deck for the next aircraft.

I was watching the aircraft clear the landing zone, when suddenly its nose landing gear started to retract and the nose dipped towards the deck! Shocked, and expecting the nose to hit the deck, just as quickly the nose lifted and the landing gear returned to fully extended!

David reported that, as his hands flew around the cockpit switches, including the hook, flaps, etc., he inadvertently retracted the landing gear handle (and managed to defeat the down-lock switch!). As soon as he felt the nose start to dip, he quickly hit the handle to the 'down' position and the aircraft stood up again! This all happened in seconds as the aircraft was taxiing forward and, from the ship's island, it looked like the aircraft 'bowed' as it taxied forward, to the astonishment of the brass on the island!

Joe Hattley

RIAT

One of the occasions in the UK was the Royal International Air Tattoo (RIAT) held at Greenham Common. Many air arms were represented, all with the biggest, 'bestest', loudest airframes to hand. The Royal Australian Navy was invited to contribute and David Ramsay, as the AWI, was invited to display an A-4G by the CO. Much thought was put into the display because of the competition. The Fleet Air Arm did not have the loudest, or the biggest, but arguably it did have the 'bestest'. Remember the A-4 was capable of lifting its own weight in fuel and stores in whatever combination you can think of up to max take-off weight.

David's solution was to hang as much off the pylons as he could and do a flat display within the airfield boundary. The aircraft was 886 and had a buddy store on the centreline, two B tanks, and two Zuni pods on the outboard pylons.

1977 snapshot

The air group embarked on 20 January for the epic cruise to the UK and many points between. It finally disembarked on 5 October.

CO VF805 remained Lieutenant Commander Barry Diamond.

Lieutenant Commander Barrie Daly was still SP. Other pilots were Lieutenants Gerry Pike USN, Nev French (LSO), Andy Sinclair, Ian Shepherd, Jack Mayfield (AWI) and David Ramsay (AWI, posted 21 October). Lieutenant Brian Rowe was Aircraft Electrical Officer and Lieutenant Bruce Hamilton the Aircraft Engineering Officer.

CO VC724 was Lieutenant Commander David Collingridge from 16 January with Lieutenant Commander Charlie Rex as SP.

The fleet stood at 16: three TA-4Gs and 13 A-4Gs.

Skyhawk 886 giving a flying display at the Royal International Air Tattoo in 1977.

The crowded hangar on Melbourne.

Chapter 14

1978: *RIMPAC 78* AND *SANDGROPER 78*

The ship's report on proceedings covering the *Rimpac 78* period was not available. It has either been misplaced or is still not released for public consumption. Peter Greenfield, therefore, opens with his experiences and provides some of the detail of yet another busy year during which wide-ranging and geographically dispersed exercises were the norm.

My logbook records a week of intensive flying beginning 11 January 1978. We needed a back-in-the-saddle programme after Christmas leave, but we also needed to work up us young ones for going to the ship. Each sortie ended with a period of field carrier landing practice, including a final night session. And then my logbook records a DLP (deck landing practice), with one landing and one cat shot. No other landings recorded, yet my memory tells me I flew three hook-up passes before being told to put the hook down. I do recall my first hook-down pass was a bolter and that my hook tore out a centreline light, but the next one was successful, and then I was taxied up the deck for my first cat shot.

I recall I hit the chocks pretty hard and had to be pushed back. But I was eventually loaded, followed the Flight Deck Officer's (FDO) directions, wound up the engine, swept out the controls, and saluted the FDO. It seemed to take an age for the cat to fire, and then, 'oomph', I was pushed back in the seat, it all went grey and then I was off the cat with the Landing Safety Officer (LSO) shouting in my earphones, 'Off the cat, ATTITUDE, ATTITUDE.' As I was told later, on your first cat shot, the ship gives you a little extra endspeed, so the aircraft tends to rotate off the cat. So that was it, I was carrier qualified! All three of us qualified on the same day, and an ABC crew filmed it all for posterity. It can be watched on *YouTube* somewhere, but is still vivid in my mind, especially the illusion the deck never gets any bigger as you fly closer.

The rest of the month was all intercept exercises/DLP to get us used to the routine. On 1 February, I flew a night approach to the ship, from a CCA (carrier-controlled approach) to a late wave-off by the LSO. The sequence finished on 8 February and we did our flying from Nowra.

No 12 Operational Flying School (OFS) began carrier qualifications (CARQUALS) straight after VF805 completed theirs in February 1978. By that stage, VF805 was flying training sorties, usually a serial of INTEX (intercept exercises) followed by a short DLP, an arrest, hot refuel, and then onto the cat for another session of INTEX and home to 'tross. We often rejoined the ship to find the circuit full of the OFS guys doing their own traps and cats.

One day, I rejoined as Lieutenant Murray Coppins declared a PAN with a utility hydraulic failure. The ship promptly told him to go ashore. I piped up and said I would escort him to Nowra. That was approved and I assisted Murray to long final for (runway) 26 before breaking off to return to the ship.

It was unusual because, in the past, the CARQUAL had been done within the air group. In this case, No 12 OFS could go straight into a VF805 workup and simply requalify with no fuss or bother. It was also unusual because they were the first to feature in *Navy News*, mainly because Lieutenant Allen Clark became the first and only Navy pilot to qualify first on the S-2E Tracker and then, after a spell at No 2 Flying Training School as an instructor, complete an A-4 OFS.

On the 27th, we returned to the ship for *Tasmanex*. On the first flight after embarking, I was on a splash target sortie, and on the first dive the aircraft vibrated like crazy. I tried again and aborted the second dive to hold overhead. I recovered back aboard to find the portside turtleback door missing, and what seemed like yards of wire streaming out of the hole where the g-recorder had been.

The maintainers worked all night to fix the aircraft and it was launched for the afternoon cycle. Young Michael [Maher] turned downwind and flew past the platform waggling his wings before disappearing into the sunset. The message came back from VC724 that he had recovered with no radios and that they would have to fix the electrical loom. So, Mike got to spend a night ashore with his new bride and came back the next afternoon with all the problems fixed. Meanwhile, I did a combat air patrol (CAP) sortie, landed on, was given a hot refuel, and promptly launched for a second CAP. I guess that is the way to make up for the loss of an aircraft and pilot from the Mayfly.

Peter Greenfield

A short explanation on G-meters from an expert at Superintendent of Aircraft Maintenance and Repair (SAMR):

A-4 AIRFRAME SUPPORT – G-METER

I arrived at SAMR, after being an instructor at HMAS *Nirimba*, and joined the Airframe Section. Among other duties, it was my task to record all the A-4 fatigue meter readings and monitor their progress towards the finite life of the type. The Skyhawk, dependent on fuel load, was capable of +8 to -3 G. When the aircraft is subject to a 'G' loading, the appropriate 'G' window in the fatigue meter will 'click' over to record that loading. The G-meter on a Skyhawk was located on the port upper engine access door.

Not an A-4 G-meter, but a very similar RN Sea Harrier G-meter. (John Bone)

Typical fatigue meters measure acceleration on the aircraft between the following 'G' readings while the aircraft is in flight: -1.5, -0.5, 0.25, 2.5, 3.5, 5.0, 7.0, and 8.0G.

The A-4 may have been designed for a 3,000-hour fatigue life but it soon became apparent, from USN fatigue testing, it was stronger than originally thought with the determining factor being the wings. If the wings were refurbished or replaced at around 4,000–5,000 flying hours then, theoretically, the airframe could continue for another 4,000–5,000 flying hours. However, while the wings were zero-houred, the airframe wasn't.

There were three main fatigue life items on the A-4 – the front, intermediate and trailing-edge spars in the wing. With the intermediate spar, there was a two-inch hole in the spar close to the edge that, historically, was of concern. After the A-4s and TA-4s were sold to the RNZAF, as a part of the Kahu avionics upgrade, there was a replacement of all three spars including using spare wings obtained through the purchase of Australian A-4/TA-4 stocks. In 2000, the RNZAF found considerable corrosion on the frame that holds the vertical fin on, resulting in some aircraft being grounded.

John Bone

AND SO BACK TO LIFE AT SEA

The days went by with lots of CAP sorties out in the middle of the Tasman. On one of them, the controller requested my state and I gave the reply 'Lamb', meaning I could stay on station until Charlie time, but did not have sufficient fuel to accept trade. About five minutes later, I was advised the tanker was being launched and I was to saunter, vector 225, meaning, turn onto heading 225 and cruise at a slow speed. About 15 minutes later, I heard the AWI call 'Heads up, 250 knots', and then he came past me with the drogue streamed. The light came on in my mind, so I plugged in and just took fuel until he turned it off. As I backed out, I got a vector for a bogey and a buster call so off I went. It was a successful intercept, but it was an RNZAF Hercules on its courier flight from Canberra to Whenuapai, plodding along at 21,000 feet and about 240 knots or so. Non-exercise traffic.

There was another intercept where I was sent off climbing to Angels 20 [20,000 feet], 'Your bogey is a shadower', meaning it was an F-111. The squadron had a method to deal with these intruders which the SP had briefed us on. It was a head-on intercept from Angels 20, and at 15 miles range future, meaning the bogey was 15 miles in front, the drill was to roll on your back and pull smartly back and descend like an avenging angel. It worked too. I saw the F-111 come out from under my nose as I passed 15,000 doing about 550 knots, and then I just pulled gently into his six o'clock, right in the centre of the Sidewinder envelope. In my intercept, the Nav must have spotted me in the last stage because the F-111 broke right, and then the fool put his wings forward. Gotcha! If he had dumped his nose and lit the burners, there was no way I would have had a missile shot.

The last intercept I had I was a little too enthusiastic. The target was at Angels 12, speed medium so probably a P-3. I had lots of fuel so I went for it and also traded my altitude for speed. As I turned in, I identified it as a P-3, but he seemed very slow. I am convinced he was on one engine because, as soon as he saw me, the pilot dumped the nose and three props started spinning up. I had too much energy, so I barrel rolled around him before settling into an escort position on his port wing.

The last tale is very amusing. I was sitting up on CAP and, being very bored, I was looking for whales. Suddenly I saw a wake, which didn't go away. I reported it to the controller as a 'poss sub'. Straight away he asked what weapons I had. 'For exercise, two Fox 2, 500 20mm'. One orbit later, he came back with 'Investigate, report'. So, off I slipped down to Angels 5 and positively identified a snort mast. Since I still had comms, I reported that and shortly after I was instructed to attack. So, I put the sun behind me, and pointed the Sidewinder at the snort-mast and almost immediately the missile started growling enthusiastically. I reported that and was then told to shoot at it. So, set up a strafing pass, and that was concluded by a full-power rotation at about 200 feet. Now, my little brother was a submariner and he told me they could hear the S-2s and helos flying around, so that would explain why when I looked back over my shoulder, the snort mast was gone. On my way back to the ship, I passed a helo nose down, tail up, going as fast as it could to the 'cert sub'. As far as I know, they got a sonar contact, but I don't know what they did with it. What I do know is the exercise umpires considered the matter, rolled their dice, and credited me with a 'sunk sub'. Howzat?!

Tasmanex concluded shortly after and we returned to Nowra while the ship returned to Sydney to refuel and do whatever the fish heads do in harbour. By 30 March, we were at sea for *Rimpac 78*. I know it began with an opposed exit from Sydney because I had gone up from Nowra by bus with the troops. The aircraft flew on about an hour out of Sydney, by which time the Sea Kings were thrashing around all over the place in a high state of excitement.

The exercise was planned as a simultaneous opposed transit from Sydney and the west coast of America. The fleet had a fairly high transit speed and we were mostly headed into wind going north-east from Sydney. We flew two strikes on Evans Head and then, a day later, two strikes on Saumarez Reef. The trip to Hawaii was pretty busy. We flew six days out of seven and often there were two sorties in one day. Unfortunately, the RAAF F-111s were grounded at Kwajalein due to their escape rocket cartridges being life expired. They would have had an enforced holiday. We saw the RNZAF A-4s get dragged past by their tankers at about 24,000 and, once, an all-black EP-3 droned past way up high.

A week went by and, as we wandered out on the flightdeck, there were ships everywhere. The fleets had joined up during the night and we moved to the amphibious phase. The US Navy had brought a complete Marine Amphibious Group and somewhere there was going to be a landing! We changed roles again and started carrying three Mk.82s to assault various targets. There was eight days of this and I guess we came close to emptying the bomb magazines.

The final event of the exercise was a cross-decking to USS *Enterprise*. Lead was the SP, No 2 me, No 3 our tame Yank, and No 4 was the AWI. I felt honoured I was part of this event, but little did I know there were other plans running in the background. The SP had a bet with the Yank he wouldn't bolter, the Yank was going to try the 'water, water, steel, steel' method of landing, and the AWI had a secret camera to record it all.[1] We had been

---

[1]   The water, water, steel, steel method was used by of all people, Sea Vixen Observers. They had no forward vision and only a little window on the starboard side of their cockpit. In between calling the airspeed, they glanced out the window in order to see how close they were to the ship. Hence 'water, water, steel, steel' and you are in the wires. Some USN people had served aboard the British carriers flying the Sea Vixen and they brought the method back to the USN. By then, the USN was flying F-4 Phantoms with Radar Intercept Officers in the rear seat and the method was often humorously referred to by senior aviators.

briefed by the US LSO that it would be a standard CARQUAL. Three hook-up passes and then a trap and a cat shot. What was missing from the brief was that everything was big, so the arrest was only about 3 G, and the cat shot also only 3 G. We made the slot in a tight four ship, did a fan break (the Yank had been training us in this) and flew our passes. The Air Boss called each of us to 'Hook down' as we turned downwind for the fourth pass.

As I came through the 90, I heard 'Bolter, bolter' as the artful SP won his bet, and that left me to make the first trap. I was used to about a 4.5-G pull out on 'Mother' so the arrest felt really soft. The director started waving me clear of the landing zone and then passed me up the deck to the next director, who passed me to the cat director. He brought me onto the cat track, and then started directing me right, except the nosewheel refused. I was pushed back and the same thing happened. The cat officer was clearly talking to somebody, and then the Air Boss said 'We are going to move you left and to the back of the pack.' And I was turned left, held facing aft watching the last two aircraft, the AWI and the SP, trap and taxi up to the cat. To my left, the Yank got shot off, and then the Air Boss explained the problem. The A-4 has a single nosewheel, but all US Navy aircraft from the F4 on had dual nosewheels. They had put a large metal ridge on the cat track that the dual nosewheels straddled and that kept them straight on launch. If the A-4 was directed the same way, the single nosewheel could not get over the ridge. Bugger, so I was first on, but last off. The cat shot was really soft, but it was 200 feet longer than *Melbourne*'s. And the approach to 'Mother' felt really weird – that small-deck illusion again. Even the Yank commented on it as we signed in. The next day, four of us flew off to Naval Air Station Barbers Point.

The author trapping on USS Enterprise. (Peter Greenfield)

Our journey home was tedious. The speed of advance was the most economical cruising speed, 14 knots. *Supply*, the fleet tanker, had broken down in Pearl so *Melbourne* sailed with two escorts direct to Hervey Bay. To make the whole journey, the ship burnt AVCAT for about ten days and every four days would refuel the escorts. We spent about a week in Hervey Bay doing Navy things. A new fuse for the Mk.82 (500-pound bomb) had to be trialled so that meant two of us loaded up with three bombs and launched with a 6-G cat shot. That was the acceleration for a 'war shot' and it felt very different to the normal 5.4-G shot. The Yank led me out past the 100-fathom line where a Sea King was hovering beside a smoke float. We then dropped our bombs one at a time near the float while a camera crew filmed the explosions. As far as I could tell, they all exploded well under the surface and no whales were injured.

The next day, I flew some high-speed passes for a crew filming Episode 2 of *Patrol Boat*. I had to fly up the starboard side at deck level between the ship and a hovering Sea King. The crew filmed both the passes and my zooms at the end of each pass. I then had to fly a hook down pass for the film crew in the 'goofers' [deck on the island where personnel would gather to watch flightdeck activity]. At about 100 feet, Boots told me to kick it around a bit and then I trapped. That bit was used by Goodyear for their tyre ad on TV the next year.

After Hervey Bay, the ship headed for Sydney.

Peter Greenfield

ENGINE CHANGE AT SEA

In the photograph below, the engine-removal dolly is in position behind the wing. The engine-moving trolley is parked under the tail of the Skyhawk on the left. The engine installation/removal trolley can be seen as a light-coloured U-shaped device beside the three maintainers. The exposed circular engine can be seen between the two maintainers standing either side of the wing.

This photograph of the engine going in shows occupation health and safety rules to the fore! Plastic sandals, shirtless and with bandanas on heads to soak up the perspiration in the hot and steamy conditions in the hangar. The engine removal/installation dolly is attached to the rear of the wing with the engine in the arms of the dolly. Note the tie-down chains everywhere. Note also how close the aircraft are parked to each other. The body in white shorts is either the AEO or the Chief Mech having a close-up inspection of the mating process.

Rob Hall

All the gear, two engines, two trolleys and a split fuselage. (Rob Hall)

MOVING A SKYHAWK ENGINE AT SEA

To my knowledge there were not many engine changes ever carried out actually underway. Most were done when in harbour if possible or ashore.

Russell Jensen and I did one at sea in 1978 on our way to *Rimpac 78*, a multi-national naval exercise, and it was a truly 'interesting' task. As seen in the previous photos, everything is lashed against the pitch and roll of the ship. Getting the engine down off the stack in C Hangar with a forklift was challenging to say the least as the forklift had a loose mast at full height and, coupled with the loose tines, the forklift has significant movement at full height. This caused it to rock, requiring coordination between the person riding the tines and the forklift driver to get the task completed. I went up on the forklift tines to release the securing chains, and rode down with it.

The engine going in. (Rob Hall)

The hangar deck on *Melbourne* was divided into three hangars and contained two aircraft lifts. The hangar layout was forward lift, A Hangar, a roll-down fire curtain, then B Hangar, a roll-down fire curtain, then the aft lift, then another fire curtain, then C Hangar. A fire at sea is the worst thing that can happen to a ship with priority given, over everything else, to saving the ship.

To move the engine, approximately 1,300 kilograms including the weight of its trolley, on its trolley to the aircraft was a significant task and not for the faint of heart. Due to limited manoeuvring space (see photo on p. 123), there was not sufficient space to simply push the engine/trolley combination from C Hangar through to the aircraft positioned under the fire curtain separating A and B Hangars. A circuitous path had to be taken. The engine/trolley combination had to go from C Hangar, up the aft lift, be towed forward along the pitching and rolling deck (wait for the pitch of the ship before moving it as you really don't need to have 1,300 kilograms loose on the flightdeck), then down the forward lift.

The next stage was to get the combination through the mass of parked helicopters in A Hangar, releasing and re-lashing the tie-down chains as you squeezed through that hangar. As the aircraft was positioned backwards (nose pointing aft) and the engine rollout gear crossed the fire curtain, preventing the fire curtain being lowered in case of a fire, we were always under pressure to get it finished.

I won't bore you with the evolutions to enact the engine change with chains and swinging loads, but it was a challenge. The entertainment really began when we were granted the use of the catapult for the engine trim/ tune up, at night. That meant being hooked up to the catapult and being restrained from moving by the holdback device. No escape gear worn or ejection possible if it all went wrong. The wind across the deck was just under 30 knots, the maximum permissible for the trim.

So, for an hour or two, with me in the cockpit and Russell on the deck, we were controlling the Fleet Air Arm *Rimpac* task force, and we had a few dramas. A hydraulic leak, an engine oil leak, and then we lost a debris guard (a removable mesh screen installed in front of the engine to prevent anything but air going into the intake) at military power. The jolt to the aircraft when we lost the starboard debris guard frightened the life out of me as I first thought the holdback device had parted and I had 97 feet to go (two seconds) before running off the end of the flight deck and into the dark and cold sea! I slammed the throttle back to idle and stood even harder on the brakes. Russell just jammed the debris guard back over the intake and he and one of the troops secured it in place. Surprisingly, there were no 'well dones' from the bridge when we finished!

Ian Scott

'You picked a fine time to leave me, Loose Wheel'

22 May 1978

We were on our way back from Hawaii after completing *Rimpac 78*, having embarked on board HMAS *Melbourne* in the beginning of March.

As we arrived back in Australian waters, a group of VIPs (mainly politicians) were ferried aboard and VF805 was asked to put on a weapons demonstration to entertain said guests. As the squadron AWI, I was tasked to organise and lead the demonstration. My memory is a little vague as how it was determined which pilot would carry which weapons but I recall that Dave Collingridge ('Cridge'), who was the squadron CO, had always wanted to lob toss a stick of 500-pound bombs (I added variable-time fuses to add to the effect) and I wanted to copy a display I had seen an aircraft from USS *Enterprise* perform just before we left Pearl; that was to load as many rocket pods as possible under my wing, approach the boat, at about 30 feet, from the stern and then, just before I got abeam the stern, pull the nose up just a little, roll on 90 degrees of bank with the belly of the aircraft toward the ship and let loose with a continuous ripple of rockets – very impressive, believe me.

The plan was to launch, form up as a five-ship, do a flypast and then disperse, and one at a time make our individual passes. As lead, I went first and by all accounts the display went over very well. I then held at a predetermined fix and the others joined me after they had done their run. Once the join up was complete we then did a low-level fan break over the ship and then we were to carry out a hook-up touch and go followed by an arrest.

As I mentioned, that was the 'plan'. Unfortunately, on my touch and go, I experienced what I believed to be a burst tyre. On touch down, and as I was advancing the thrust, the aircraft yawed to the left quite violently, but with a boot full of right rudder, a little right aileron and the normal amount of back stick, I became airborne. I called 'Paddles' and suggested I might have a blown tyre; his response was 'It's a little worse than that.' As it turned out, my left main wheel had come off and transited up the axial of the flightdeck, missing the FDO by a matter of inches.

I was not privy to this next bit, but I was told the display the flightdeck crew put on for the 'guests' was quite something. Because my stub axle had damaged one of the arresting wires, both it and its paired wire had to be removed. Apparently, the fastest way of doing this is with axes and blocks of wood. After my No 3 (Cridge) had inspected my aircraft and given me the bad news, the remaining four aircraft were told to Charlie but, as two of the five wires were missing, this took a little longer than normal with a number of hook skips.

In the meantime, I was holding overhead with my gear down (I had a utility hydraulic light flicker a couple of times and I was reluctant to raise my gear until it was decided what was to be done) and starting to run low on fuel. After the last aircraft had trapped, I was informed by Wings that they were planning a barricade landing for me. I was not all that impressed with this idea and my response got me into a 'little' bit of hot water later. By now, fortunately, Cridge had landed, parked and made his way up to flyco. He asked what my thoughts were (he may have heard my response to Wings). I had enough fuel (just) to make Mackay if I left immediately but would have little or no assistance there and no time to have a good look at the runway on my arrival. I figured, if I could refuel, I could easily make it to Amberley where all sorts of assistance was available.

The tanker was duly launched and I elected to refuel with the gear down – just in case, for reasons unknown, I could not take on any fuel (as it turned out the tanker pilot was not familiar with the buddy store and had to be talked through the operation). Once I had refuelled, I raised the gear, it was confirmed by the tanker pilot that everything was okay, and I headed off to Amberley.

The transit to Amberley was uneventful and I was surprised to speak with a Navy air traffic controller, Russ Dowrick, who was attached to Brisbane air traffic control (ATC) at the time. I arrived in the circuit at Amberley with plenty of fuel and they gave me the choice of runways. I elected to use the short runway (22) because, on my previous landing on the long runway (15/33), I found it to be very rough and, as I was planning a wheels-up landing, on the B tanks that were on the aircraft, I figured this was important.

At this stage, I should point out that, a couple of months prior to this event, I had read a report by a US Navy

Skyhawk pilot who had successfully carried out a partial gear-up landing. Armed with this knowledge, plus the NATOPS [Naval Air Training and Operating Procedures Standardization] checklist, I requested the runway NOT be foamed. From what I had read, foaming just lubricated the runway and increased the stopping distance. I asked for a pilot with a radio to be positioned at the touchdown end of the runway with instructions that he inform me if I was going to land short. As it turned out, this was a good idea for I made a number of practice approaches and he was able to give me an idea how each one looked. As the approach was very flat, I had to negotiate my way around a tree at about a mile and a half from the threshold and it took a little practice to get it right. What I wasn't aware of was, because of the flat approach, I was passing over the city of Ipswich each time and this had the effect of stopping most of the traffic in the city centre – an impromptu airshow!

After about four practice approaches, I told the tower I would land off any approach that looked good from that point on. As it transpired, I was comfortable with the very next approach, so I elected to land. My approach speed was a little slower than a normal approach and, as I crossed the threshold, and immediately prior to touchdown, I put in full back trim and stop-cocked the engine. The aircraft touched down very softly in ground effect on the back end of the fuel tanks, about 200 feet from the runway end, and slowly rolled to a level attitude. I was able to steer it by use of the rudder and it came to a stop after just 1,400 feet. There was an audible bang when the tanks wore through, and the trapped fuel ignited, but there was no fire. After the 'bang', the nose of the aircraft dropped, very slowly, and skidded along the ground. Once the aircraft came to a complete stop, I disarmed the ejection seat, released my seat harness and then stepped out; it was quite odd stepping out of the cockpit on to the ground. The fire trucks, which for some reason had positioned themselves at the touchdown end of the runway, were now speeding down the runway, foam cannons at full blast spraying in front of them and reducing their forward vision. I had to move quite quickly so as not to be run over.

Skyhawk 887 after the wheels-up landing by Barry Evans at RAAF Amberley on 22 May 1978. (Seapower Centre)

I was taken to the sick bay where, even after I tried to explain that it was one of the smoothest landings I had ever done, I was subjected to no less than 32 x-rays. Having been medically cleared, the OC of RAAF Amberley then approached and 'ordered' me to speak with the waiting media, of which there were quite a few. I figured I would not get a warm reception because I had not permitted the news helicopters into the circuit to film the wheels-up landing; I figured they were just one more thing to worry about and I didn't need the distraction. I informed the OC that Navy Instructions (NIs) did not allow me to have anything to do with the media so, unfortunately, I would not be carrying out his 'orders'. He stormed off and within five minutes I received a phone call by someone purporting to be Director of Naval Air Power (DNAP). Now I won't say I didn't know who it was but, as I had no way of confirming his identity, I respectfully declined his 'orders' as well. Within minutes, I received yet another phone call, this time from Zork Rohrsheim (not sure of the spelling here) who was Naval Officer in Charge Queensland at the time and an acquaintance. He explained that perhaps it would be in my best interests to go speak with the media and said he would explain to DNAP why I was not willing to accept his 'orders'.

By the time I did my first interview, a Sea King from the ship had arrived with all the necessary parts and a crew to carry out the repairs, and Neville French who was to fly the aircraft on to Nowra, the lucky B— (remember, we had been at sea for quite a long time by now and Neville was to arrive home about a week before the rest of us). The interviews were going well; I figure I did around three or four TV channel interviews but the first question the first radio station interviewer asked was if I was the same pilot that had ditched an aircraft in the South China Sea five years earlier.[2] Then everyone wanted to redo their interviews and it went downhill from there.

On my return to the ship, I was instructed to report immediately to the captain with my CO. Commodore RC Swan was not pleased (and that is putting it extremely mildly) I had performed the interviews and it was his opinion that not only had I contravened Naval Instructions, he was my immediate chain of command and I should have received permission from him. I tried to explain I had been given orders from an authority above his position and he was not available at the time, but it fell on deaf ears; on top of that, I had been somewhat out of line in my radio call to Wings when it was suggested I would be landing into the barricade.

I consider myself extremely lucky I had the support of my CO (Cridge) during both the decision to do the wheels-up landing and the aftermath at the ship.

The reason the wheel had come off was because the thread on the stub axle for the main nut had been over machined, causing the nut to come off with any form of side load. The oleo had only just been replaced so I was just lucky enough to be the pilot who had drawn the short straw.

Barry Evans

(Authors: the troops were all singing a new refrain in the ship's cafeteria that night – 'You picked a fine time to leave me, Loose Wheel.')

REMOTE MAINTENANCE AND 887

Returning from *Rimpac 78*, the 'big war canoe' spent a couple of days operating in Hervey Bay, before sailing south to Sydney. My job was overnight rectifications and servicing, usually getting to bed around 0330. Was awoken at around 0730 and told that Skyhawk 887 had lost a wheel and brake unit during a touch and go and was flying around getting a drink from the buddy store aircraft before recovering at RAAF Amberley!

In the next couple of hours, I collected a bunch of spares and a toolbox. Along with Lieutenant 'Buzz' Garrett, Chief Petty Officer ATA Russ Jensen, Chief Petty Officer ATC

The drop tanks that did their job. (Ian Scott)

Ron Cook and about half a dozen other sailors, we were loaded on a Sea King and flown to Amberley. The RAAF had thoughtfully placed the aircraft on Mirage jacks, using jack pads that VC724 prepositioned in years past.

We did airframe/engine/undercarriage inspections in accordance with the aircraft maintenance manual, changed the starboard undercarriage leg and brake, radome, chin antenna, repaired holes in the flaps, and removed the two 150-gallon Bravo external tanks, or rather the halves that were left after Barry gently lowered them onto the airstrip.

Using a Mirage hydraulic rig, we carried out undercarriage retractions. An engine ground test run and bye, bye 887 to *Albatross*, 18 hours after we arrived. A Caribou was slated to take us to *Albatross* the next day, however, Buzz hooked us a ride with a tactical C-130 which landed at *Albatross* around 2130 with no runway lights or

---

[2]   This was the loss of Skyhawk 889 in 1973 off Singapore after a failed catapult launch, as detailed in Chapter 8. Barry Evans was the pilot.

ATC. Taxied to J Hangar and dropped us off. We reported back on *Melbourne* two or three days later when she docked. I recall Buzz got a smack for not waiting for the Caribou, but we loved it!

Investigation later revealed that, while the axle nut thread was manufactured undersize, it could still be torqued up to specification and it would hold. This undersized nut, coupled with the force of a deck landing, could and did enable the wheel bearing to flex and force the wheel nut outwards, shearing the lock pin and resulting in the wheel and brake assembly falling off the aircraft. A quality check of the wheel nuts installed and in the air stores resulted in finding only one or two of the maximum-size nuts. However, a fleet wide change of nuts was instigated to reduce any errors in measurements.

Ian Scott

OILS AIN'T OILS

It was an early morning start and, as I walked into J Hangar, I noticed a young Air Technical Aircraft (ATA) sailor on the wing of an aircraft. He was topping up the hydraulic system as part of the before-flight inspection. There were lots of empty oil cans on the deck.

The conversation went something like this:

Me – 'What are you doing?'

ATA – 'Topping up the hydraulic system.'

Me – 'Is this the oil you are using?'

ATA – 'Yes.'

Me – 'And you have topped up the hydraulic system?'

ATA – 'Yes.'

Me, in a panic – 'PO you gotta see this!'

So, while the aircraft hydraulic and engine oil systems had child-proof connections on them to prevent inadvertently connecting the wrong rig to the wrong system, the rigs themselves do not stop you from putting the wrong oil in the replenishment rigs. The young sailor had successfully managed to top up the hydraulic replenishment rig, and therefore the hydraulic system, with engine oil. The young ATA was sent to the junior sailors' galley to give him a break from his present career.

T-BIRD MATS

It was about six months later and the young sailor was returned to the squadron. However, there was a little bit of apprehension within the senior sailors' crew room and the question was what to do with this sailor. It was recommended he be given a task not too difficult and surely one that could not do any damage to an aircraft, like take the mats out of the two-seat TA-4 training aircraft (also known as the T-bird), wash them and then reinstall. That should be a simple task and relatively harmless.

Time passed and eventually the young sailor appeared in AMCO pretty proud of himself. A conversation followed:

ATA – 'All done!'

PO – 'What's all done?'

ATA – 'I've washed the T-bird's mats.'

PO – 'Are they back in the T-bird?'

ATA – 'No, PO.'

PO – 'Where are they?'

ATA – 'Outside, drying in the sun.'

PO – 'Outside, where outside?'

ATA – 'Outside on the bins, drying.'

PO – 'Bins, what bins?'

ATA – 'You know, the garbage bins!'

PO – Speechless, shattered, and that look of disbelief.

So, at this point it was almost (I said almost) funny watching two Petty Officers, a chief followed closely by the AEO, running very fast across the hangar, through the hangar doors and out to the area where the bins were kept. However, the only thing that could be seen was the rear end of a garbage truck disappearing over the hill and down to the dump. A crew was sent down to the dump to try to find the mats but all that was left were smouldering leftovers in no condition to be fitted back into the T-bird. New mats were acquired after a short time and the T-bird flew high once more.

THE LOST CSD KEY

As I remember it, I was on the 724 Squadron flight line for the day when the word was passed around that an 805 Squadron Skyhawk was on its way to *Albatross* as there was an unaccounted tool, a constant-speed drive (CSD) key. On arrival, my Petty Officer asked me to conduct a search of the aircraft, particularly the forward engine bay access area (fwd hell hole) and in the area of the CSD control mechanism.

I searched for about an hour and cannot remember if a second independent inspection was carried out; needless to say, the CSD key was not found. When I reported back to the PO that I could not find the key and that I didn't believe it was in the aircraft, he asked if I was sure. 'Yes, I'm sure,' was the reply. So, the aircraft was then dispatched back to the ship. On arrival, and after shut down, the forward hell hole was opened up; as is the usual case, the wayward CSD key fell out onto the deck.

Steve Fuller

SANDGROPER 78

At the end of October, eight aircraft flew to RAAF Pearce via Edinburgh to participate in Exercise *Sandgroper 78*. We had two T-birds and six A-4s with 805 and 724 joining forces. Both COs were on detachment, with the SPs remaining behind to catch up on administration, I suppose. My drama involved my oxygen mask. It decided not to work, so the SE guy handed me the squadron spare. After the pitstop in Edinburgh, where the pilots turned the aircraft around, we departed in two waves about 15 minutes apart. About an hour into the cruise, I noticed that my oxygen was already down to five litres. When I dropped my mask, a bunch of plastic bits dropped out. It was busted. We were cruising at 26,000 feet and the cockpit altitude was about 18,000 feet. After some discussion with the Boss, I descended to 18,000 feet; that put the cockpit altitude at a more reasonable 13,000. I had a nice flight sans mask although it was a bit hard gazing up at the others. Once on the ground, the Boss fined me a beer for not checking my mask properly. Fair enough, you can't win them all.

RAAF Pearce was awash with aircraft. There were eight USAF F-4s from Clark in the Philippines, the eight of us, and four F-111s. The USAF had even flown in a mobile arresting gear staked out on the approach end of 36. We had two sessions of dissimilar air combat training with the F-4s which was a hoot; one of them went supersonic, breaking some windows at New Norcia. On the first ship strike, we were led by a pair of F-4s. The Boss was on the left side and I was on the right as we flew low level down a wide valley to the sea. The F-4s accelerated and we tried hard but could only get about 550 knots with the F-4s slowly running away from us. All of a sudden, there was a bright red light in my cockpit and, as I squinted at it, it read 'FIRE'. The adrenalin hit like an electric shot and I pulled the nose up and rolled toward the south. At about 4,000 feet I gasped out 'Fire warning' and the Boss called out 'No smoke'. At 10,000 feet, I pulled the throttle back to 85% and then the Boss was able to catch me up and look me over. I dialled in the TACAN [tactical air navigation system], headed for Pearce and let the plane level off at 20,000 feet. At this stage, I still had a fire warning, but no smoke, so I told the Boss I was headed for Pearce and an arrest. He escorted me home and I arrested. I think he went round and landed on 18. The next thing was the ATC jeep arrived with an ATC officer and the duty boy, both in a state of excitement. Apparently, an F-4 had a hydraulic failure and needed the wire, so we had to shift the A-4. The arrestor crew helped us push the A-4 backwards towards the operational readiness platform [an area at both ends of the runway where fast-response aircraft can park, removing the need to taxi from the flight line] and, when it was mostly clear of the runway, the lads reset the wire just in time for the F-4 to arrive and trap. The recovery crews worked hard to clear the runways for the other F-4 to land and it rolled past the two broken airplanes dragging its 'chute.

Back at Nowra sometime later, the SP started to get the squadron ready for a pilot changeover and a change-of-command. We flew a period of air-to-air gunnery, before starting on the essential skill of air refuelling and navigation. There was a long navex led by the SP where we refuelled at top of climb (4,000 lbs offload by the tanker to the flight of four). The SP then led us to Broken Hill and north-east up the Darling River towards Lightning Ridge, except my fire light repeated itself abeam Bourke. The nav was abandoned and we followed the railway line back towards Nyngan and thence Nowra at 20,000 feet. Once more into the wire. A few days later, I was No 3 to the Yank on a navex around southern New South Wales that was supposed to finish with a range slot at Beecroft, except the Yank had a fire light in the western wastelands and I offered him Canberra or Nowra. He chose Canberra and the ATC guys saw three A-4s approach with one landing and two of us overshooting for home.

The sequel; there is always a sequel. The Yank shut down on the runway, which is sensible. The firies rolled up but refused to get close to his aeroplane because it was fitted with six practice bombs and a rocket pod. So, he had to get out of the cockpit, go back to the LOX Bay, get the pins out and safe the pylons and pin the gear. Sometime later, a helicopter arrived with a recovery team, by which time the RAAF had found a tow bar and moved the jet to a ramp area. The maintenance troops tightened up the jet pipe adaptor and the Yank flew the aeroplane home. When it was brought into the hangar, the jet pipe was pulled and the adaptor was very carefully examined. It was cracked and the AEO opined that when we flew around long enough at low level, enough hot gases escaped to overwhelm the fire warning loop.

Peter Greenfield

The change-of-command occurred in December with Lieutenant Commander Collingridge being replaced by Lieutenant Commander Kavanagh. A magnificent flypast was performed by Lieutenant Ridgeway Corbin III USN – 500 knots right over the parade between H and J Hangars. The flying programme was strictly weaponry and then it was Christmas leave.

1978 snapshot

The carrier air group embarked on 27 February and disembarked on 31 May after a busy period at sea.

CO VF805 was Lieutenant Commander Collingridge from 16 January to 11 December when Lieutenant Commander Errol Kavanagh assumed command.

Skyhawk pilots for the year were Lieutenant Commander Barrie Daly as SP (posted off June), Lieutenant Commander Keith Johnson (SP from June), Lieutenants Kevin Finan USN, John Siebert, Peter Greenfield, star of the nightly news Barry Evans (AWI, posted 7 November), Nev French (LSO, posted August to VC724), Kim Baddams (LSO), and Sub-Lieutenants Col Tomlinson and Mick Maher (posted 19 July to LSO Course).

Lieutenants Bruce Hamilton and Brian Rowe continued in their roles as AEO and Aircraft Electrical Officer respectively until posted out on 4 September and 30 November. They were replaced by Lieutenants B Garratt (from 20 August) and Larry O'Neill (from 15 December) respectively.

CO VC724 was Lieutenant Commander Clive Blennerhassett with Lieutenant John Hamilton as SP.

The Skyhawk fleet, happily, remained at 16: three TA-4Gs and 13 A-4Gs.

Chapter 15

1979: THREE LOSSES IN A YEAR

It was a new year with a new CO, Lieutenant Commander Errol Kavanagh, and an almost completely new line up of pilots. January 1979 saw the team complete a back-in-the-saddle (BITS) refresher before starting a squadron workup. The new guys had carrier qualified the previous year and all that was required was a renewal of skills. While January was a busy start to a busy year, within nine months the Skyhawk fleet was short three A-4Gs.

Oops!

In January, we began another BITS with two general flying practice sorties followed by a formation sortie over the first three days. The Senior Pilot (SP) must have been keen to get us back in the instrument flying practice (IFP) groove because we flew four IFP sorties over the next four days. We then moved to an air combat manoeuvre (ACM) phase which began with a tanker to practice the art of aerial refuelling. So, when the CO briefed our afternoon sortie, he swapped me into the tanker and the tanker pilot became his No 2. I was given a TACAN [tactical air navigation system] fix and he briefed a 'No Radio' rendezvous. This was quite prescient of him.

The weather was deteriorating as I started and taxied first. By the time I got to the end of the runway, it was raining quite hard and, as I pushed the throttle up, a fountain of water gushed out of the air conditioning vent.

My radio failed as the gear came up and I went on instruments at 400 feet. I changed frequencies and transmitted normally and just flew out to the TACAN fix. As I orbited there, I saw the two aircraft emerge from the clouds and close on me. As the Boss stabilised on me, I signalled 'no radio' and he responded with the signal to start the package, and then stream the drogue.

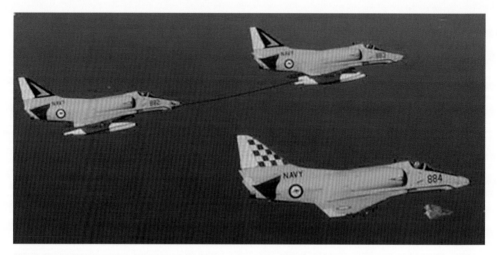

Two VC724 A-4s practice air-to-air refuelling with a VF805 Skyhawk alongside.
(Peter Greenfield)

The Boss slid behind me and I saw him take 500 pounds and then cross to my left wing. No 2 slid behind me and also took 500 lbs before he slid out and stabilised outside the Boss. I then descended towards the cloud tops and, when level, the two refuelling aircraft repeated the sequence. The Boss signalled to stow the drogue and then shut down the package. With that done, he gave me a thumbs up and blew me a kiss, before taking his wingman off to do their ACM thing.

I tracked off to the 150 radial at about 30 miles, and flew the left-hand triangle a couple of times, then started a High TACAN for Runway 21. I kept changing to the expected channels and turned up the volume and pressed the squelch, with no luck at all. Inbound to the runway at about 15 miles, there was a crackle on approach and I transmitted my callsign. The crackly reply was to switch to ground-controlled approach (GCA). That worked and I was given a GCA down to just above the minima.

After I taxied in, both a VC724 staff pilot ('Shep') and the Aircraft Engineering Officer (AEO) were at the foot of the ladder. The staff pilot told me the wingman had ejected, and the AEO told me my plane was impounded so the drogue could be officially examined, just in case.

Peter Greenfield

Sub-Lieutenant Col Tomlinson had ejected from 870. There was the usual inquiry, report and so on. For once, the wreckage could be recovered and examined in detail. Most of it was brought back by truck, but a Wessex was tasked with lifting the engine from the bottom of the crater and returning it to Nowra for examination.

THE FLIGHT OF MY LIFE

Little did I know (or do you ever) that I was in for the flight of my life as I entered the cockpit of 870 on 23 January 1979. On completion of start and post-start checks, I taxied No 2 to my Boss for an ACM and air-refuelling sortie. The tanker aircraft had departed to the south and we followed him at one-minute stream intervals into an overcast sky. On climb, we established the tanker had lost his radio transmitter, so we re-joined him at the pre-briefed rendezvous and commenced our tanking practice. We each made two dry plugs at 20,000 feet then descended and made two more at 10,000 feet without incident. Lead obtained a clearance for the tanker to make a TACAN approach back to the naval air station and he departed for home.

We then commenced the ACM phase of the sortie. After approximately 10 minutes of Battle Formation practice, we set up for our first level split. The split commenced and shortly after gaining sight, the Boss indicated that he had experienced a possible compressor stall whilst nose high and slow and was checking the aircraft. Following him through his various manoeuvres at 180 knots with military power set, I too experienced a slight compressor stall. Reducing the throttle, I regained level flight and informed lead. He had deduced that his drop tank pressurisation was the source of his concern and, as my aircraft was operating normally, we set up for a second split.

We had just commenced manoeuvring when my aircraft gave an almighty bang and started to vibrate. Calling the flight off, I reduced the throttle and regained level flight. The aircraft was chugging and stalling but this reduced as the throttle was retarded. Throttle was reintroduced and the chugs re-appeared at 80%. Again, the throttle was reduced and they died away although the aircraft was still vibrating. The throttle was again moved forward and the chugs and stalls started again at 83–84%. Shortly after, the oil low quantity light illuminated and the oil pressure dropped to 20 psi, flickered to 35 psi, then decayed rapidly to zero.

Lead was informed and he advised that I had smoke coming from the rear of the aircraft and suggested that I prepare for ejection. I repositioned the seat to an optimum position while he made a MAYDAY call on GUARD. Almost straight after, the fire light illuminated and the realisation that I was really in an ejection situation dawned on me. The whole process had only taken 1 to 1½ minutes and I was too busy to be thinking about anything else. The right rudder pedal gave way and simultaneously I started to get a slight smell of smoke through the LOX [liquid oxygen] system. I heard the Boss calling that I was on fire: 'EJECT, EJECT'. The sudden realisation that it was really time to go hit me and I reached for the blind hoping like hell it would work.

The blind came to about eye level and I was gone instantaneously with an almighty crash. At this stage, the starboard side of the aircraft was on fire; I was blacked out by the force of the ejection but, after a short time, came to with the sensation of looking through the top of my head at a white mass that was rotating at a tremendous rate.

Next came the great opening shock of the 'chute. The ballistic spreader, now incorporated in the seat, threw the risers out instantaneously and I slowed from 260 knots to zero in approximately 0.5 seconds. My whole body felt like a piece of rag being whiplashed as the opening shock rippled through it. I was in the 'chute within approximately 1½ seconds as advertised and felt myself sinking into the torso harness with the helmet rotated forward and oxygen mask held tightly around my throat. It slipped down through the ejection and opening shock and had to be released before I could look up and check the 'chute. I felt dazed for a few seconds and a feeling of nausea developed in my stomach.

The RSSK-8 (dinghy and survival pack) was becoming increasingly uncomfortable, and I released one side of it to relieve the pressure, also hoping that, after descending through the cloud, I would come out into a clear area and be able to release the pack just above ground so it would not injure me on landing. Not long afterwards, the tops of the clouds (approximately 7,000 feet) started to engulf me and the white mass that took away the bright sunshine and blue sky felt very pleasant for some reason.

I broke out of the cloud about 500 feet above heavily timbered rainforest country and, taking a quick look around, all I could see was the surrounding hills covered in cloud and drizzle. I reached down and with the aid of my legs was able to pull the RSSK-8 back up as the trees now came rapidly towards me. It took some time to relocate the RSSK-8 connections and while doing them up I noticed a small clear area of about 20 feet in diameter below. Attempting to steer into it by pulling on the rear risers, I was only successful in slowing some of the drift over the ground and landed into the top of a 100-foot-high tree on the edge of it. Crashing through the top of the tree, I hoped that the 'chute would not tangle and hold me stranded 100 feet high, but luckily it didn't. I continued through the foliage, breaking off branches as I went. Luckily, the foliage broke my fall, and I landed quite safely onto the rainforest floor.

I released the 'chute and RSSK-8, and activated the SARBE [personal locator beacon]. I then calculated that it would be at least 30 minutes before a helo would get to the area, so I switched it off. I looked around at the thick undergrowth that surrounded me and mentally prepared myself for a long wait before rescue. I decided I would re-activate the SARBE in 10 minutes in case there was anyone else in the area. I noticed a large fallen log protruding out of the undergrowth about 20 yards away in the clear area I had seen. Dragging the RSSK-8, I repositioned myself on the log and took off my gear. Just as I was taking out the foliage penetration flares, I heard the faint sound of a helo approaching. Switching the SARBE back on, I couldn't believe my ears and wondered how the hell they got there so quickly as I had only been on the ground for ten minutes. I fired a pen-gun flare, then another, and another. The sound continued to come closer, and I was able to make contact with them.

I could only see about 30 meters through the heavily timbered trees, so I was very relieved to have the Iroquois hovering above. An attempt was made to lower the strop, but it became entangled in the treetops, so the ball and hook only were lowered. It stopped about half a metre above me, so I had to reconnect my torso harness

Skyhawk 870 in happier times. It was lost after Col Tomlinson's ejection on 23 January 1979. (Seapower Centre)

and jump to grab the hook. After pulling myself up and connecting the hook through my D ring, I was able to message that I was ready to be pulled up. Apparently, the winch was only working to 120 feet (normally 160 feet) which gave us an indication of the tree height! I was winched up into the helicopter through the foliage. It was a very welcome sight for me to see the crew!

Col Tomlinson

FEBRUARY – MAY 1979

February was a busy month. I was the only nugget left from the previous year. Young Michael [Maher] was on a Landing Safety Officer (LSO) course, the other member of our Operational Flying School (OFS) was recovering in hospital from compression fractures. The Air Warfare Instructor had gone back to 724 Squadron, and the Senior LSO had also left for 724. The CO had brought his team across from 724 and only The Yank, the junior LSO and I were left. We were working up to re-embark on 'Mother'. There was lots of weaponry programmed including a splash target towed by an escort. Two live weaponry missions were scheduled to Puckapunyal for the Army's annual Joint Service weapons display.

Refuelling on the flight deck with the engine running, known as 'hot' refuelling. (FAAAoA)

In the next month, there was a lot of weaponry sorties and, unusually, I was programmed to deliver 886 (our favourite tanker) to Qantas Engineering for deep maintenance. The sorties continued with a night FCLP where we helped the troops out; after 30 minutes of bouncing, I taxied in and they gave me a hot refuel before I taxied out to do it again. Some of the maintenance guys had never done it, so the senior guys wanted them to practice it ashore. Towards the end of the month, we started working with the ship.

By May, the squadron was partially embarked, with one aircraft ashore awaiting a test flight. The pilots and maintainers were working hard conducting flight operations in accordance with the ship's workup programme.

Peter Greenfield

MY SHORT CAREER

My short career on the A-4 from mid-1977 until the end of 1979 had an unbelievable amount of action packed into such a short period. Looking back through my logbook was a bit of an eye opener.

February 3, 1978. My first day heading out from Nowra to a rendezvous with HMAS *Melbourne* for my first taste of the deck was in my favourite jet, 888. I can't remember who I went out with, but we nearly always tasked as pairs. The first few approaches to the deck were touch and goes with the hook up. Once the LSO ('Paddles') was happy with our form, he instructed us to lower the hook for the next pass. After touchdown and applying full power as always, the deceleration from the wire catching the hook was dramatic. I came to a stop with the engine still roaring at full power, and it was only after the LSO over the radio told me I was safely caught that I reduced the power. I had very little time to collect my thoughts as the flightdeck marshaller was directing me onto the catapult track after I was clear of the arresting wires.

Within minutes, I was rushing down the track, unable to move as the longitudinal G force pinned me to the back of my seat. The force of the cat shot had to be extreme to get a high-performance jet to minimum flying speed in the short distance available. *Melbourne* had not been designed with A-4s in mind.

Back to Nowra for a refuel and then back to the ship in the afternoon. It was an awesome day at work!

Later that year, now in 805 Squadron, I was leading another pair in a navigation exercise that took us low level through the Snowy Mountains. As I was enjoying myself immensely, it was a bit of a shock when the fire warning light came on.

We abandoned the low-level fun stuff and headed for the moon. I remember declaring an emergency (not sure who to, as the A-4 was not fitted with a VHF radio to talk to civilian air traffic control). We headed for Canberra where I landed safely. My wingman followed me until I landed, then flew a low overshoot and headed home to Nowra.

I was welcomed to the RAAF side of the airfield by being told I could not enter the officers mess as I was in a flying suit. No kidding, Sherlock. Some more friendly RAAF pilots escorted me to the back bar (flying-suit friendly), fortunately out of the hearing of the 'Blunt' who was mess president.

The next morning, a truck arrived from Nowra with some 805 Squadron saviours. They quickly found the hot air leak in the engine and fixed it. All that was left was for me to do a full power run while they checked their work and then I was free to depart. We found a compass-swing concrete circle in a quiet corner of the airfield. After the run was completed, the maintainers seemed to be in a hurry for me to depart. There was lots of waving of hands and thumbs up, so off I went.

Unbeknown to me, the concrete circle was surrounded by another circle of bitumen dust seal, a huge section of which was ripped up and hurled into the adjacent grass by my jet blast. I didn't actually see the damage, but I never heard another thing about it!!

May 23 was a sad day in one respect but a happy one in retrospect. I was tasked with some 20-degree dive bombing on a splash target, followed by some DLP (deck landing practice). The splash target went as well as I expected, (i.e., not brilliantly) and the DLP was going as expected. My fearless leader was our US Navy exchange pilot, Kev Finan. With only the two of us in the landing pattern, if one successfully arrested, he would foul the deck for the other until he was marshalled forward onto the catapult.

As Kev proceeded to successfully hog the deck time, I kept getting waved off. I remember flying the downwind leg watching Kev touch down as I flew abeam the ship, secretly hoping he would bolter (miss the wire with his hook), not something he usually did. On this occasion, he started to slow down after touchdown, but then kept going, not seemingly fast enough to my eye. Sure enough, as the jet reached the end of the angled flight deck, the canopy blew off and Kev ejected.

Not something you witness every day. My favourite jet, 888, lost forever to the deep. Happily, Kev was plucked out of the sea moments later by the rescue helo. The rest of my landing pattern was going well except all I wanted to do was get down on the deck safely. I assumed Kev had a problem with his aircraft. It did not occur to me at the time that the ship was the problem (the wire he caught broke after slowing him to a speed from which he couldn't get airborne again).

The LSO wouldn't talk to me, until I was on late final approach. I guess he was busy and had other priorities! Finally, he remembered me as I flew through Kev's smoke cloud. The instructions were pretty clear to wave off and recover to Nowra. When I landed back in Nowra and parked the aircraft, I had to be helped out of the cockpit by 'Hammo' as delayed shock had started to take hold and my legs didn't seem to want to work.

Murray Coppins

Bye Bye 888

It was a wire break, but an unusual one. The wire snapped at the first sheave from the arresting engine. The aircraft pulled the wire all the way through the intervening sheaves to the flightdeck, fatally slowing the aircraft. As the Skyhawk ran over the angle at about 80 knots, The Yank initiated ejection and within 1.5 seconds was in a fully developed 'chute. The seat did what it was intended to do – save a pilot from a deck-edge ejection. Kev was in the water for less than a minute before Pedro was over the top, and all he had was a sore neck!

And so, 888, the trials aircraft and a good 'un, sank, fully serviceable, after two minutes. RIP 888.

The ship and embarked aircraft continued working up to a warmup exercise, before embarking on Exercise *Sea Eagle* in the cold and miserable Tasman Sea.

KEV FINAN'S EJECTION

During the ship's workup phase prior to participating in Exercise *Sea Eagle*, we sailed to our training area off the east coast in the Sydney area; I was tasked to lead a three-ship formation to conduct air-to-air tactics. My No 2 was our US Navy exchange pilot and 'Top Gun' graduate, Kev Finan, and my No 3 was Murray Coppins.

We had planned to complete our airborne manoeuvres and then return on board to undertake 'hot refuelling', then taxi straight back on the catapult for a continuation of the airborne exercises.

The moment of ejection for LCDR Kevin Finan USN. (RAN)

Hot refuelling was conducted abeam the island area, clear of the landing area, and involved fuel being transferred via the refuelling probe while the engine was still running. It was a very efficient way of reducing the turnaround times.

I was the first to land and caught the 3 wire. I might point out that the target wire for the A-4 was No 4. This gave the best hook/ramp clearance without compromising the probability of a successful trap.

On this occasion, I had already commenced refuelling when Kev landed and caught No 4 wire. The next thing I heard was the LSO screaming out over the radio, 'EJECT, EJECT, EJECT'.

Naturally, this caught my immediate attention and although from the cockpit I could not see the aircraft disappear over the port side following the wire break, I did look up to see Kev and his ejection seat flying parallel to the ocean perhaps only a hundred or so feet above the water.

When flying we always wore a knee pad which held various briefing notes etc and I distinctly recall seeing these trailing behind Kev and his seat. With heart-in-mouth, I witnessed the seat release, the parachute bloom and, with perhaps only a couple of swings, Kev entering the sea. The plane guard (safety) helicopter, Pedro, was quickly on the scene and within a few minutes a drenched but otherwise uninjured Kev Finan USN was back on *Melbourne*.

Coincidently, during an on-deck delay earlier, Kev and I had gone through the same practice exercise to determine which handle we would 'pull' if we needed to eject in a hurry. While using the upper handle would provide more head protection and help keep the upper body straight, the lower handle was easier and quicker to grasp with one hand, with the other hand supporting the wrist.

Kev credited this practice with saving his life. My guess is that a mere tenth of a second delay in pulling that lower handle would have seen him bouncing across the ocean with little or no chance of survival.

Allen Clark

Skyhawk 888 disappears under the waves following Kevin Finan's ejection. (Seapower Centre)

Lieutenant Allen Clark also contributed the following regarding a man overboard incident and the loss of Skyhawk 886:

MAN OVERBOARD

There is rarely a dull moment on board an aircraft carrier and Monday 24 September 1979 was no exception with a particularly exciting and dramatic conclusion. We were in the final days of Exercise *Sea Eagle*. The following is a partial extract from the ship's report of proceedings (ROP) for that day:

'The very strong feeling of well-being which permeated the ship took a powerful downturn on the morning of Monday 24th, however, when it all went sour. The weather had become very unpleasant the night before, during a front from the south but I considered the conditions to be still suitable for flying. At 0805, while preparing to move aircraft in readiness for the launch of a strike, an A-4G (No N13-154907) broke loose and flipped over the starboard bow of the ship under the impetus of very heavy roll. Able Seaman ATWL ER Krenn (S 118640) was in the cockpit at the time as the brakeman … After only 11 minutes in the water Able Seaman Krenn was safely onboard HMAS HOBART where he had a number of stitches inserted in two gashes in his forehead … He was later charged by the Commanding Officer HMAS *Hobart* with improperly leaving HMAS *Melbourne* and with being absent from place of duty for 11 minutes.

At least the CO of *Hobart* had a sense of humour!

I'm not entirely certain of the outcome and conclusion of the subsequent Board of Inquiry, suffice to say the ROP does not tell the full story. Further, in the excellent biography of Sir David Martin, the then CO HMAS *Melbourne*, the incident is discussed but the real circumstances are not fully or accurately recorded.

I happened to be the squadron duty officer that day. The weather was marginal and the swell, at times, on the limit for Skyhawk recoveries. I happened to meet Captain Martin on my way to flyco and he sought my opinion on the suitability of the conditions for launch. I suggested we could launch the strike but have an aircraft on standby with the buddy store (external fuel tank) rigged and ready for launch to refuel the aircraft, if needed, for a delayed recovery. In a worst-case scenario, I pointed out that Amberley was within range and the aircraft could recover there and await improved conditions before returning to the carrier. He agreed with this assessment and, I assume, after discussions with CO 805, Commander Air and Little F (Air Boss), the plan was put into action.

The first action required was to move the A-4 (886) to the centre of the deck in order to carry out a proving cycle of the buddy store. This involved deck crew manually extending the refuelling basket and hose to check the serviceability of the equipment. At that time, 886 was chained down close to the deck edge on the starboard side of the forward deck with the tow motor attached.

From memory, the wind had turned southerly, but the large swell was out of the north-west. Consequently, on our then course, the ship was experiencing significant roll.

I was in the flightdeck office and heard the instructions given to the flightdeck crew that the ship was about to commence a turn to starboard and, once the ship had steadied on her new course, the A-4 could be moved as required.

I then proceeded to the bridge and heard the navigator instruct the officer of the watch (OOW) to commence a turn to starboard and take up a course of (from memory) 130 degrees, putting the swell directly astern. Obviously, the OOW misheard the instruction and had the ship roll out on a course of 030 which happened to be directly across the swell. The navigator immediately shouted to the OOW words to the effect, 'I said 130 not 030.'

It just so happened that the ship did indeed steady momentarily on the 030 course and, coincidently, there was a brief lull in the swell and roll. The flightdeck crew, seeing a steady ship and with little roll at that moment, assumed the ship had completed its manoeuvre and ordered the chains to be released in preparation for moving the aircraft.

At that very moment, with the aircraft still attached to the tug, the ship rolled heavily to starboard. I was running down the ladder from the bridge to the flightdeck at the time and recall the ship's roll, which was the worst I'd ever experienced. I almost fell down the ladder! The roll was recorded at 20-degrees starboard (as an aside, I was later advised the roll caused the dental chair to break from its floor mountings).

The aircraft toppled upside down into the gun sponsons and then did another flip to land upright in the water alongside the ship.

I believe Able Seaman Eric Krenn was quite concussed from the blow to his head and was still sitting in the cockpit when the aircraft passed abeam the starboard after boat space. Kev Finan later told me he witnessed the aircraft floating past with Krenn still in the cockpit looking very dazed. He yelled at him to get out of the cockpit and inflate his flotation vest. Whether he heard and responded to this is unknown, suffice to say, that is what he did and he disappeared into the enormous swells.

HMAS *Hobart* had been ordered to the rescue station and just happened to be in the right place at the right time and miraculously spotted the sailor in the very rough seas (no mean feat). I was later told one of *Hobart*'s crew jumped over the side of the ship with a rope tied around his waist and somehow managed to get hold of Krenn. At that moment, a huge wave hit the side of the ship and the two sailors disappeared into the depths. When the ship rolled again and the swell had passed, the *Hobart* rescuer emerged still with a vicelike grip on his fellow sailor. An absolutely amazing rescue and a positive ending to what was a somewhat disastrous day.

Allen Clark

In Eric's own words:

On 24 September 1979 at 0805, on HMAS *Melbourne* and 160 miles off the coast of Newcastle, we were in severe weather with very high waves. We needed to bring Skyhawk 886 back from in front of the bridge to the rear of the flightdeck for repairs.

I was ordered into the Skyhawk several times by the flightdeck Petty Officer but declined due to waves breaking over the flight deck and a 60-knot wind blowing. The saltwater spray would have damaged many of the instruments in the cockpit and there was a real fear the canopy would have ripped off. I explained this to the flightdeck officer who then told me to get in when the wind died down.

At the time, we were sailing into the waves. The ship changed course and the crew (except for the flightdeck) was warned the ship would list severely. After the change of course, the wind died down to about 20 knots so I was told, 'Get in now while you can.'

I got into the Skyhawk and closed the canopy, all the chains were taken off and I was attached to the aircraft power cart, an NC2A. I looked out to the starboard side and was amazed at how rough the water was and noticed a huge wave coming. I then looked out the other side and saw the Petty Officer with a horrible look on his face and noticed also that the wing was high off the deck; it was at this point I knew I was in trouble. The aircraft rolled off the ship onto the gun sponson, from there it did a complete flip and landed right way up facing astern in the water.

In the water, I thought I had awoken from a lousy dream until I saw *Melbourne* sailing past me. After what seemed like minutes to me when I was in the cockpit, I smashed my way out of the already broken cockpit glass (I am vague on that thoughI somehow got onto the wing and heard and saw heaps of people shouting at me from three decks to inflate my life vest which I then did, and I think I then jumped away from the wing into the water; the weather was freezing cold at the time. I was told that from the time the plane hit the water to it disappearing was only five seconds, which I still find hard to believe.

In the water, I was swearing at the ship, shouting that I knew it was too dangerous to move that Skyhawk at that time. The lifebuoy sentry was so stunned seeing me floating past the ship that he forgot to throw the lifebuoy with the flare on it until I was far away. Most of the time I couldn't see until a wave hit me, it was not until then that I noticed I was being blinded by my blood. I felt my head and then noticed a deep laceration.

It was here that I tightened my life jacket in the hope my body would be found because I knew there was no way of living through that head wound that far from land and certainly no one could find me in this water. After what seemed to be over an hour (was only 11 minutes), a wave hit me, clearing away the blood and I saw HMAS *Hobart* right in front of me. I thought that was great for a moment, then the blokes on *Hobart* pointed to behind me. A huge wave had formed behind me and many of the sailors later told me they went back inside because they believed no one could survive that wave. The wave hit me and I was underwater for a long time getting thrown around; in the end I couldn't take it anymore and breathed in what I thought was water but had at this stage come back on top of the water. I'll never forget that breath as long as I live.

HMAS *Hobart*'s ship's diver, Martin Lang, then jumped in the water, swam to me and pulled me alongside *Hobart* where I was then winched on board. I thought I was alright but ended up collapsing and they carried me to the sick bay.

In sick bay, the medic, Peter Laylor, now had the task of suturing me up. This was almost as bad as the accident because getting sutured above the eyes with the ship, and both of us, rolling on the deck every which way was really scary. After an hour, Peter said he couldn't do any more as he was tired. Even so, he did a great job.

The young man himself, ABATWL Eric Krenn, who survived being swept overboard in the cockpit of Skyhawk 886 on 24 September 1979. (Eric Krenn)

We then sailed to Sydney; I thought I was very privileged to be on the captain's boat till I noticed there were heaps of officers in front of me. This was undoubtedly so no media could get a picture of me or get near me.

At the hospital, the doctor told me that, due to my severe injuries, I would be there at least a month. Somehow, two days later, I was at the naval enquiry on *Melbourne*. They asked me if I had put on the brakes and I told them '… any harder and I would have gone through the floor, and did you guy's notice that the aircraft went sideways not backwards or forwards?' I think they were trying to stitch me up for the blame.

It was a long weekend and they also generously gave me one other day off. We sailed the next Tuesday. With sutures still in place, a Chief Petty Officer (CPO) then ordered me to ride brakes; I think I told him no. This then went to the squadron CO who probably told me six times that I had to obey orders; orders are orders. I told him he had two choices: either charge me with disobeying an order or order the CPO not to order me to ride brakes. The squadron CO was really annoyed about that but not as much as the CPO who then, in front of everyone, called me a coward.

Eric Krenn

Exercise *Kangaroo III* found VF805 embarked, but VC724 was deployed to RAAF Amberley in support.

AMBERLEY DETACHMENT – WHAT'S IN STORE?

So, one time on a *Kangaroo* exercise in the late-1970s, 724 Squadron Skyhawks were based at RAAF Amberley in Queensland, operating out of No 12 Squadron's Chinook helicopter hangar. Meanwhile, 805 Squadron was embarked on HMAS *Melbourne* offshore for the exercise.

After a week of long days flying and maintenance around the clock, we had a couple of days and the night off. The officers retired to the mess for wining and dining and the troops cleared out one of the accommodation block rooms to make a nice 'party space' named 'el Cabino Royale' for all to enjoy with music, Uckers and copious amounts of beer!

Late in the evening, the party was roaring and we were a bit surprised to see the Squadron Weapons Electrical Engineering Officer (WEEO) standing at the door, a little worse for wear and trying to catch our attention. I spoke to him he said, '805 have contacted us and they need a canopy system desiccator cartridge tomorrow morning, there is an aircraft flying in to collect it.' 'No problem,' I said, confidently sipping my beer, 'I have a couple in the

FAK (Flyaway Kit).'

He looked at me intently and then said, 'Let's go and check.' I responded, 'No, no, no need to do that, I packed it myself, it's all good,' and had another slug of beer.

'No, we will go and check.' He was getting very insistent now and obviously not going to take no for an answer. The WEEO then drove us to the flight-line security post and explained we needed access to check some spares and the RAAFie on duty shook his head as two tipsy Navy guys – the WEEO in casual clothing and I resplendent in a T-shirt, shorts and a pair of runners – entered the deserted flight line.

It was quite dark and dead quiet as we walked between the hangars, heading to the 12 Squadron area. We chatted as we went along when suddenly a bloody BIG German Shepherd guard dog leapt out barking at us and looking like he was going to eat both of us in one bite! HOLY HELL! We were screaming and then the dog's chain caught and he froze in mid-air about a metre from both of us, now flat up against a hangar wall!

The dog-handling RAAFie guard had obviously been sitting down and taking a snooze against one of the hangars when we staggered along. Startled by the racket, he looked bewildered at the sight of us! 'Wh, wh, wh, what the HELL are you doing here?!' was all he could get out. Lucky he was still holding the other end of the dog's leash!

A little nervous explaining and showing ID cards ensured we weren't going to sabotage the hangar and we were permitted to proceed. We quickly scuttled into the hangar, got the aircraft part confirmed and got out of there as soon as possible!

The car ride back to the blocks was very quiet and we saw the party was still in full flight. I said to the WEEO, 'Would you like a beer?' His response was, 'Yes, I think I need one' and we re-joined the party, now stone-cold sober and needing something strong to calm our shattered nerves. Early the next morning, I marshalled in the 805 Squadron aircraft, put the desiccator cartridge in the LOX Bay bag and watched it roar off back to the ship.

Another exciting Skyhawk squadron adventure and all before breakfast.

Joe Hattley

Meanwhile out in the 'oggin', 805 needed some LOX bottles refilled for the next day's flying.

'Too slow, mate, I've already done 'em!'

It's mid-October 1979, post mini-refit, and after a brief workup period. We were now undertaking *Kangaroo III*, of nearly three weeks' duration, in the Coral Sea. Underway off the north Queensland coast, the ship's squadrons were flying hundreds of sorties.

I was a leading hand on a two-year draft to Air Engineering Department (AED), HMAS *Melbourne* – February 1979 to February 1981. One of my many duties was as Liquid Oxygen Plant Operator (LOX), requiring inspection and replenishment of the ten-litre LOX converter vessels/bottles from VF805 A-4 Skyhawks deployed on board. LOX converters were found in a small compartment of the Skyhawk's aft fuselage, starboard side, below the speedbrake, and were part of the aircraft's larger oxygen-supply system providing breathable oxygen for aircrew.

The LOX Servicing Plant Bay and entry compartments on *Melbourne* were located in 3J Port with an Upper LOX Generation/Refrigeration Room at 2J Port. It was overseen by a Petty Officer MTP (Marine Technical Propulsion) Supervisor as part of the larger Catapult and Arrestor Party within the ship's Engineering Department. Access was via port side of B Hangar just near the hangar fire curtain between A and B Hangars.

Kangaroo III was well underway and, after a long sea day of normal workshop activities, I returned to my birdies' mess 3D Port, had a tubs, enjoyed scran (a meal), and retired to the mess for further chat with mess mates, some TV and reading before sleep. Around 2130 in comes a squadron member calling out my name via the aft entry to 3D Port mess from the 3E Port Boat Space. What the hell? What's going on at this hour?! 'We need you to come down and charge some converters for our early morning strike sorties tomorrow! We're dropping them off now.'

'Well, I 'spose I've got no choice,' I think to myself, and I leave the mess and head aft to the AED Workshop via A, B and C Hangars. At the workshop, I changed into overalls and put on safety boots, made my way forward via C and B Hangars to the LOX Servicing Plant Bay at 3J Port. At the entry compartment, I change yet again into the usual white, hygienic LOX operator overalls and enter and close the compartment door to the actual Servicing and Charging Plant Bay, where I find to my surprise the POMTP is doing the refill job right then and there, and in the process of finishing off the fourth and last converter. All converters were charged now, cold as ice with condensation and sitting on the servicing bench.

He turned towards me, smiled, and said through his safety face mask, 'Too slow, mate, your converters are all done! Just do the serviceability tags now, will ya?'

Taken aback somewhat, I slowly grab some green serviceable labels and proceed to fill out and sign, ready for the squadron boys.

The POMTP says to me, 'All's well, mate. I just got on with it as I was already here doing a double check of the Plant Room, before hitting the rack.'

I reply something like, 'Geez mate, you didn't have to do that! But thanks, 'cos I was already in mine. Do they check out, okay? Alright then, I'll just finish these tags off and then go and let the squadron boys know they're good to go.'

I then reverse the clothing sequence, changing out of the white safety overalls, into my regular overalls and was on my way back to AED Workshop, dropping into 805 AMCO [Aircraft Maintenance and Control Office] in C Hangar to let them know the converters were ready for collection.

I changed back into my 10As and returned to my 3D Port mess, thinking, 'Now that I'm wide awake, do I go down to the galley to grab a cup of kai?'

PJ Fleming

P Allen (Nobby) Clark Skyhawk stories

To avoid any confusion, my actual first name is Philip but, ever since I can remember, my parents called me either Alan (spelt how my parents wrote my name) or Al. According to my mother, I was their fourth child and, after three boys, they were hoping for a girl and had planned to call me Phyllis after my mother.

However, nature had other plans, so my parents amended this idea and selected the nearest equivalent, Philip. So it wasn't until I joined the Navy and discovered my birth certificate that I realised that, a. my first name was actually Philip (one 'L' not two as I was led to believe), b. my second name was Allen (not Alan as they addressed me throughout their lives) and, c. to top it off, after always celebrating my birthday on 21 January (according to my parents, the actual day I was born), I discovered the birth certificate showed my birthday as 22 January.

Thankfully, as soon as I joined the Navy I, like many Clarks, was awarded the nickname 'Nobby' although that in itself could be confusing with so many 'Nobbies' about. Even during my two-year posting to RAAF Pearce as a flying instructor there were two of us; we became known as 'Navy Nobby' and 'Air Force Nobby'!

So, to my Navy flying days. My first posting after completing pilots' course was to the S-2E Grumman Tracker. So off to VC851 in July 1969 to undertake OFS with fellow graduates Owen Nicholls, Clark Stitz and George Harvison.

We completed the Tracker course in mid-1970 and were then posted as supernumerary crew with VS816 on board HMAS *Melbourne* for an exercise to Western Australia. Not a lot of fun and very little flying but we did manage to discover quite a lot about the workings of an aircraft carrier with visits to every department onboard.

I was then posted to VS816 and subsequently gained my CAPC rating (carrier airplane commander). I then completed several operational tours in the Tracker, undertaking anti-submarine and surveillance exercises with SEATO and *Rimpac* forces.

But I never lost an overwhelming desire to fly the A-4. I reasoned my first step was to undertake the Flying Instructor Course with the RAAF at East Sale. However, the normal pattern was 'prop' guys were posted to train as instructors on Winjeels before being subsequently posted to No 1 Flying Training School (FTS) at

RAAF Point Cook while 'jet jocks' trained on the MB326H Macchi and could expect to be posted for advanced instructional duties at No 2 FTS at RAAF Pearce. Therefore, I needed to secure a posting to East Sale and the Macchi, not Point Cook and the Winjeel.

Much to my delight, this eventuated and I subsequently spent two very demanding but thoroughly enjoyable years plying my instructional skills in the Macchi. During this time, I continued to apply for an assignment to the A-4 Skyhawk and, thanks to the then Aircrew Posting Officer, Errol Kavanagh, at the completion of my tour of duty at Pearce in 1975, I received a very much appreciated posting to VC724 to undertake the A-4 Skyhawk OFS.

My first carrier landing in the A-4 was completed in February 1978. Although I had accumulated over 120 Tracker traps, the exhilaration of landing a fast jet on the smallest operational aircraft carrier deck in the world was exciting, horrifying and amazing all at once. After carrier quals, I could now lay claim to being the only Navy pilot to gain operational flying status on both the Tracker and Skyhawk.

CHASING THE F-111S

VF805 was embarked for Exercise *Kangaroo III*, which was being conducted off the Queensland coast. During the early phase of the exercise, we had received a number of attacks from the F-111s but our A-4s had not been able to counter these with any effective intercepts.

The successful raids on the fleet were invariably conducted at first light so I suggested to our then squadron CO, Lieutenant Commander Errol Kavanagh, that we should have two aircraft prepared on deck before first light, engines running with one aircraft on the cat ready for launch. As soon as we received intelligence a raid was inbound, we could have two aircraft airborne within a minute or so.

I'm not at liberty to reveal how we discovered an inbound raid was imminent (maybe something to do with airborne helicopters being advised to maintain a particular altitude), but Errol was immediately airborne and climbing through low broken cloud, and I followed moments later.

As I climbed out, and just a few miles straight ahead of the carrier, I spotted through the broken hazy cloud a very low F-111. Immediately, I rolled into a tight right-hand dive and accelerated to maximum speed, latching onto the tail of the raider.

With only Sidewinder missiles on board, the A-4 was capable of over 600 knots at sea level and, assuming the F-111 was simulating a bombing attack, its speed at that stage would have been subsonic and slower than my aircraft.

When conducting a Sidewinder attack, the indication of a successful 'lock on' is listening for a 'growl' (which can be heard through the helmet headset) from the infra-red sensor located in the nose of the missile. When the missile is launched (real or simulated), the call over the radio is 'Fox 2' (Fox 1 being 20-mm cannon). In this instance, just before we flew over the flightdeck, I locked on and made my Fox 2 call. Meanwhile, in the Operations Room, the Fighter Flight Ops Director was being monitored by the exercise umpire.

The probability of achieving a 'kill' was determined by the simple throw of a dice. I'm unsure what number coincided with a successful attack, but in this instance the radio call came back saying the shot was a miss which necessitated another launch.

By now, the F-111 had started to 'sweep' its wings and was accelerating away from me but, in cognisance of the strong growl in the headset and my eyeball estimate of distance, I was confident I was still within Sidewinder range.

Again, I made the Fox 2 call and, from what I was later told, the director was yelling 'Roll the dice, roll the effing dice'. The call then came over the radio saying I'd achieved a kill. This resulted in a heated complaint from the hierarchy at RAAF Amberley questioning the integrity and professionalism of the Skyhawk pilots!

My guess as to what brought this about was the fact a second F-111 had just completed an attack on an outlying warship approximately ten miles to my port side (possibly HMAS *Supply*) and was turning to join his companion. By the time he saw me and his buddy, there is little doubt my target had accelerated away at supersonic speed and I would have been well and truly out of missile range.

The resulting story of our successful attack against the raiding F-111 was promptly recorded in the Brisbane newspapers and it was this story that infuriated the boys in blue and led to their 'nastygram' to the fleet commander. Ah, the fun and games of inter-service rivalry.

CAP MISSION

We were approaching Hawaii for a *Rimpac* exercise in early 1980 and steaming towards the main island of O'ahu which bristled with fighter bases, including the US Navy at Barbers Point, the US Air Force at Hickam and the Marines at Kaneohe. I was on CAP and was vectored via the ship's radar to targets to the north of the fleet, where I encountered a number of A-4s approaching at medium altitude and immediately engaged. What surprised me was how relatively easy it was to manoeuvre onto the tail of two of the incoming aircraft. The ensuing 'battle' lasted about ten minutes; I then returned to 'Mother'.

Subsequent to our arrival to Pearl Harbor, we invited the pilots from VC1 to visit the ship. I then met two of the pilots I had intercepted a few days earlier. Their names were Andrea Rice and Lucy Young. The following is an extract from the *Navy News* article dated 21 March 1980:

'The war games currently being played on and over the sparkling blue waters around Hawaii generally follow a similar pattern to those of previous *Rimpac* exercises. But for individual participants, there can still be surprises as Australian Fleet Air Arm pilots from HMAS *Melbourne* can testify following what started out as routine air combat manoeuvres between Australian and American jet fighters some 350 nautical miles west of Hawaii.

Thirty-three-year-old Allen Clark, a highly experienced naval pilot with 3,000 hours in his logbook, was flying a Combat Air Patrol at 15,000 feet when he spotted four 'bogeys' coming into attack the fleet at about 6,000 feet. They were USN tandem-seat TA-4J Skyhawks from Hawaii's Naval Air Station at Barbers Point.

He swung his aircraft over into a deep dive to intercept and, for about eight minutes, the sky was a jigsaw of Skyhawks wheeling and diving, trying to gain the upper hand in combat tactics, which are the 'bread and butter' of a fighter pilot's life.

What Lieutenant Clark didn't know at the time, only learning later when he landed back on the carrier, was that the first aircraft he 'jumped' was flown by a US Navy WOMAN PILOT.'

The article then gave some background into the women flying with the US Navy and in particular Lucy ('Juicy Lucy') and Andrea (can't recall callsign). They were among the first female US Navy pilots to train on jet aircraft but were not permitted to be attached to an operational squadron. In fact, they were not trained specifically in ACM, they were restricted to naval support missions. However, the other squadron pilots had undertaken some unofficial dogfight manoeuvres to teach them the ropes.

IADS EXERCISE

In late 1979, VF805 was invited to attend an International Air Defence Exercise based out of what was then the dual RAAF and Malaysian base at Butterworth in northern Malaysia.

We ferried the Skyhawks to Butterworth via Darwin and Bali. At the time, the RAAF had Mirages based at Butterworth and these conducted simulated attacks on Singapore and Malaysia. It was local

A colourful USN TA-4 refuels from a VF805 A-4G with a 'buddy' refuelling tank during a Rimpac exercise in the late 1970s. The USN TA-4s are from VC1, the same squadron from which Allen Clark intercepted two female pilots in 1979. (Seapower Centre)

government policy that Republic of Singapore Air Force (RSAF) aircraft would not simulate attacks on Malaysia and, similarly, Malaysian Air Force aircraft would not 'attack' Singapore.

Our task then was to initially fly down the Malaysian Peninsula at high altitude (around 30,000 feet) then drop to very low altitude (below 500 feet) to make a simulated attack on Singapore's international airport. We could expect to be intercepted by RSAF fighter aircraft (F-5s) once inside Singapore's airspace.

As it prevailed, the weather throughout the flight was typically equatorial with storms, low cloud and poor visibility. The radar was next to useless as a weather radar but, somehow, I managed to make my way high then low level down to Singapore.

Air traffic control were very much aware of our planned 'attack' and kept all civilian aircraft clear of the island while I was making passes over the airport. I made a couple of dive attacks then headed back to Butterworth, low then high level again, through the storms without ever seeing an RSAF aircraft. One up for the A-4s.

It was during this time I had the opportunity to engage in DACM against the F-5s of the Malaysian Air Force. The key to success in aerial combat is knowing the strengths and weaknesses of both your adversary and your own aircraft and then operating your machine to its absolute limits.

'Pulling G', and thereby achieving high rates of pitch, is part and parcel of ACM but the amount of 'G' is limited not only by the aircraft's structural limits but also by the aircraft's current speed. The A-4 was capable of pulling 7G at light weights but the only way of determining if the aerodynamic limit was close was to 'feel' the onset of pre-G-stall buffet.

Insofar as roll was concerned, there was virtually no limitation provided the manoeuvre was conducted with an awareness of potential adverse aerodynamic effects (departure).

In the case of the F-5, the aircraft had a superior pitch rate but, with its stubby, almost square, wings, the roll rate was poor compared to the A-4 which (from memory) was in the order of 720 degrees per second.

On this occasion, and knowing the poor roll rate of the F-5, it was not too difficult to engage in a 'rolling' battle to overcome its superior pitch. On each encounter, I was able to successfully achieve a 'firing' position on the tail of the F-5 simply by countering his pitching manoeuvre with a tight roll.

Allen Clark

SINGAPORE DIVERSION

During my short time with the frontline A-4 squadron, we participated in *Sandgroper 78*, *Tasmanex 79*, *Sea Eagle 1*, *Kangaroo 3* and IADS 5 and 6/79.

The flights to/from Malaysia for the IADS [Integrated Air Defence System] deployment were memorable for two reasons. The first was on the Bali to Butterworth leg (six-ship formation), when I suffered a Utility Hydraulic failure somewhere over Indonesian jungle. I was acutely aware of the note in the flight manual: 'Be alert for fire.'

After advising my flight leader, his response was predictable: 'Look around, maybe pressing on to Singapore is the obvious choice.' So, my pair departed the formation and diverted to Tengah. With no brakes or nosewheel steering, an arrested landing was called for. Apart from the ground crew initially not understanding that I couldn't raise the hook after stopping, the diversion all went swimmingly.

As I waited for the C-130 and squadron ground crew to arrive, I contemplated an unscheduled overnight in Singapore. Sadly, the SP was in the Herc. He assumed the role of 'pilot remaining with the broken jet' and despatched myself and the majority of ground crew and the C-130 to continue to Butterworth, where we arrived just as the welcome party was winding up!

The second reason was the flight from Townsville back to Nowra which was my last in the A-4 (887). An all too short A-4 career. My own fault really. While at Nowra, Caro and I bought a block of land and built our first house, which pretty much guaranteed that, as soon as it was finished, I was posted to the Qualified Flying Instructor's course, never to return to the Nowra area.

Murray Coppins

Being part of HMAS *Albatross*, VC724 fell under the purview of the admiral in command of Support Command. In 1979, the admiral and his staff came to *Albatross* for the annual inspection known as Admiral's Rounds. In J Hangar, Chief Petty Officer Peter Welsh was running the Air Refuelling Store Maintenance Section.

AIR REFUELLING STORE MAINTENANCE

During his inspection of HMAS *Albatross*, Rear Admiral Guy Griffiths and I were talking about air refuelling store maintenance and the maintenance of its propeller. While the Admiral looked intently on, I was explaining to him how I was able to strip and rebuild an In-flight Refuelling Store Propeller Assembly without a jig and thereby save six months of downtime when the damaged units were required to be returned to the USA. The Lieutenant Commander was looking very apprehensive as he thought I would get a rocket for not following procedures. The Admiral's comment was 'Well done Chief, keep up the good work.'

Peter Welsh

Peter Welsh (right) in conversation with Rear Admiral Guy Griffiths (left), as related in the story above. The bearded lieutenant commander is the apprehensive staff air engineer. (Peter Welsh)

1979 snapshot

The air group embarked on 22 May for a short stay, leaving on 30 May. It returned to *Melbourne* on 18 July and remained on board for almost four months, disembarking on 14 November.

CO VF805 was Lieutenant Commander Errol Kavanagh.

The pilots to fly the embarked aircraft were Lieutenant Commander Keith Johnson (SP), Lieutenant Commander Kevin Finan USN, Lieutenants John Hamilton, Kim Baddams (LSO), Al Clark, Murray Coppins and Mick Maher (LSO), and Sub-Lieutenant Ray France.

CO VC724 remained Lieutenant Commander Clive Blennerhassett.

The fleet was now down to 13 aircraft: three TA-4Gs and ten A-4Gs.

This A-4 has its main landing gear in 'tram tracks' which were devices introduced during the 1979 cruise to assist with deck parking. They had been invented during WWII for use with Seafires. (Allen Clark)

Chapter 16

1980: THE BEGINNING OF THE END

On 14 January 1980, Lieutenant Commander Clive Blennerhassett assumed command of VF805. It was a long time since he had completed No 1 Operational Flying School back in 1968. The Senior Pilot (SP) remained Lieutenant Commander Keith Johnston until mid-year. The carrier was programmed for an Indian Ocean deployment later in the year, but there was a long, intermediate docking after it returned from *Kangaroo III*. However, the writing was almost on the wall with the loss of another three aircraft and catapult problems, while the search for a replacement carrier and fixed-wing fleet competed with other Defence procurement projects.

At this point, HMAS *Melbourne* was the only Royal Navy (RN) designed aircraft carrier still operating high-performance fixed-wing jet aircraft in the conventional way. HMS *Ark Royal* had paid off, and the Argentinian and Brazilian carriers of the same class were no longer operating their jets. The Indian Navy, with their INS *Vikrant*, was actively pursuing Sea Harriers; their Sea Hawks and Breguet Alize aircraft were no longer going to sea, just their helicopters.

The two companies who had built the steam catapult (Brown Brothers) and the arrestor gear (MacTaggart-Scott) were no longer supporting these items. HMAS *Melbourne*, when commissioned, was one of the first aircraft carriers with a steam catapult (a BS-2). Commissioned in 1956, the ship had primarily operated in Australian waters ever since.

The catapult itself was a hybrid. It was a combination of parts from HMCS *Bonaventure* and USS *Coral Sea*. Documentation, if it ever existed, must have been seriously out of sync with the machinery. The Navy had relied on the skills and knowledge of the dockyard staff and ship's staff to keep it working. In fact, while the ship was involved in the Spithead Review in 1977, the catapult engineer was in the dockyard at Portsmouth, finding parts to repair the catapult.

The arrestor system was a similar story. MacTaggart-Scott built them in the mid-fifties and, with the demise of conventional carriers in the RN, both it and Brown Brothers closed shop. At one stage, the US Navy had sent experts to physically review the catapult; their advice had been to use the monitoring systems built into the catapult.

A review of the ship's reports of proceedings (ROP), for the years prior to 1980, shows there were continual problems with the spline valves, particularly Nos 1 and 3. Another problem existed too; the Board of Inquiry into the catapult 'cold shot' and loss of 885 revealed a serious lack of documented operating procedures. In other words, the operators relied on accumulated knowledge and 'handover briefs' as they posted in. That led to the developing problems the Navy had in manpower management – retention and sailors' postings.

In between the embarkation for *Rimpac 80* and the Indian Ocean deployment, VF805 was operating ashore from HMAS *Albatross*. It was a time for pilot changeovers and continuation flying to maintain skills. This contribution from 'Nobby' Clark describes the ejection of his leader at the conclusion of one of those multi-role flights – a formation sortie and aerial refuelling.

ANDY'S EJECTION

It was 28 April 1980. VF805 had disembarked to Nowra a few weeks earlier following the successful completion of *Rimpac 80* in Hawaii. The flying, however, never ceased and it was at the conclusion of an air-display practice sortie that Lieutenant Andy Sinclair and his VC724 TA-4 (878) parted company.

Andy was the designated flight leader of the mission, which included an air-to-air refuelling session, and I was his No 2. We had completed our practice and returned to Nowra in an echelon three-plane formation. The normal joining procedure was identical to that employed for embarked operations. That is, approach via an 'initial point' around 5–10 miles downwind from the active runway at a comfortable speed (this was generally around 300 knots but could be a much higher speed for tactical reasons) and then carry out a formation 'break' into the circuit.

On this occasion, as I recall, we entered upwind at 300 knots and, as briefed, carried out a formation three-second break onto downwind. In order to achieve a neat symmetry, my count for three seconds was 'one banana, two banana, three banana' then break. And, again to achieve that all important (and neat) level formation break, No 2 and, in turn, No 3 needed to keep the leader level with the horizon.

On this occasion, I noticed Andy had lost some altitude in the break and, dutifully, I tried to match his elevation by dropping the nose a little. Very shortly after rolling wings level downwind, I then heard those dreaded words 'Mayday, Mayday, Mayday, Engine Failure'. Andy had lost engine thrust and was unable to maintain altitude.

Attempting to force land (glide to the runway) was definitely out of the question. The swept/delta wing of the A-4 gave it the gliding performance of a brick. A forced landing at an airfield would require something in the order of 6–8,000 feet overhead the field to have any chance of success.

So, there we were, downwind at around 800 feet when Andy pulled the ejection handle and I had a bird's eye view of the two ejection seats firing, with Andy safely out of his disabled TA-4 (he didn't have a backseat passenger on this occasion).

The aircraft continued to descend downwind and then erupted into a huge fireball as it ploughed into the ground a few miles south of the field. I'd never witnessed an aircraft crash and all I could think was: 'How could I have saved that aircraft, maybe fly underneath and give it a lift to the runway?' I know, a stupid thought, but here was this beautiful TA-4 gracefully gliding to its inevitable demise right in front of my eyes. Thankfully, Andy survived the ejection relatively uninjured.

I presume there was an investigation into what caused the engine failure, but I'm not aware of the outcome. I do recall some discussion regarding the possibility the engine may have suffered what is known as an 'idle undershoot'.

All A-4 pilots were briefed and trained not to rapidly reduce thrust to idle without subsequently 'cracking' the thrust lever forward a little so the engine maintained positive (above idle) thrust. If not, there was a potential problem with the fuel-control unit whereby the engine revolutions would roll back to a sub-idle speed. If this did occur, the engine would not respond to any increase (forward) in throttle movement and would stagnate at sub-idle. The only way to recover from this situation was to shut the engine down and carry out an in-flight relight. Knowing the glide capability of the A-4, this would be impossible unless the aircraft was above 10,000 feet. Below this altitude, an ejection was the only option unless located more or less directly over a suitable landing field.

Andy was a very capable and experienced A-4 pilot and I have little doubt he would have followed the standard break procedure, so what caused the engine failure remains a mystery as far as I know.

Allen Clark

TA-4G 878 seen during an Amberley deployment in the mid-1970s, with the chequered VC724 marking on its fin. The aircraft was lost after Andy Sinclair was forced to eject near Nowra on 28 April 1980. (FAAAoA)

Shortly after, 'Nobby' was posted to the Director of Naval Air Power (DNAP) office in Canberra. There he was the V/STOL (vertical/short take-off and landing) Project officer, and he offers this contribution:

THE V/STOL PROJECT

The Sea Harrier was a derivative of the Hawker Siddeley Harrier built by British Aerospace and operated by the Royal Navy (RN). It was developed to replace the RN's fixed-wing jet (F-4) aircraft following the retirement of their conventional carriers (*Ark Royal* finally decommissioned in 1979).

It was designed to operate from the new class of 'through-deck-cruisers', RN ships *Illustrious, Invincible* and *Ark Royal* which had neither a steam catapult nor wire-arresting systems. The aircraft required a short take-off run (hence the 'ramp' at the bow of the ships) but could land vertically by vectoring the engine thrust through nozzles which rotated to the vertical position.

Following *Rimpac* in May 1980, I was posted to the position of V/STOL project officer located within DNAP. My task was to produce the Staff Requirement Paper which would be presented to Defence for the acquisition of a replacement for the A-4s. Our target aircraft was in fact the AV-8B, which was an upgraded version of the Sea Harrier and operated by the US Marine Corps.

The Replacement Aircraft Carrier team led by 'Toz' Dadswell was working feverishly to convince Defence that, on mothballing HMAS *Melbourne*, we purchase a V/STOL-capable aircraft carrier along the lines of the Italian Garibaldi-class or the Spanish equivalent.

As all and sundry would be aware, the Australian Government was offered the opportunity to purchase HMS *Invincible* which the British Government saw as surplus to their requirements. Then came the Falklands War and suddenly we were back to square one.

There was no disputing the fact the Sea Harriers performed an excellent job during the Falklands clash. The squadron only lost four aircraft, two were shot down by ground fire and the other two lost as a result of accidents during recovery.

There have been a number of excellent books written about the Harriers in the Falklands War and the consensus appears that the Sea Harriers accounted for between 20–23 Argentinian aircraft, principally A-4 Skyhawks. It's a fair assumption the British fleet would have suffered significant losses but for the presence of the Harriers.

Meanwhile, in Canberra, we were busy beavering away with our own endeavours to acquire a V/STOL aircraft. Simultaneously, the Air Force was seeking to replace the Mirage; consequently, there was a huge battle for funds from the Defence budget.

I cannot vouch for the veracity of the rumour at the time that all Air Force staff in Canberra were encouraged to undermine, at every opportunity, the Navy's proposal to purchase both a replacement aircraft carrier and V/STOL aircraft. An example of this occurred after the Falklands adventure. The press had reported on the massive success rate of the Sea Harriers and sought comment from our military experts.

Nobody from Navy Office (in particular DNAP) was interviewed. In fact, it was a wing commander (if my memory serves me correctly) from the Mirage replacement team who was interviewed and asked for comment. Sadly, the response did our cause no favours.

Allen Clark

Meanwhile, VF805 was at sea. This contribution comes from the older and wiser Michael Maher, by now the Squadron Landing Safety Officer (LSO):

WIRE BREAK!

On 16 September 1980, I had just completed a Probex[1] with (to the best of my memory) Sub-Lieutenant Eamon Lines and came back to recover on a fairly calm day somewhere in the Indonesian archipelago. After a normal break into the circuit and approach (an okay 3 wire), I touched down and initially felt normal retardation; I was just about to close the throttle when I felt the retardation completely cease. Fortunately, I still had the throttle at full and the stick full back; the aircraft accelerated and, as I approached the end of the deck, the nose started to lift back into the flying position.

As I left the deck, there was some sink, but I had good speed, attitude and power; the aircraft stabilised just below deck level and then climbed away. I left the gear and flaps down and had the other pilot do a damage check. He reported all looked good, so we entered holding and waited on a decision to land or divert. We were directed to land – the 3 wire was removed – and we both landed without further incident.

Good points: flying procedures and checklists worked perfectly and no adverse outcomes resulted. Bad points: the newly installed rubber matting installed to protect the deck from the arresting gear knuckles slamming into it was not positioned properly. The three wire knuckle had been hitting the raised metal edge around the matting; this had been noted by deck personnel but the significance of the damage to the knuckle was not understood. When I landed, the knuckle sheared, resulting in the wire break. The matting was newly installed for this cruise. Clearly the misplacement of the mat, and the lack of understanding of the consequences of the damage to the knuckle, caused this incident.

Mick Maher

In Singapore, the ship was about to enter a self-maintenance period (SMP). The fixed-wing aircraft were not flown off for essential continuity flying as essential spares had been flown in for required aircraft maintenance. The rotary wing aircraft did fly off the deck during the SMP but disrupted essential maintenance activities on the catapult and arrestor systems.

The ship berthed in Sembawang at 1000 on 17 September and remained alongside until the 30th. On 1 October, *Melbourne* departed Sembawang for a passage through the Malacca Straits en route to Cochin. Catapult defects prevented any Skyhawks exercising with the RAAF Mirages based at Butterworth on the first day at sea. It was not a catapult issue, however, that led to the second Skyhawk loss of the year.

[1] A Probex was essentially a flight out ahead of the ship for about 30 minutes searching visually, then turn, climb to 15,000 feet and radar search back towards the fleet.

Commander John Crawley was the Aircraft Electrical Officer of VF805 back in 1976. He maintained a deep interest in aviation safety and in retirement worked for the Directorate of Flight Safety for the RAAF. He compiled this report on the loss of 875:

LOOKING BACK – A BAD MONTH FOR THE BEAN COUNTERS!

On the 2nd October 1980, VF805 Squadron Skyhawk N13-155062 (875) suffered an engine failure during a catapult launch from HMAS MELBOURNE in the Andaman Sea, 35 nm north of Sumatra, Indonesia. The pilot, fortunately, was able to eject and was rescued by 'Pedro', the search and rescue helo. The aircraft sank in 1,279 metres of water and was lost.

Skyhawk 875 was the first of two Skyhawks to be lost off the same catapult during the same month. On the 21st October, SBLT David Baddams also ejected, this time into the Indian Ocean 100 nm south-west of Colombo, Sri Lanka, escaping with only minor injuries after his aircraft, N13-154906 (885), received a 'slow' catapult shot.

These two launch attempts proved to be among the last at launching Skyhawk aircraft from HMAS MELBOURNE [885 was the last A-4G catapult]. The ship was to later go into refit and shortly after in early 1983 the new Federal Government announced the intention to cease fixed-wing flying in the RAN and dispose of the aircraft carrier. The following account of the loss of the first Skyhawk, 875, is from an interview with CMDR Clive Blennerhassett and the Board of Inquiry (BOI) Report.

At 1708 hrs local on the 2nd October 1980, Skyhawk 875 was recovered onboard HMAS MELBOURNE following a normal training sortie. The pilot for this sortie was Captain Tom White, USMC. Following the landing, the aircraft was positioned for an engine-running or 'hot' refuel prior to the next launch. Captain White remained in the aircraft during the refuelling operation and then handed the aircraft over to [the then] LCDR Clive Blennerhassett, Commanding Officer of VF805 Squadron, and pilot for the next sortie [Clive is simply known universally as 'BH']. Let's begin with his account of the final flight of 875.

THE PILOT'S REPORT

I was briefed for an INTEX/DLP [intercept exercise/deck-landing practice] sortie with LEUT Andy Sinclair. I was due to take aircraft 876, but it became unserviceable and so it was arranged for me to do a hot fuel and hot pilot switch with one of the Skyhawks that was already airborne. That switch was due to occur at 1705. Andy manned his aircraft and launched at 1645 or thereabouts and I waited for my aircraft to arrive back. About five or ten minutes later I went down to the deck ready to get in the aircraft, and I suppose it finished its hot refuel (4,600 lb) about five minutes later.

Captain White climbed out of the aircraft and I climbed in. I strapped in, turned all my avionics on and then just sat there for a while and made sure that everything was up and running okay. I then went through a TAFFIOHHHC[2] check while I was still in the chocks, which is a very comprehensive check for take-off flight actions. Once I'd completed that, I called 'On deck'. Almost immediately, I was taxied forward loaded on the catapult without any problems.

Virtually as soon as I was tensioned up, I was told to go to full power, which I did. The EPR [engine pressure ratio] provided earlier was 2.42 which agreed with the EPR on my gauge, oil pressure was just above the lower limit at 41–42 psi, EGT [exhaust gas temperature] was 650°C and rising, oil quantity was 20–80%, trims were indicating 6° nose-up and zero rudder, and flaps were full down. I checked the fuel-control panel – the aircraft was in primary fuel control, drop-tank pressurisation was off, as was emergency fuel transfer. I lowered the catapult grip, wound up full friction on the throttle and saluted the FDO; away I went!

The launch felt quite normal, and the aircraft rotated normally off the end of the ship, but at that point I noticed that everything suddenly went very quiet and my rate of acceleration reduced quite markedly. I was looking out at that stage, adjusting the aircraft's attitude and when I looked back inside the cockpit I noticed the RPM gauge winding down through 72% or thereabouts – this was merely an observation of the main needle, a position rather than a physical reading.

---

[2] TAFFIOHHHC: Trims, Airbrakes, Flaps, Fuel, Instruments, Oxygen, Hydraulics, Harness, Hatches, Controls.

TIME TO GO

So, I elected to eject – probably about two seconds after I realised something was wrong. I ensured the aircraft was in a nose-high position – and I had plenty of elevator control to achieve that – but I felt that the aircraft was sinking. I reached down with my left hand and pulled the seatpan handle. Next, I saw the canopy go and almost immediately the seat fired. It was a reasonably gentle ride up while I looked down and saw the A-4 'sinking' underneath me. I tumbled in the seat a couple of times before ending up facing backwards along the shroud lines. I saw the parachute streaming but not inflated. I then turned around again to face forwards at which point the parachute canopy ballooned with a reasonable but not large shock.

I don't recall the remainder of the descent into the water. My next recollection is of hitting the water and submerging two or three feet. I floundered to the surface confused but I had no trouble staying afloat even though my Mae West was not inflated. The parachute had collapsed by this time, so I searched for and found the actuating handle for the Mae West and it inflated okay.

I was worrying heaps about sharks at about this time until I realised I was having trouble breathing. I tried to get rid of my oxygen mask but the stoles on my Mae West had inflated to such a degree where they were bearing against my chin and I was having difficulty reaching the mask fastening clips. I eventually got the right clip unfastened and pulled the mask away from my face. What a relief – but just then the bow wave from the ship hit me and I went under again gulping in not air but seawater!

A lot of things started happening about this time. I saw a ship making for me (the rescue destroyer), Pedro (the SAR helo) was hovering nearby, I was coughing up sea water just as the SAR diver (Leading Seaman Rick Newman) jumped from the helo to assist me.

I owe that guy heaps, he jumped into a known shark-infested area to assist me. After ascertaining that I was reasonably okay, and after a rather fruitless attempt to partially deflate the over-inflated Mae West, Rick wrestled me into the winching strop. From here it was clear sailing and, after Rick was winched up, we landed back on board the carrier for the mandatory medical check. Total time from 'go' on the catapult to landing back on board was only four minutes, but it seemed much longer!

WHAT CAUSED THE ACCIDENT?

The Board of Inquiry (BOI) assisted by ship's staff, carried out an exhaustive analysis of the accident and considered the full gambit of possible causes: sabotage, human error, catapult malfunction, environmental conditions, catastrophic mechanical failure within the aircraft's engine, fuel contamination, Flight Control System malfunction and accessory failure.

After a lengthy and detailed investigation, the Board concluded that the accident was caused by a significant loss of engine thrust as, or soon after, the catapult fired and this thrust loss was attributed to a fuel system malfunction. In the absence of actual physical evidence, the precise nature of the malfunction could not be determined; however, the cause was deemed to be (in order of most likely) either: an FCU [fuel-control unit] failure, a throttle linkage failure, an engine-driven fuel pump failure, a manual fuel shut-off valve closure due to mechanical failure or a fuel line rupture.

The Board noted that HMAS MELBOURNE's records show that there had been 8,834 A-4 Skyhawk launches since 1969. As far as could be determined, no previous unexplained cases of abrupt power loss during the catapult stroke had been experienced nor had any abrupt power losses occurred during full-power base runs. They were well aware that, in the absence of definite physical evidence, their findings were, to some degree, speculative. Nevertheless, after thoroughly considering the available evidence, they recommended that this accident be regarded as 'an isolated case of fuel system malfunction'.

Commander John Crawley

Fixed-wing flying was suspended during the passage to Cochin while the Board of Inquiry deliberated. The suspension was reconsidered after the CO VF805 requested an interview with the fleet commander. He represented himself as the senior jet aviator and must have been persuasive. After the time alongside in Cochin, the suspension was lifted and flying resumed for the two-day passage to Colombo. The squadron flew several sorties on the 11th and 12th for general flying practice, deck landing practice, and task unit support.

MICK'S FLICK

After a short period of flying on 1, 3 and 11 October, I was conducting a formation and instrument flying practice sortie on the 12th and again came back through a normal break and circuit; approach was normal and engaged a wire (I believe it was the 5 wire) – while there was some retardation, it certainly was not normal. I had pulled the throttle back to idle and, as the end of the ship was approaching fast, I reached down for the ejection handle with both hands; there was a severe stop and the aircraft was catapulted backwards (as the wire had reached its full pull out and obviously stretched and shot me backwards). As I was holding the ejection handle, I could not press the nosewheel steering button and the nosewheel castored as the aircraft went backwards.

Skyhawk 876 going sideways on the deck on 12 October 1980. Note the angle of the front wheel and the wire underneath. (Phil Thompson)

This resulted in the aircraft turning 90 degrees, so now I was going backwards towards the side of the ship; I put on the brakes, which then caused the nosewheel of the aircraft to lift into the air. Then it all stopped, the nosewheel came back onto deck and the aircraft stopped moving. This incident was again caused by someone not doing their job properly. The five wire arresting-gear system did not have any oil (which normally dampens and regulates the pull out of the wire) in the system so it just 'free wheeled', so to speak, until it reached full throw. This system had been drained in Singapore but never refilled. Again, the ship's crew's inexperience, and the lack of checklists and procedures caused this incident.

Mick Maher

Michael had clearly come back from his LSO course older and wiser. While the ship was in Sembawang, the Arrestor Party had dockyard assistance to replace the No 1 spline valve. This valve controlled the wire runout using oil regulated by the spline into a holding cylinder. Work on the spline valve meant the system had to be drained and, as the spline valve was made good, it had to be refilled. The whole arrestor unit should then have been tested with low drag and then high-drag pull outs.

But there was more to come. At 1400, the SP, Lieutenant Commander Peter Clark, experienced a utility hydraulic failure. He had no speedbrakes, no flaps, the gear had to be extended manually, and every station included a store, including the buddy store on station 3. The ROP recorded he recovered uneventfully via flapless recovery. That was a masterful understatement.

The successful flapless approach by Lieutenant Commander Peter Clark in October 1980. Note the stores on every station.

The arrestor gear had a capacity of 108 knots for an aircraft at maximum landing weight.

That meant the wind over the deck had to be 20 knots for an aircraft approaching at 127 knots. With no flaps, the optimum speed is increased by approximately 12 knots. Speedbrake loss had no effect. The approach speed would therefore be approximately 140 knots for an on-speed indication. The ship, therefore, had to generate 32 knots wind over the deck which, in HMAS *Melbourne*'s case meant into a wind of 12 knots at a ship's speed of 20 knots. Not great, but at least doable. The real question was how much fuel did he have as he crossed the ramp?

Loss of A-4G Skyhawk 885

Tuesday 21 October 1980 was the first day of scheduled fixed-wing flying operations following the Fleet visit to Colombo. A period of eight days had elapsed since the last fixed-wing flying was completed. Not quite three weeks after the loss of Skyhawk 875, on this day Skyhawk 885 was lost at sea from HMAS *Melbourne* during catapult operations, southwest of Sri Lanka. The pilot, Sub-Lieutenant David Baddams, ejected and was rescued uninjured. Wessex helicopter pilot Dick Chartier relates the following story of the incident:

THE RESCUE OF SBLT DAVID BADDAMS

The rescue of SBLT David Baddams is etched in my memory and I guess will be for the rest of my life. However, 21 October 1980 was a long time ago, so the routine parts of that day are somewhat fuzzy.

The aircraft carrier HMAS *Melbourne* had two Wessex Mk.31B helicopters embarked as SAR and utility aircraft. For this particular sortie, our aircraft side number was 834. I was aircraft captain, Leading Seaman Ray Cully my aircrewman, and a member of our maintenance crew, Rick Newman, was the SAR diver. We attended the fixed-wing briefings, most of which involved much hand waving and tactical terminology that was complete gobbledygook to us, so we just sat 'glazed over' until it was our turn to brief.

When compared to pre-flight briefings of today, those in 1980 were pretty casual. The purpose of plane guard, as the name suggests, was to act as rescue helicopter for carrier fixed-wing take-off and landing operations by either S-2 Trackers or A-4 Skyhawks. It was a given we would be airborne solely to rescue ditched aircrew, so we just discussed what we would do if either of us ditched; the same as every other plane guard sortie.

It's probably worth explaining that plane guard was probably the most mundane and boring flying one could do, so if you'd flown one, you'd flown them all. It involved a launch, typically from six spot (the most aft helo spot on the ship) and then a quick transit to a 40-foot hover, maintaining a position about 400m off the ship's port quarter. On completion, a radio call 'Pedro to Six Spot' was our signal to return. Sortie duration was based on the time it took for fixed-wing take-off/landing operations to be completed and many were recorded as just 0.2 hrs (12 mins).

Despite the mundane nature of this task, we paid particular attention to all of these activities. Each landing was slightly different, with some landings involving much wing waving or anxious calls from the LSO. Not all intended landings resulted in an arrest but could involve a 'wave off' or a 'bolter' – where the arrestor hook skipped over the five arrestor wires and the aircraft would apply full power and get airborne to try again.

By very nature, the fixed-wing circuit with the possibility of a 'wave off' or 'bolter' on landing meant the plane guard position was restricted to the port quarter. However, for sorties that involved just take-offs, I would often sneak up to a position about 100m abeam the catapult in order to watch the launches, adding some interest to an otherwise brain-numbing flight. On this occasion, as it only involved A-4 launches, I decided when airborne to move to abeam the catapult to watch.

On this particular launch, all proceeded as normal apart from the catapult launch itself which should have hurled the aircraft airborne in about two seconds flat. Instead, the aircraft just moved slowly down the catapult track and my heart immediately went into overdrive! While the two guys in the back could see what was happening, I instinctively yelled to them 'Get ready, guys!'

SBLT Baddams' ejection as captured by Melbourne's deck camera. (Jack Mayfield)

As the doomed Skyhawk approached the edge of the flight deck, the radio came alive with an urgent, 'Eject! Eject! Eject!' This was LCDR Errol Kavanagh who manned the tower and watched everything. Immediately the aircraft canopy flew off very closely followed by the ejection seat shooting skywards. I distinctly remember arms and legs flailing as the seat ascended before the parachute canopy with its ballistic spreaders blossomed.

It's amazing how many things run through your mind in situations such as this. I immediately realised that we were way too close. Why? I had the very strong perception that the pilot in his parachute was going to drift into our rotor disk. I realised that this was why the plane guard was really supposed to be stationed off the port quarter. I immediately flew away to the left into an orbit with the intent of returning to where the pilot would be waiting to be rescued; meanwhile the ship kept travelling forward. Returning to where the pilot would be, we were perplexed to find no sign of anything and flew another orbit to locate him.

Returning to the hover and scratching our heads as to what had happened, Dave Baddams, looking somewhat dazed, suddenly appeared at the surface. I descended to about 20 feet for Rick to drop into the water to assist Dave into the rescue strop, while Ray prepared for winching. The expectation was for this to be completed relatively quick, but time dragged and Ray and I were surprised at how long Rick was taking in the water.

Finally, Rick was ready. He and Dave winched aboard in the double lift harness and we recovered to the ship. Whilst inbound, Rick explained that Dave had been completely tangled in his parachute shrouds and it had taken him all that time to cut Dave loose. Of course the ship was ready with the medical team poised for action and, upon landing abeam the island, Dave was whisked away to the sick bay for examination.

Looking at my logbook, I reckon the rescue took around 45 minutes as I had recorded it as 1.0 hrs. This was exceptionally long for a routine plane guard sortie. I later learnt that following Dave's ejection he actually landed on top of his aircraft. Dave's parachute shrouds then snagged on the aircraft and proceeded to pull him down with it as it sank. This certainly explained why we were unable to see him when we'd completed our initial orbit, and also why he had become so entangled in his parachute shrouds. He was a very lucky fellow.

Dick Chartier

PILOT'S ACCOUNT OF ACCIDENT

Pre-flight briefing began at 0830 for a two-aircraft launch with LEUT Mike Maher as flight lead and myself as No 2. The sortie was briefed to be FRU [fleet requirements] and INTEX and was very thorough due to us both not having flown for seven days. At the completion of the formal brief, a standard squadron brief was carried out by Mike, which included a comprehensive emergency section taking special note of ship-oriented emergencies such as hold-back failure, 'soft catapult shot' (how appropriate), broken arrestor gear, hydraulic problems etc.

We suited up 40 minutes prior to planned take-off time to enable plenty of time for precise pre-flight actions and for the completion in slow time of all relevant checks and procedures. Strapping-in was carried out normally with emphasis placed on tightening the harness lap straps due to problems I had experienced on arrestment in a previous sortie with loose straps. Cockpit checks and start-up were completed without incident, all indications being normal. After-start checks were also completed and the aircraft systems were operating normally. During the final external checks on the aircraft, I completed two sets of thorough TAFFIOHHHC checks as well as two sets of placard pre-take-off checks. At the thumbs-up given by ground personnel, I acknowledged their signal and radioed 'On deck' to flyco some five minutes after Mike in 876.

I was taxied first, the brakes operated normally as did the nosewheel steering. The taxi to the catapult chocks was uneventful. On reaching the chocks, I noticed ground personnel observing something at the rear of my aircraft. Meanwhile, I selected full flap and lowered the catapult grip.

The chocks were lowered prior to the shuttle being brought back and after a short period of time I was given a thumbs up and green flag from the Flight Deck Officer (FDO). He waved me forward and tension was taken on the catapult. I noted that in tensioning, instead of several small jolts pulling the aircraft nose down, there was only one large jolt.

However, this had occurred to me before and I assumed it was a relatively normal occurrence. The FDO then waved his flag indicating a wind up to full power. I selected full power and ran through the pre-take-off vital actions written on my knee board. The engine instruments were all indicating normal, I rechecked full flaps, catapult grip down and selected full throttle friction with my right hand. At this stage, I transferred my gaze to the other side of the cockpit and noticed that my horizontal stabiliser trim was fractionally off 6° nose-up. Whilst correcting for this, I experienced a jolt and realised I was moving along the deck.

I immediately assumed a premature hold-back failure and retarded the throttle to idle and applied full brakes. This action seemed to have no effect, so I moved my left hand to the lower ejection seat handle and pulled seemingly in conjunction with an 'Eject, Eject, Eject' call from flyco.

My body posture at ejection, given the time available was as close to optimum as possible. The lower handle pulled out very easily. I felt pain from the initial ejection shock, I suspect this was due to the heavy braking raising my bottom slightly from the seat. It seemed that, instantaneously after the initial ejection shock, the ballistic spreader inflated the chute. Immediately after this, my next action was to grab for the two dinghy release handles; I grabbed them and pulled.

The next conscious thought I had was of being in the water facing the direction of the ship's travel. I don't remember sinking on initial entrance into the water. I looked right and saw the ship about 20 feet away with the last bits of my aircraft submerging about halfway between me and the ship. I then inflated the Mae West and tried to release the parachute risers, but the latter proved unsuccessful – and then I was hit by the ship's wake.

It seemed now as though I was being pulled head first down into the water. I noticed that I couldn't breathe and my efforts to release the parachute Koch fittings were futile. I soon became panicky and started flailing wildly, pulling at anything my hands happened to come into contact with. After what seemed like an eternity, something jerked free – as if I had broken away from it. My swimming for the surface was quite frantic as I still was unable to breathe.

When I broke surface, I removed my oxygen mask and discarded it. Although I still experienced some difficulty in breathing, I eventually got some air. But I was still in a lot of trouble, hopelessly entangled in my parachute risers. The SAR diver, Rick Newman, then magically appeared and started to untangle me.

At this stage, I began to relax as I felt very safe with him there. He talked me through releasing all my Koch fittings (RSSK-8 seat pack included) and then the oxygen hose. After this, he was finally able to clear the parachute and let down my Mae West to enable the winch strops (double) to be fitted, and we were then winched up together. I had to take some of my weight on my hands during the hoist as my lower back was hurting. Once in the helo, Rick and the aircrewman (Leading Seaman Ray Cully) proceeded to remove my torso harness. Once back on the ship, I was placed in a stretcher and carried off to sick bay.

Isolating the accident cause

With plenty of witnesses to the accident, it soon became apparent that, unlike the accident involving Skyhawk 875 earlier in the month, a perfectly serviceable aircraft had been dispatched off the end of the ship.

The BOI was quickly satisfied that the pilot was properly briefed and authorised, and that he was competent to complete the flight. The Board was further satisfied that the aircraft was fully serviceable and that the weather was suitable. Clearly, something had gone horribly wrong with the catapult launching process. Normal aircraft start-up occurred at 0950 and the aircraft subsequently taxied forward towards the catapult at 1003. The catapult loading sequence was delayed momentarily as the catapult crew were not ready to accept the aircraft; however, very shortly thereafter the catapult crew indicated to flyco that they were ready to proceed.

The Assistant Flight Deck Officer (AFDO) then took charge of the launch. Aircraft loading varied from normal in that it was taxied into the catapult chocks, the hold-back fitted and then the chocks lowered with the shuttle forward. The shuttle was then retracted, the launching bridle attached and the tensioning sequence completed. The AFDO, having received visual confirmation from the catapult CPO [Chief Petty Officer] that the catapult was ready for the launch, then proceeded to signal the pilot to wind up to military power. Then, with the aircraft at military power, but with no launch acceptance signal having been made by the pilot to the AFDO, the tension bar parted and the shuttle commenced towing the aircraft down the track.

The rate of aircraft acceleration was abnormally slow and it soon became apparent that, irrespective of any pilot action, the aircraft would leave the flight deck well below flying speed. Flyco, rapidly assessing the situation, transmitted to the pilot to eject. Pilot ejection was initiated just as the aircraft nose wheel dipped onto the bridle recovery platform and was followed by normal seat separation and parachute deployment.

The aircraft departed the flight deck, slewing slightly to starboard before impacting the water close to the bow and subsequently passed quite close down the port side of the ship. Pilot splashdown occurred on the port side in close proximity to both the ship and the aircraft. A few parachute shroud lines were observed to be draped over the aircraft tail plane, the parachute canopy still partially inflated.

As the SAR helicopter, piloted by SBLT Dick Chartier, manoeuvred for the rescue, the downed pilot was observed to be suddenly jerked underwater (although his Mae West and dinghy were inflated), surfacing some seconds later. The SAR diver, Rick Newman, was 'despatched' to assist in what proved to be a difficult recovery due to the tangled parachute shroud lines. After disentangling the pilot, a double-lift recovery followed and the pilot was returned safely onboard.

The aircraft sank a few seconds after impact with the water, and although the rescue destroyer HMAS *Perth* was quickly on the accident scene, nothing of value was salvaged.

Commander John Crawley

This was the last loading of an A-4G on HMAS *Melbourne*'s catapult. A-4G operations from the ship were immediately suspended.

1980 snapshot

The air group embarked on 20 January and disembarked on 16 April following its *Rimpac 80* deployment. It returned to the ship on 17 July and disembarked sometime in November.

CO VF805 was Lieutenant Commander Clive 'BH' Blennerhassett.

The pilots flying the squadron's A-4s were Lieutenant Commander Keith Johnson (SP, posted 6 June), Lieutenant Commander Peter Clark (SP, 6 June until 2 July 1982), Lieutenants Mick

Maher (LSO until 14 December 1981), Allen Clark (posted 4 May), Murray Coppins (posted 14 July), Bob Stumpf USN (14 January until 2 June), Ray France (posted 14 July), Gary Osmond (posted 5 September), Andy Sinclair (AWI until 19 January 1981), Tom White III USMC (6 June 1980 – 12 June 1981), and Sub-Lieutenants Eamon Lines (7 July – 2 July 1982) and Dave Baddams (to 2 July 1982).

CO VC724 was Lieutenant Commander Barrie Daly.

The Skyhawk fleet had dwindled to an almost unworkable number, 10: two TA-4Gs and eight A-4Gs.

Skyhawk 885 taxiing forward in the initial stage of being loaded on the catapult. Note the plane guard Wessex in the background, positioned approximately 400 metres off the port quarter as described by Dick Chartier. Note also the camouflage. By 1980 the Melbourne embarked a mix of camouflaged and non-camouflaged Skyhawks. The scheme had been first applied on a VC724 A-4 at Nowra in 1977 using washable paint. After formal approval, the scheme was applied by Qantas as airframes were overhauled. (Seapower Centre)

Chapter 17

1981: THE YEAR THAT WASN'T

Lieutenant Commander Gary Northern assumed command of VF805 on 19 January 1981. The unit was in limbo; Skyhawk operations from HMAS *Melbourne* were suspended indefinitely. There weren't really enough aircraft to operate on the scale the squadron was used to, but in Navy style they had to do the job with what they had. The pilots of VF805 had some deck time during *Melbourne*'s workups but were limited to touch and goes.

The carrier remained alongside the Fitting Out Wharf throughout January and February in an assisted maintenance period (AMP), but the focus was on aircraft support systems, notably the catapult and the arrestor gear. A report on these systems was received on Friday February 20, and the captain, Commodore Mike Hudson, drily noted that action was in hand to implement the report's recommendations, where it was within the capability of ship's staff to do so. On the following Tuesday, the 24th, there was a three-way discussion between the CO, Commander Australian Fleet and the author of the report (Commander GD White). The next day, Hudson and White travelled to HMAS *Albatross* to give a pre-embarkation briefing to the aircrew, and the results and recommendations of the Aircraft Support Systems Report.

The S-2G Tracker crews appeared to have confidence the ship would be able to operate the aircraft safely. However, delays in the catapult repair due to rewiring problems in the catapult control console, and industrial problems, precluded any catapult trials in February. Spline valve A, removed from arrestor unit 1 during the previous deployment, was found to have damaged seals requiring extensive work; final replacement was not expected until March.

During the first week of March, deadload trials on the catapult and fast pull-out trials on the arrestor gear were successfully conducted. On 11 March, HMAS *Melbourne* proceeded to sea. The aim was to qualify the rotary wing pilots and then the fixed-wing pilots of VS816 by 20 March. It was noted that Lieutenant Commander RD Mummery led a team of engineers from the Directorate of Naval Training to commence development of a training programme for catapult and arrestor gear personnel. This was a recommendation from the Aircraft Support Systems Report. Lieutenant Commander AW Criddle SO (Air) from the Directorate of Naval Safety also joined the ship to review the ship's flight-safety organisation.

The catapult and arrestor systems appeared to work reliably during the workup, and deck time was offered to VC851 and VF805. However, the Skyhawks were limited to touch and goes (really hook-up bolters). The ship recorded 106 A-4G movements during the period. During slow pull outs of the arrestor gear on 18 March, the spline valve of No 3 unit was observed to be acting erratically. Close observation of the valve showed fluid leaks during operation,

Skyhawks 883 and 887 show the final incarnation of VF805 markings applied while Lieutenant Commander Gary Northern was Commanding Officer in 1981. Consistent with the overall low-visibilty camouflage, black 'knight' markings have been added to the fin. The knights maintained the squadron chess theme dating back to the Checkmates display team. (Seapower Centre)

indicating defective internal seals. This valve was removed by the dockyard; it was anticipated the repaired valve would be returned on 8 April.

During the workup, there were two catapult 'hang fires' separated by 20 launches. Flying ceased and airborne aircraft diverted ashore as the ship made for Sydney. The catapult staff investigated the problem thoroughly and discovered two small loose bolts within the electrical relays controlling the firing sequence. After these were removed, the catapult operated successfully. Unfortunately, although the repaired No 3 arrestor gear spline valve initially operated successfully, it was found to be suffering excessive air ingress.

The ship carried on with its exercise programme which included an Exercise *Compass Beacon* off Western Australia, and then a cruise through the Indonesian archipelago to Manila, arriving on 31 March. An exercise, *Oriental Express*, was conducted there before the ship and its escorts made their way to Hong Kong. Once alongside HMS *Tamar* on 4 June, HMAS *Melbourne* entered a self-maintenance period planned to last until the 19th. The work was proceeding well but was interrupted by the approach of a typhoon from the South China Sea which required the ship reducing to four hours' notice for sea.

From Hong Kong, the ship proceeded south through the South China Sea, making for the exercise areas off Malaysia. Late in the afternoon of the 21st, an S-2G returning from a surveillance patrol sighted a crowded boat. *Melbourne* despatched HMAS *Torrens* to investigate, recovered the S-2G and, while doing so, despatched a medical officer by helicopter to *Torrens*. *Melbourne* arrived shortly after dark to find the survivors numbered 99 and their boat was unseaworthy. The decision was taken to bring them on board and destroy their vessel as it was a navigation hazard. The survivors were medically examined, provided food and water, clothing as required from stores, and accommodated on the forecastle, the only space available.

The ship continued to Singapore, exercising en route. On arrival at Sembawang, United Nations and immigration officials came on board to process the refugees and transfer them to a refugee camp. A decision must have been made somewhere in high levels of authority, because the ROP drily noted again that the process of culling A-4 stores had begun.

From Sembawang, *Melbourne* sailed south-east through Indonesian waters, on the way to Darwin. Flying was conducted to retain currency for the S-2 crews. On Monday 13 July, the ship gathered its escorts and conducted a ceremonial entry to Darwin Harbour. The carrier remained at anchor until the 15th, offering an opportunity for guests to visit and sailors to go ashore for sporting activities.

On leaving Darwin, the ship gave a mini 'Shop Window' to civic dignitaries before flying them ashore by Wessex. Crossing the Gulf of Carpentaria, fixed-wing flying was carried out before entering the restricted waters of the Barrier Reef. The ship anchored off Fitzroy Island to conduct Admiral's Divisions on both *Melbourne* and *Torrens*. Late in the afternoon, the ships weighed anchor and proceeded on a night passage to Cid Harbour, anchoring at 0700. Formal Rounds of both ships were conducted during the day after which they weighed anchor and proceeded independently.

Melbourne anchored off Great Keppel Island next morning on 21 July, and the formal Admiral's Rounds were completed. A Wessex carried the admiral off for air passage from Rockhampton, while *Melbourne* weighed anchor. At sunset, *Torrens* rejoined and both ships made ground on the journey home to Sydney. At 1000 on the 21st, the S-2Gs were flown off to Nowra and, the next morning, at 0915, *Melbourne* entered Sydney, berthing alongside the Fitting Out Wharf.

After a shortened AMP, HMAS *Melbourne* proceeded to sea for a workup. During this period, deck time was made available to VF805 and the Skyhawks managed to run up a total of 129 hook-up bolters. The bad news in the ROP was a report on the ship's double bottoms, first raised the previous year. They had continued to deteriorate, leaking water into the fuel storage. Two further double bottoms had been taken out of use, making the total loss of storage equivalent to 310 tons of furnace fuel oil.

The ship proceeded to sea for a short workup before pre-exercise briefings for *Kangaroo 81*. The air group remained the same with six S-2Gs, six Sea Kings and two Wessex embarked. No fleet tanker was available for the exercise, so this forced the carrier to refuel its escorts and visit Brisbane twice to refuel to maximum capacity. This was compounded by industrial unrest in southern Queensland which made the process difficult. On the first occasion, two S-2Gs were flown ashore to RAAF Amberley to maintain surveillance operations in the exercise area.

The captain, Commodore Hudson, was very pleased with the performance of the air group as he claimed it was both flexible and responsive. It exceeded planned flying hours by a good margin and, importantly, the aircraft support systems had only had minor defects, which were quickly repaired.

> In my view, the ship performed most creditably and met all her operational commitments. However, the absence of organic air-defence aircraft was most noticeable and highlighted, once again, the needs of an afloat commander to be able to respond at very short notice to a fast-developing air threat. On too many occasions, land-based air assets were not available when and where required.

The ship paid a visit to Brisbane with a very successful open day, and visits and return calls with various dignitaries. On the final day of the port visit, the ship took on board some local VIPs for the trip downriver. Lines were cast off at 1500 on 9 November and the ship proceeded slowly downriver. The guests were flown off by Wessex to Brisbane Airport, and the ship made its way to sea.

The passage south was very quiet compared to the preceding month. The major activity was purging the AVGAS tanks, before flying off the six S-2Gs to return to Nowra. Rather presciently, the commodore observed:

> It was a sad moment seeing them go and knowing, on present planning, this would be the last time *Melbourne* would see them for at least twelve months. Indeed, if media speculation proves to be correct, then it was the last time *Melbourne* would launch her fixed-wing aircraft.

Unfortunately, he was correct. On 25 February 1982, the Minister for Defence made a statement that ended the speculation. HMAS *Melbourne* was to be placed in contingent reserve. And so ended the operational life of our aircraft carrier, the home for so many over the years.

Ironically, the 1980 cruise had triggered actions that should have been taken, probably, in 1971. It appeared the catapult and arrestor gear had been reliable throughout the operations of the Trackers in 1981.

Lieutenant Commander Gary Northern was the last Commanding Officer of VF805 in the Skyhawk era. The squadron decommissioned on 2 July 1982.

The VF805 decommissioning crew. Left to right. Lieutenant John Bartels, Lieutenant Commander Gary Northern CO, Major Chuck Smith USMC, Lieutenant Commander Peter Clark SP, Lieutenant Gary Osmond, Sub-Lieutenant David Baddams, Sub-Lieutenant Paul Kalade. (Phil Thompson)

Chapter 18

1982–1984: THE END OF RAN FIXED-WING AVIATION

This chapter covers the period from January 1982 through to the closure of fixed-wing flying in the RAN. It was the end of an era, and a hard time as morale in the squadrons, and at HMAS *Albatross*, changed as rumours spread through the community.

A JUXTAPOSITION – FROM BEING A JUNIOR MEMBER OF THE SENIOR SERVICE TO THE SENIOR MEMBER OF THE JUNIOR SERVICE!

I had always wanted to fly the A-4 Skyhawk. As a kid, my dad used to take me to the HMAS *Albatross* airshows and I used to love watching the A-4 aerobatic team displays and the A-4s dropping practice bombs onto the Western Pad using Divisional Attacks.

I was privileged to be one of two graduates from No 106 Pilots' Course selected for A-4G conversion and commenced No 14 Operational Flying School (OFS) at the end of 1979. I loved flying the A-4G and never forget my first solo in 884. It was the fact you didn't just get into the A-4 but seemed to 'put it on' that I loved. The cockpit was tight, but you quickly forgot about that. It was a very capable day visual fighter and attack aircraft and taught me a lot about flying fighters. I spent a year in VC724 and one in VF805 but only ended up getting 420 hrs of A-4G time.

In mid-1981, during a Directorate of Naval Officers Postings visit to *Albatross*, I was asked if I would be interested in doing an exchange with Air Force flying the Mirage IIIO. I was amazed at the time to learn this would be a first. Not much happened for a few months, but towards the end of the year a message came out posting me to No 77 Squadron at RAAF Base Williamtown. I was looking forward to a two-year stint at Newcastle, then returning to Nowra.

I started my Mirage conversion in January 1982 with a bit of trepidation. While I had good friends from my course flying the aircraft, and was confident in my skills, I didn't want to let the A-4G community down. Despite the issues at high levels playing out between the Air Force and Navy, I was well accepted into the community – quickly gaining the callsign of 'Boatperson' or 'Boat' for short. I soon demonstrated I could more than handle myself in the air-to-air environment and could consistently drop an accurate bomb in the attack/strike role. Flying the A-4G, and the mentoring from some great A-4G pilots, had been great preparation.

The Mirage and A-4G had similar weapons at the time. Mk.82 Lo- and Hi-drag weapons were the mainstay in air-to-ground, but the A-4 had a better selection of other weapons. The Air Force didn't have 2.75-inch or 5-inch rockets, which proved to be a limitation for many years to come, and the Mirage wasn't fitted to drop illumination flares. In air-to-air, both forces were transitioning out of the AIM-9B Sidewinder missile – the Air Force to the Matra R550 Magic and Navy to the AIM-9L. The Mirage's 30-mm cannons were more potent than the A-4's 20mm and packed a punch in both air-to-air and air-to-ground.

The Mirage also had the advantage of the Cyrano radar and Matra R530 combination, giving it an all-weather intercept capability. However, R530 serviceability was not trusted by many and difficult to employ, so it was not widely used tactically. That being said, in the second year I was flying the Mirage, we started emphasising the use of it in some scenarios. While the radar provided the Mirage with an all-weather day and night-intercept capability, in a dynamic multi-aircraft fight it was normally only useful in close cooperation with very capable Air Force intercept controllers for positioning during the initial tactic; however, after that, manoeuvring was predominantly visually cued.

In performance, the A-4 had longer range, could carry more ordnance and was more manoeuvrable than the

Mirage; however, the Mirage had a speed advantage and in the air-to-air environment could rapidly time compress an adversary with speed and large altitude manoeuvres.

What rapidly became apparent during my exchange was that, when flying the Mirage, we did more day-to-day training in larger multi-aircraft operations than in the A-4G. What was also noticeable was that the Mirage squadrons were more advanced than the Fleet Air Arm in assessing the evolving surface-to-air and pulse doppler equipped air-to-air beyond-visual-range threats and developing and testing tactics to improve survivability and effectiveness in those environments. This led early on to me discussing with my COs the chances of me completing a Fighter Combat Instructor (FCI) course prior to returning to Nowra. I

Mark Binskin and his Mirage cockpit in 1982. (Mark Binskin)

wanted to bring the lessons and tactics the Mirage squadrons were developing back to the A-4 world. However, by the end of my first year flying at Williamtown, the Federal Government had already decided the fate of the fixed-wing part of the Fleet Air Arm.

I subsequently did complete the FCI course, part of it while still in the Navy, and was always sad to see our old A-4s whenever I deployed to New Zealand.

Mark Binskin

Crash Investigation

On 23 January 1979, single-seat A-4 870 crashed due to turbine failure/engine fire 24 kilometres south-east of Braidwood (as described in Chapter 15).

The pilot, Sub-Lieutenant C Tomlinson ejected and was picked up by an RAAF helicopter. The engine was picked up by Wessex N7-200 on a 150-foot strap and returned to Nowra. In 1982, Lieutenant Commander John Crawley summoned me and Chief Ian Scott to go to a house near Braidwood/Captains Flat to talk to a timber cutter who had dug up some remnants of 870. It appeared this bloke had spent his holidays digging around the crash site and had rung the base and mentioned what he had found. So, Scotty and I drove down to his place to find a tarp laid out on his front lawn; on the tarp was a lot of crushed black boxes. He mentioned about digging these bits up and ringing the base as he thought they may be important. Scotty and I looked deeply at this pile of smashed black boxes and made the appropriate noises about them being valuable and that they should be taken back to *Albatross* for further examination. After gathering the bits up and putting them into the back of the station wagon, we went inside for a coffee into what was, apart from my mother's house, the most spotless place I had ever seen. Clearly a very house-proud woman. After asking them if they would like to take a tour of the base if in the area, and saying our goodbyes and thanking him for his efforts, we went off to the Captains Flat RSL for dinner. After dinner, we drove back to *Albatross* and just made it back with a nearly flat tyre, having nearly rolled a tyre off its rim due to just about missing a corner in heavy rain and muddy dirt road conditions. The next morning, after talking to Lieutenant Commander Crawley, we took the smashed and mangled bits straight to the rubbish dump. At some later stage, I received a phone call that the family was at the main gate and I took them on a comprehensive tour of the base.

David Prest

V/STOL encounters

In January 1982, I returned to HMAS *Albatross* (Nowra), posted as Senior Pilot of VC724 with Lieutenant Commander Keith Johnson as CO. By then I had a foreboding outlook on the future of naval fixed-wing flying which crystallised following the 1983 Federal election which saw the Labor government installed in Canberra.

One of the first Defence decisions made by Labor was to completely disband the fixed-wing squadrons of the FAA (the HS748 gained a short reprieve). The Defence Minister, Gordon Scholes, announced VF805 was to be decommissioned immediately and its Skyhawks transferred to VC724, which was scheduled for decommissioning in mid-1984.

We continued to perform our squadron functions, principally fleet support and Army support, under somewhat trying circumstances. Towards the end of 1982, HMS *Invincible* paid a goodwill visit to Australia and VC724, now under the command of Lieutenant Commander Peter Clark, took the opportunity to arrange some dissimilar air-combat manoeuvres (DACM) missions against the Sea Harriers. After all the success experienced in the Falklands, I wanted to see whether the aircraft could in fact out-manoeuvre the A-4. DACM was scheduled for three separate occasions – 20 November for 1v1 and 13–14 December for 1v1 and 2v2.

One of the 'party tricks' of the Harrier is what is known as 'viffing', or vectoring-in-forward-flight, whereby the jet exhaust nozzles are rotated to the slightly forward position. It can be used during ACM, but is regarded as an emergency manoeuvre and, from what I have read, was not used during the squadrons' battles in the Falklands.

During my first 'dogfight', our two aircraft were engaged in a 'scissors' manoeuvre and I deliberately allowed the Sea Harrier to get into a position whereby the pilot would likely use the viffing technique (we were already at low speed). It was somewhat eye-watering to see the deceleration and the Harrier was briefly able to get on my tail.

However, having witnessed the manoeuvre firsthand, it was relatively simple to devise a counter. After viffing and decelerating so much, the Harrier lost all energy and there was only one way to go and that was to point the nose at the ground to accelerate.

The 'counter' to the viffing was simply to pull up vertically with as much pitch as possible before getting into a very slow speed situation. Immediately the Harrier dropped its nose to accelerate, the A-4 could easily slide onto its tail. I was able to do this on all our following engagements. It proved the manoeuvring capability of the Skyhawk could certainly match the Sea Harrier.

Reflecting on the success in the Falklands, the Sea Harriers had no need to engage in close air combat as they were able to rely on radar vectoring from their ships in the area and their own air-to-air radar to release their AIM-9L Sidewinders. On the other hand, the Argentinian aircraft were operating at extreme range and therefore had minimal time on task (reports indicated around five minutes over the islands).

The Harrier was a brilliant and futuristic concept which led the way to bigger and better V/STOL aircraft such as the AV-8B and, most recently, the F-35B. My point here is simply that the A-4 Skyhawk, although designed in the mid-1950s, was an extremely capable and versatile aircraft and, with proper handing, could hold its own in ACM with any other fighter aircraft (then) operating around the world.

Allen Clark

Lieutenant John Bartels was the 'O' who kept showing up with a huge camera and begging rides from the Senior Pilot of VC724 back in 1976. He took great photographs and the best seemed to come from his trip on Exercise *Kangaroo III* in 1976 and *Rimpac 76*. The day he received his posting to pilots' course was one of great joy!

THE TRICKS OF THE TRADE

I joined the Navy in July 1973, for an observers' course that was due to start a couple of months later. Being an observer wasn't my first choice, though, as it turned out, it was probably a good avenue for me. After a delay, the 'O' course eventually started in January 1974, and at the end I was posted to HT725 for the Wessex anti-submarine warfare OFS. We'd barely finished that course when the Sea Kings arrived in Australia, and I was posted to the Sea King flight. So, the last Wessex observer OFS, and the first Sea King. The flight morphed into HS817 and we were soon off to HMAS *Melbourne*, initially for *Kangaroo 76* and then *Rimpac 76*.

All through this period, I'd watch the A-4s flying with great interest and a fair bit of jealousy. I started to investigate the chances of being posted to a pilots' course. It had happened in the past, but not recently. So, I started writing letters, and trying to enlist my COs to help the cause.

I was then posted to Canberra to a desk job. Not a place that I enjoyed, but the posting people were there, so

I continued my quest. After Navy Office, I was then posted to 723. There I was the token observer and my job was to teach some navigation to the new aircrewmen. At 723, I found a group of pilots who were quite happy to let me have a 'pole' of the Wessex and Iroquois.

During the period in Canberra, I'd done some flying with the local aero club and had gained a restricted licence. Somehow, presumably in the bar on a Friday afternoon, I managed to convince John McCauley and his CO, to let me have a front seat ride in a Macchi.

Things started to move then, with calls to attend various parts of the pilot selection system, and in early 1979 I got that sought-after posting, with the posting to Point Cook for 109 Pilots' Course. I found the course to be enjoyable; hard work, but lots of fun too. At the end, on Posting Night, I got the pot of gold, with the direction to VC724 for the A-4 OFS.

Back at Nowra, I joined Dave Coote and Mark Boast in waiting for the A-4 OFS. The squadron had plenty for us to do in the interim, with a mini Macchi OFS (basic tactics and weaponry) and lots of fleet support. Eventually, the long-awaited day for the start of the OFS arrived.

One rather important item was missing from our OFS though. In October 1981, there had been two A-4s lost off HMAS *Melbourne*. 'Blemish' and 'BH' had both ejected after launch accidents, so there was a hold on operations from the ship. We didn't get the chance to deck qualify but figured it would happen soon enough. How wrong we were.

Because I was the most senior of the three of us on the course (I'd done the pilots' course as a lieutenant, not a midshipman), I was posted to VF805. It was destined to be a short posting. We had the high of the Government announcing they were buying HMS *Invincible*, and with it the chance of Sea Harriers, to the low of it all being cancelled, and 805 being decommissioned.

I was posted back to 724 and flew there until I left Nowra in early 1983. My last A-4G flight was an epic beat up of the base, something that the observer who started at the helicopter end of the flight line would have loved. After this, it was off to RAAF East Sale for the QFI course. While A-4 people weren't generally posted to the CT/4 Airtrainer, I'd put my hand up, as it was the same QFI course and, with all of the uncertainty, it seemed a good idea to have a qualification that would be useful in the future. A couple of final jaunts in the TA-4 were to come after I flew a No 1 Flying Training School CT/4 to Nowra and hitched rides. And at that point, on 27 September 1983, my A-4 journey was over, only a bit over two years from the start of the OFS.

There were, of course, lots of moments in that two years, including cheating in the bombing competition. This came about because 805 suddenly had a load of war-shot bombs to use. The CO (Gary Northern) decided that, instead of having a couple of bombs each, he'd divide the squadron pilots into two teams, and the winners would take all. So, Team A was the Boss, Peter Clark (PC) and Gary Osmond. Team B was everyone else. We figured we were toast. So, we had to work to improve our scores above theirs. Unlikely. The next idea was to lower their scores and that seemed more promising. Bribing the people doing the scoring was considered and discarded. So, we brainstormed ideas for ruining their drops. In the end, we decided that bending the fins of a practice bomb sounded like it might work.

On the day, we needed the complicity and assistance of the ground crew, who basically looked the other way (and never gabbed) as we approached their aircraft from the rear and adjusted the fins on half of the SP's and Air Warfare Instructor's bombs. We left the CO's alone. The outcome was exactly as we hoped with the CO having a reasonable result, and the other two being all over the place. It didn't work though; PC didn't believe he could have such a terrible score and figured we'd cheated somehow.

After my QFI course, I spent two years instructing at Point Cook. During that time, Qantas started a major recruitment effort and I joined them in March 1985. My luck continued to hold, with the opportunity for a long haul Boeing 767 command coming up in 1992. In 2004, a 747-400 command, and then, 2009, off to the A380. In 2008, I had a momentary flash of fame when a 747 decided to have an unheard-of oxygen explosion. Mostly though, it was quiet airline flying, and we'd fill in the nights with tales of prowess in our previous lives.

John Bartels

The last one

John Hamilton seemed to have been flying Skyhawks forever. He was on No 3 OFS (see Chapter 20) and I met him on his first embarkation. He had an incident on the range in Hawaii and impressed everyone with his coolness in dealing with it, successfully landing off a short-field arrest.

After the cruise, he returned to VC724 where he went off for a QFI Course and, in the fullness of time, became an Instrument Rating Examiner, a Maintenance Test Pilot, and a Forward Air Controller. John was then posted on exchange to a US A-7 Squadron, returning to VC724 in 1977. That is where I met him again.

To me, as a neophyte Skyhawk pilot, he was the font of all knowledge. John, to his credit, freely offered advice when asked and rarely criticised. He was full of fun and could laugh at himself as well.

Several years later, I spent most of a night sitting on the steps of his RAAF flat at Pearce, discussing the ins and outs of where the Skyhawk fleet was going. I had chosen my path, civilian life, and he was the Senior Naval Officer at RAAF Pearce. Much later, after the disappointment of the Government's decision, I felt the Navy was very lucky to have John to see the aircraft into retirement.

John chose, as did all the other commanding officers, not to make a contribution and simply directed me to the Navy History website. I have tried to write respectfully of his composed dealing with what must have been a very difficult time for him, having given so much.

Peter Greenfield

The Last CO

Lieutenant Commander John Hamilton joined Fleet Headquarters in 1983 as the Command Aviation Officer before returning to HMAS *Albatross* to assume command of VC724 on 3 December 1983.

This proved a dark time for those serving in the Fleet Air Arm and in the broader Navy as the Government had made the decision not to replace *Melbourne* and to discontinue fixed-wing operations from 30 June 1984. All the Skyhawks were now concentrated in VC724 which, together with the eight Macchis on strength, made for a big squadron. It took great effort on the part of the entire unit to maintain integrity, safety and morale through those melancholy months. Such a time can only successfully be navigated with leadership from above, the CO.

Screech! The final flypast of TA-4G 880 on 30 June 1984, crewed by John Hamilton and John Da Costa. (John Hamilton)

VC724 detachments to RAAF Edinburgh in support of Army Rapier trials, to RAAF Amberley for joint exercises, in addition to providing ongoing fleet requirement services, saw the conclusion of an amazing era in the history of the Royal Australian Navy.

The final Skyhawk aerial display for those at HMAS *Albatross* on 30 June saw TA-4G 880 with John Hamilton (the last CO 724) and Commodore John Da Costa RAN (Rtd) (the first Skyhawk

CO) exhibit what they described as 'The magnificence of this marvellous little aircraft in RAN FAA colours.'

It later fell to John to conduct maintenance test flights on all ten remaining Skyhawks before they were handed over to the RNZAF. VC724 was decommissioned on 31 August 1984, which was to prove a very sad day for its last CO, with the irony of the disbanded squadron having to prepare the Skyhawks to be flown out by the RNZAF.

1982–84 snapshot

Lieutenant Commander Keith Johnson assumed command of VC724 on 19 December 1980.

CO VC724, the remaining Skyhawk squadron, was Lieutenant Commander PL Clark from 23 August 1982. He in turn was replaced by Lieutenant Commander John Hamilton AFC on 3 December 1983. Lieutenant Commander Allen Clark was the SP from January 1982 until July 1983, when Lieutenant Ray France succeeded him.

There were ten Skyhawks remaining at the time of the disbandment.

Tracker and Skyhawk crews during the final decommissioning ceremony at Nowra in June 1984. (John Hamilton)

Kiwis *can* fly – backwards!

When the fixed-wing elements of the Fleet Air Arm were disbanded in 1984, 724 SQN had the job of preparing all the remaining A-4 Skyhawks for sale to the Royal New Zealand Air Force. It was a sad time to be readying our well-loved aircraft for sale to a new owner, however, in true squadron spirit, 724 stepped up to the mark and decided that we would give the Kiwi's the best aircraft, all in tip-top shape! At the same time, the squadron Macchi aircraft were being prepared for transfer to the RAAF and the Macchi guys were equally as busy.

We were told to prepare all our available spares for handing over to the Kiwis as they were flying over their Andover aircraft to pick them up. The aircraft arrived and, with its unique 'squatting' landing gear, we piled in as much as we could fit into the cargo hold. Everything that wasn't tied down got packed, spares, tooling, anything we could find. The Kiwi's certainly got a good deal when they bought the Skyhawks as they got a bunch of extra equipment thrown in for free!

As the preparation of the aircraft continued, one job that had to be done was the painting out of the kangaroos on the aircraft roundels and spraying on the kiwi logos for their flights to New Zealand, as they would be New Zealand military aircraft for the Tasman crossing. We did this in batches as groups of aircraft departed to their new Kiwi homes.

The final batch of aircraft included one aircraft I had worked on for my entire career, both ashore and embarked on HMAS *Melbourne.* Skyhawk 876 was one of my 'babies' and I was the PO in charge of prepping her for the trans-Tasman flight and the painting on of the dreaded kiwi logo. The troops on watch were busy spraying out the kangaroos and diligently spraying on the red kiwis. Animal logos, such as kangaroos or kiwis have a specific position when placed on aircraft identification roundels. They are always placed feet down (on vertical surfaces, such as the fuselage) or inboard (on horizontal surfaces such as wings) and always facing forward.

As 876 was being painted, I was chatting to the troops as they grumbled about 'damn kiwis' and other comments about the Federal Government at that time. Then someone came up with a brilliant idea. 'What if one kiwi was to fly home backwards?' 'No, no, you can't do that, it's against the rules … BUT, it could happen entirely accidentally!' Later, I came by again, and there on the starboard fuselage of 876 was a lovely red kiwi, painted on backwards, bum to the wind! The troops were very happy!

We towed 876 down to the flight line and I felt privileged to complete the final engine run and test the fuel transfer system on all three drop tanks, ready for the ferry flight to New Zealand. It was ready to go, complete with the backwards kiwi!

The 724 SQN CO signed over the aircraft to the New Zealand pilots with a ceremony and they conducted their pre-flight walkaround, checking all the flight controls and the aircraft condition before flight. I wandered around behind the Kiwi pilot of 876. As he went around the rear of the aircraft, he spotted the backward kiwi. I held my breath for his response.

After a long second or two, he burst out laughing hard, pointing to the hapless bird! I said 'Sorry, little mistake there …' He knew immediately it was no mistake and laughed all the way to the cockpit ladder.

Before he climbed in, I said, 'That's a good bird, take care of her.' 'I will indeed', he said and we shook hands. After conducting the final engine start-up and control checks, 876 was off to her new home.

The poor kiwi was flying home backwards …

Joe Hattley

Skyhawks 877 and 876 prepped for their trans-Tasman flight. The kiwi in the roundel on the left is in the correct position, while the one on 876 on the right is facing backwards. (Joe Hattley)

Chapter 19

THE SKYHAWK SQUADRONS

Note: this information is sourced from https://www.navy.gov.au/history/squadron-histories.

724 Squadron

Formed at RNAS Bankstown on 10 April 1945 as a naval air communications unit under the command of Lieutenant (A) JHL Evans RNVR, 724 Squadron received two Expeditor C.IIs from 723 Naval Air Squadron which had been operating the communications flight until their arrival.

The squadron operated out of the nearby civilian airport at Mascot, as the grass surface at Bankstown was unsuitable for the heavy twin-engine aircraft, and received an additional two Anson Mk.Is. They operated regular flights to Melbourne, five times a week, and to RNAMY (Royal Naval Aircraft Maintenance Yard) Archerfield three times, carting passengers and light stores. In the new year, the range and frequency of services was increased; the Archerfield service was extended, after an overnight stop, the aircraft continued on to RNAS (Royal Naval Air Station) Maryborough, the most northern of the RN sites in Australia, a 1,400-mile round trip. The Melbourne service became a daily one and, from June, six days a week, a twice daily service to the air stations at Nowra and Jervis Bay began. At its peak, the squadron operated as many as 20 aircraft, each wearing its Australian radio call sign on the rear fuselage above the roundel – VJAAA to VJAAZ were allocated.

When RNAS Bankstown was closed on 31 March 1946, the squadron moved to nearby RNAS Schofields but was disbanded there two months later on 31 May.

The unit recommissioned into the Royal Australian Navy (RAN) at Naval Air Station Nowra on 1 June 1955, carrying out fixed-wing conversion training for the Fleet Air Arm's front-line squadrons. Commanded by Lieutenant Commander Lionel Robinson, the squadron flew a variety of aircraft including Commonwealth Aircraft Corporation CA-16 Wirraways, Hawker Sea Fury Mk.11s, Fairey Firefly AS.6s, and de Havilland Sea Vampire Mk T.22s, and took delivery of three Fairey Gannet T.2s in May the following year.

In 1958 it became an all-jet squadron flying Sea Vampires and Sea Venoms. In 1968 it received its first Skyhawks followed by Macchi trainers two years later when the Sea Vampires and Sea Venoms were retired. The unit decommissioned at NAS Nowra on 30 June 1984.

805 Squadron

First formed as an RN Fleet Air Arm squadron in November 1940 at the RAF aerodrome at Aboukir in Egypt, 805 Squadron operated Fairey Fulmars in the convoy protection role in the Western Desert until January 1941, when it transferred to Crete. A short time later, it returned to Egypt where, at Dekheila, it re-equipped with Brewster Buffalo fighters. In June 1941, these were replaced by the Grumman Martlet III. The squadron disbanded in January 1943. It recommissioned in the UK for service in the Pacific campaign, equipped with Supermarine Seafires, but saw no further service prior to the end of the war.

In August 1948, 805 Squadron was reformed as an RAN squadron operating Hawker Sea Fury Mk.11 aircraft. The squadron formed part of the 20th Carrier Air Group embarked on HMAS *Sydney*. During September 1951, 805 Squadron deployed to Korea, flying sorties for 64 days. Three 805 Squadron pilots were killed during the campaign. The battle honour 'Korea 1951–52' was awarded for this deployment. Following the retirement of the Sea Fury, the unit was disbanded on 26 March 1958.

It reformed at Nowra three days later on 31 March, now equipped with the de Havilland Sea Venom FAW.53 all-weather night fighter. The squadron later embarked on HMAS *Melbourne* as part of the 21st Carrier Air Group. The squadron was again disbanded on 30 June 1963 and its aircraft transferred to B Flight, 816 Squadron.

On 10 January 1968, 805 Squadron reformed, equipped with the McDonnell Douglas A-4G Skyhawk fighter. The VF805 designation was used to conform with the US Navy squadron naming system during the Skyhawk era, under which 'VF' referred to fixed-wing fighter aircraft, denoting the fleet-defence role of the squadron's aircraft. The unit operated from *Melbourne* until 1981 and was decommissioned on 2 July 1982.

On 28 February 2001, 805 Squadron was reformed once again, equipped with Kaman SH-2G(A) Super Seasprite helicopters to be operated from the new Anzac-class frigates. The squadron completed First of Class Flight Trials aboard HMAS *Parramatta* but did not reach operational status due to difficulties with integrating the helicopters' avionic systems. Following technical problems with the new helicopter, the squadron was relegated to minimal duties in 2005, grounded in 2006, and faced possible scrapping in early 2007. Efforts to rectify the technical problems were not successful and the project was cancelled in early 2008. As a result, 805 Squadron was disbanded on 26 June 2008.

Chapter 20

THE PILOTS AND THEIR AIRCRAFT

No 1 OFS (VF805) January 1968

Students standing, left to right: LCDR Fred Lane, SBLT Ralph McMillan, LEUT Barrie Daly, LEUT Barry Diamond, LCDR Bill Callan, LEUT Clive Blennerhassett and SBLT Keith Johnson.

Staff seated, left to right: US civilian contractor, LEUT Reg Elphick ALO, LEUT Jim Firth SO, LCDR Grahame King SP, LCDR John Da Costa CO, LEUT Mike Gump USN, LEUT Brian Dutch SAWI, LEUT Jim Lamb AEO, and US civilian contractor.

Special Note: Jim Firth was the squadron's Staff Officer. Most of the RAN pilots had come from Sea Venoms where they had crewed with observers. The A-4 was a single seater, so Jim Firth's job was to make sure the pilots did not embarrass themselves geographically. He also took care of the administration because there were only three pilots, all instructors. He loved to gloat in later life, as SOBS on HS817, that he had been the only SOBS for a single-seat fighter squadron.

The pilots were instructed by John Da Costa, 'Dusty' King and Mike Gump. So, this group was special: No 1 OFS and the VF805 plank holders. This group includes five officers destined to be VF805 COs.

OFS No 2 1969
Back row, left to right: SBLT Ken Palmer, SBLT
Gary Northern and MIDN Peter Cox. Front row,
left to right: LEUT Errol Kavanagh and LEUT
Dave Collingridge. This group includes three officers
destined to command VF805.

No 4 OFS (VC724) late 1970
Left to right: LEUT Charlie Rex, LEUT Rick Symons
and LEUT Murray Smythe.

No 3 OFS (VC724)
January 1970
Left to right: LEUT Barrie
Daly, LCDR Col Paterson,
LEUT Peter McNair, ASLT
Phil Thompson and ASLT
John Hamilton.

No 5 OFS (VC724) 1971
Rear, left to right: SBLT Graham Donovan and SBLT Tony DerKinderen.
Front, left to right: LEUT George Heron and LEUT Tom Supple.

No 7 OFS (VC724) 1972
LEUT Peter Clark was injured in an ejection from a Macchi shortly before the OFS commenced. He was given a special OFS for one student.

No 6 OFS (VC724) June 1972
Left to right: LEUT Graham Winterflood, SBLT John Siebert and LEUT Jack Mayfield.

No 8 OFS (VC724) early 1973
Left to right: SBLT Jerry Clark, SBLT Barry Evans and SBLT
John McCauley.

No 9 OFS (VC724) June 1973
Left to right: LEUT Dave Ramsay, SBLT Ian Shepherd, SBLT Leigh Costain (broke leg and DNF),
SBLT Andy Sinclair and SBLT Nev French. Ian Shepherd and Andy Sinclair were both removed
from the OFS, due to budgetary constraints, and sent to sea to gain a Bridge Watchkeeping
Certificate. They joined No 10 OFS the following year.

No 10 OFS (VC724) mid-1974

Left to right: SBLT Ian Shepherd, SBLT Andy Sinclair, MIDN Kim Baddams and MIDN Mal McCoy. This OFS were posted to VF805 immediately after completion. On the right is Mal McCoy who was tragically killed in a mid-air collision over Beecroft Range in July 1975. In a strange quirk of fate, his ex-instructor at Pearce was giving author Peter Greenfield an instrument rating test as the news was released. He was naturally very upset and we discontinued the flight. He thought very highly of Mal and considered him to be very promising.

No 11 OFS (VC724) May 1976
Left to right: MIDN Mick Maher, SBLT Col Tomlinson and LEUT Peter Greenfield.

THE PILOTS AND THEIR AIRCRAFT

No 12 OFS (VC724) mid-1977
Left to right: SBLT Mark Measday, LEUT Allen Clark, LEUT Murray Coppins and SBLT Alan Bradtke.
Mark Measday chose to leave the RAN when the OFS was completed and became an anaesthetist, now sadly deceased. Alan Bradtke was medically grounded shortly after the OFS was completed.

No 13 OFS (VC724) mid-1978
Left to right: SBLT Gary Osmond and SBLT Ray France.
The world famous 'Mondo Brothers', so christened by John Hamilton.

No 14 OFS (VC724) 1980
Left to right: MIDN Paul Kalade, MIDN Dave Baddams, ASLT Eamon Lines, MIDN Mark Binskin and LEUT Rob Bradshaw RN. Dave Baddams became a QFI and later transferred to the RN. He served for 20 years, flew both marks of Sea Harrier, and became a squadron CO. Mark Binskin went on exchange to the RAAF on Mirages, was selected as the first F-18 Display Pilot and made a career of the RAAF. He attained the final rank of Air Chief Marshal and the position of Chief of the Defence Force. Rob Bradshaw was the first RN fixed-wing exchange pilot since the 1960s. As things got worse in early 1982, he was recalled to fly Sea Harriers.

No 15 OFS (VC724) July 1981
Left to right: ASLT Dave Coote, ASLT Mark Boast and LEUT John
Bartels. John Bartels was a former Sea King observer who transferred
successfully to become a pilot. He was also a keen photographer. Many of
the aircraft photos in this book are from his lens.

OFS No 16 (early 1982)
Left to right: SBLT Mark Pearsall, SBLT Adrian Wilson, FLTLT Gary Standen RAAF, LCDR
Hugh Slade RN and SBLT RAY Wittman. Hugh Slade was recalled to the UK around Easter
as he was required for operations in the South Atlantic. Gary Standen was the only RAAF
pilot to have officially flown the A-4G Skyhawk.

Royal Australian Navy Skyhawk pilots

	NAME	CALLSIGN	QUALIFICATION
1	Da Costa, John		AWI
2	King, Grahame	*Delta*	QFI
3	Dutch, Brian	*Lambda*	AWI
4	Lane, Fred	*Sinbad*	
5	Callan, Bill†	*Top Cat*	
6	Blennerhassett, Clive	*Chalkboard*	QFI
7	Diamond, Barry	*Buckeye*	QFI
8	McMillan, Ralph†	*Falcon*	AWI
9	Daly, Barrie	*Shamrock*	AWI, QFI
10	Johnson, Keith	*Baron*	LSO
11	Collingridge, David	*Victor*	AWI
12	Northern, Gary	*Zebra*	QFI
13	Cox, Peter†	*Nomad*	
14	Kavanagh, Errol†		
15	Palmer, Ken		
16	Paterson, Colin†	*Hawk*	
17	Hamilton, John	*Eagle*	QFI
18	Thompson, Phillip	*Sinbad/Lucifer*	PI
19	McNair, Peter	*Black*	
20	Smythe, Murray	*Viking*	
21	Symons, Rick T	*Taipan*	
22	Rex, Charlie†		
23	Olsson, Chris		
24	Marshall, Peter†	*Pegasus*	AWI
25	Hickling, Alan	*Spastic*	AWI
26	Heron, George	*Jumbuck*	
27	Donovan, Graham†		
28	Supple, Tom		
29	Derkinderen, Tony	*Springbok*	
30	Winterflood, Graham	*Vondo/Panther*	
31	Siebert, John	*Campaign*	LSO

	Name	Callsign	Qualification
32	Mayfield, Jack	*Cheetah*	AWI
33	Clark, Peter†	*Cowboy*	AWI
34	Clark, Jerry	*RamRod*	QFI
35	Evans, Barry	*Jackass*	AWI
36	McCauley, John	*Satan*	QFI
37	Ramsay, David†	*RamsDog*	AWI
38	Shepherd, Ian	*Panther*	QFI
39	Sinclair, Andy	*Archie*	AWI
40	French, Neville	*Frogman*	LSO
41	Baddams, Kim	*Dingo*	AWI, LSO
42	Flynn, Michael		Flight Surgeon
43	McCoy, Malcolm†		
44	Maher, Mike	*Fearless*	LSO
45	Tomlinson, Colin	*Sandpiper*	QFI
46	Greenfield, Peter	*Ranger*	
47	Measday, Mark†		
48	Clark, Allen	*Nobjob/Python*	QFI
49	Coppins, Murray	*Trojan*	QFI
50	Bradtke, Alan	*Bobcat*	
51	Osmond, Gary	*Wizard/Merlin*	
52	France, Ray†	*Dodger*	
53	Binskin, Mark	*Snoopy*	
54	Lines, Eamon		
55	Baddams, Dave	*Blemish*	QFI
46	Kalade, Paul	*Tarzan*	
57	Bartels, John	*Trashcan*	
58	Boast, Mark	*Wombat*	
59	Coote, Dave	*Bandi*	
60	Wittman, Ray	*Magpie*	
61	Pearsall, Mark	*Percy*	
62	Wilson, Adrian	*Wipeout*	

Exchange Pilots

	Name	Callsign	Qualification
1	Nordeen, Mike	*Nordo*	USN
2	Hart, Joe		USN
3	Park, John		USN
4	Gump, Mike		USN
5	LaMay, Tom†		USN
6	Finan, Kevin	*Findog*	USN
7	Pike, Gerry A		USN
8	Corbin, Ridgeway	*Junkyard*	USN
9	Hershberger, John		USN
10	Stumpf, Robert	*Ripper*	USN
11	O'Brien, Paul		USN
12	White, Tom	*Too Tall*	USMC
13	Smith, Chuck		USMC
14	Davis, Don		USMC
15	Hanner, Robert		USMC
15	Bradshaw, Robert		RN
16	Standen, Gary	*Stando*	RAAF

Royal Australian Navy A-4G Skyhawks – Synopsis of airframe history

This list shows all 20 RAN Fleet Air Arm Skyhawks and a brief synopsis of what happened to each one during their lifetime. Note they are in chronological order of their demise. First batch was acquired in 1967, second batch in 1971. The trainers were, sequentially, 878, 879, 880, and 881, in the middle of the side-number series.

Build No	Type	Side No	Batch	Aircraft History
N13-155060	A-4G	873	2nd	5 June 1973 Crashed 20nm E RAAF Williamstown NSW. Turbine shroud failure. SBLT Derkinderen.
N13-154910	A-4G	889	1st	8 November 1973 Ditched HMAS *Melbourne*. Catapult failure near Singapore. LEUT Evans.
N13-154648	TA-4G	879	2nd	16 May 1974 Crashed into sea 64km NE of Nowra. Possible pilot disorientation/ disablement. LEUT McMillan.
N13-155055	A-4G	872	2nd	17 July 1975 Crashed Beecroft Head, Nowra. Mid-air collision. SBLT McCoy.
N13-155051	A-4G	870	2nd	23 January 1979 Crashed 24km SE Braidwood NSW. Engine fire. SBLT Tomlinson.
N13-154909	A-4G	888	1st	23 May 1979 Crashed over side HMAS *Melbourne* 90km E Jervis Bay. Arrestor wire failure. LCDR Finan.
N13-154907	A-4G	886	1st	24 September 1979 Rolled off deck HMAS *Melbourne* during storm 355km E Australia. Handling failure.
N13-154647	TA-4G	878	2nd	28 April 1980 Crashed 5km S Nowra. Engine failure LEUT Sinclair.
N13-155062	A-4G	875	2nd	2 October 1980 Ditched off HMAS *Melbourne* in Andaman Sea. Engine failure on launch. LCDR C Blennerhassett.
N13-154906	A-4G	885	1st	21 October 1980 Ditched off HMAS *Melbourne* 200km SW Colombo. Catapult failure. LEUT Baddams.
N13-154903	A-4G	882	1st	To RNZAF July 1984 as NZ6211 Crashed Nowra 16 February 2001 during airshow rehearsal. SQNLDR Neilson.

Build No	Type	Side No	Batch	Aircraft History
N13-154912	TA-4G	881	1st	To RNZAF July 1984 as NZ6256 Crashed into sea off Perth 23 March 2001. LEUT Barnes.
N13-154911	TA-4G	880	1st	To RNZAF July 1984 as NZ6255 Donated by RNZAF to RAN Fleet Air Arm Museum, Nowra.
N13-155061	A-4G	874	2nd	To RNZAF July 1984 as NZ6216 Now displayed at Omaka Museum, NZ.
N13-154904	A-4G	883	1st	To RNZAF July 1984 as NZ6212 Sold to Draken International in 2012. Registered as N142EM.
N13-154905	A-4G	884	1st	To RNZAF July 1984 as NZ6213 Sold to Draken International in 2012. Registered as N143EM.
N13-154908	A-4G	887	1st	To RNZAF July 1984 as NZ6214 Sold to Draken International in 2012. Registered as N144EM.
N13-155052	A-4G	871	2nd	To RNZAF July 1984 as NZ6215 Sold to Draken International in 2012. Registered as N145EM.
N13-155063	A-4G	876	2nd	To RNZAF July 1984 as NZ6217 Sold to Draken International in 2012. Registered as N146EM.
N13-155069	A-4G	877	2nd	To RNZAF July 1984 as NZ6218 Sold to Draken International in 2012. Registered as N147EM.

Chapter 21

TRIBUTES

The body of pilots who flew the A-4G Skyhawk throughout its years in service with the RAN is quite small. We would like to pay tribute to those who have died. Only two pilots were killed flying the Skyhawk; they are presented first. The second group are pilots who contributed greatly during their time in the RAN but, with the passage of time, have since left us.

Lieutenant Ralph McMillan

Lieutenant Ralph McMillan

Ralph McMillan was born on 7 April 1947, at Cooroy on the Sunshine Coast of Queensland, and subsequently enlisted in the RAN as a Midshipman (Aircrew) at Brisbane on 18 February 1965. Together with other midshipman trainees, he joined the former aircraft carrier HMAS *Sydney* in July 1965 for initial sea training.

In October, McMillan transferred to RAAF Point Cook to begin his Basic Flying Training Course. Just over a year later, on 14 December 1966, he was made a 'probationary pilot' and awarded his provisional flying brevet (wings). He then transferred to RAAF Pearce for conversion to jet aircraft.

In February 1967, he arrived at HMAS *Albatross* to commence an Operational Flying School (OFS) course. He reported at 724 Squadron in February 1967 where he began his training, flying de Havilland Mk T.22 Vampire and DH Sea Venom aircraft.

In November 1967, McMillan was selected for conversion to the newly acquired A-4G fighter-bomber. A short time later, he joined VF805. Although records are unclear, it appears he spent time on HMAS *Melbourne* with VF805, gaining a reputation as a skilful pilot and a popular officer.

On 7 March 1969, McMillan was promoted to Lieutenant (P) and in April 1970 spent time with VC724. As his records moved to Electronic Data Processing in 1970, further details are not available.

On 16 May 1974, Ralph lost his life in a Skyhawk TA-4G which crashed into the sea 64 kilometres north-east of Nowra during a mock attack on HMAS *Melbourne*. He was 27 years old.

David Collingridge shared squadron life and an Air Warfare Instructor (AWI) course with Ralph McMillan. They became firm friends. David was airborne from the carrier when Ralph was lost at sea.

We began flying together on VF805 Squadron (CO, John Da Costa), embarked on HMAS *Melbourne* between February and July 1970, deployed around Papua New Guinea, the Philippines and Singapore. Ralph always impressed in the briefing room and in the air. He was calm, focused and loved what he did in A-4s – flying with a passion. On disembarkation at Nowra, we both hit the jackpot when we were posted to the Royal Navy's AWI Course in the UK.

In October 1970, with an introduction to the Hunter GA.11 and some ground school on bombs, bullets and ballistics at HMS *Excellent*, we joined 764 Squadron, Lossiemouth, and proceeded to have the most fun possible squirting guns, missiles and bombs at targets around the snow-covered hills and waters of the north of Scotland and in the south of France.

For Christmas in the UK, he loaned me his 12-year-old £100 Ford Anglia to drive from Scotland to Cornwall to visit friends. It could do 40 mph on the M1, any faster and the front wheels wobbled uncontrollably. On my return in the new year, Ralph generously donated the car to be helicopter dropped on Air Day and drew great applause.

We flew against each other on several occasions back home – on 805 and 724 – most commonly strike training missions or trying to stop such flights reaching their target at sea or among the hills on the South Coast. It was on one of those missions that I last flew against Ralph.

In May 1974, I joined 805 for a couple of months as AWI and embarked with the squadron. On 16 May, Ralph was in a 724 Squadron strike group off the coast looking for *Melbourne*. His TA-4 was being chased by several A-4s when I last saw him at around 500 feet over the sea, turning hard against his attackers. Within seconds of having rolled away from the melee, I heard the report on the radio that he had flown into the water.

For me he was the quintessential fighter pilot; clever, knowledgeable, sure of himself, but never cocky. He was a great shipmate, entertained all with such good humour and was popular with everyone.

He was missed by us all from the day we lost him.

David Collingridge

Acting Sub-Lieutenant Malcolm McCoy

Malcolm Keith McCoy was born on 23 October 1955. Having completed his schooling, McCoy enlisted in the RAN on 19 February 1973, as a Recruit Midshipman (Aircrew). Two months later, he began basic pilot training at RAAF Point Cook, prior to conversion to jets at RAAF Pearce. After completing the course in July 1974, McCoy was posted to HMAS *Albatross*.

Acting Sub-Lieutenant Malcolm McCoy

McCoy began his naval aviation training with VC724. Initially flying Macchi advanced trainers, he then converted to the A-4G Skyhawk. On 7 July 1975, having accumulated some 397 hours flying time, McCoy transferred to VF805.

On 17 July, McCoy was flying A-4G Skyhawk 872 with two other Skyhawks on a practice bombing run at Beecroft Weapons Range near Jervis Bay. At about 1030, his aircraft struck the underside of the aircraft above him and crashed into the ground, killing him.

On 22 July, a memorial service for ASLT McCoy was held at Westminster School, Adelaide; fellow 805 Squadron officers attended. On 15 September, McCoy's funeral service was conducted at St Nicholas Chapel, RANAS Nowra, with his ashes laid to rest at the Naval Memorial Cemetery in Nowra.

The sudden death of ASLT McCoy, aged 19, was a sad end to a promising career serving his country.

Captain David Ramsay

David John Ramsay was born into a naval family in Sydney on 14 January 1948. He was the son of Commodore Sir James Maxwell Ramsay KCMG KCVO CBE DSC, who became Queensland's 20th Governor.

In January 1963, David joined the Royal Australian Naval College as a Junior Entry Cadet Midshipman. On graduation from the Naval College in 1967, he completed his midshipman's sea time in HMA Ships *Yarra* (III) and *Sydney* (III). After attending courses in the UK, he joined HMAS *Brisbane* (II) in May 1970 and served during the RAN's final deployment to Vietnam.

Captain David Ramsay

In 1972, David began flying training with the RAAF, before a posting to HMAS *Albatross* where he completed a conversion course on the A-4 Skyhawk. He then joined VF805 and was soon embarked on HMAS *Melbourne* (II).

In the latter half of 1976, Lieutenant Ramsay completed an AWI Course, before joining VC724 to instruct students in the finer points of air-combat and weapons-delivery techniques. After serving in several other FAA roles during the late 1970s, David was sent to the UK to fly Sea Harriers and in 1981 spent time on the carriers HMS *Invincible* and HMS *Hermes*.

Returning to Australia in 1983, Commander Ramsay re-joined HMAS *Albatross* as Commander Air, where he experienced the demise of the RAN's fixed-wing jet capability. For the next decade, he served in a variety of senior naval roles, including as commander of HMAS *Creswell* and HMAS *Success*.

For the remainder of his full-time service, Captain Ramsay undertook language training before being appointed as the Australian Naval Attaché to Indonesia until his retirement in 2001. He subsequently served in a variety of diplomatic roles in Indonesia. On 4 September 2012, while attending a ministerial conference in Jakarta, David Ramsay was taken ill and died unexpectedly later that afternoon.

As surmised by his fellow Knox Grammar school friend and fellow RANC Classmate Roger Cawthorn:

> David lived life to the fullest – to him, sleep was a waste of time.

Commander Errol Kavanagh

Errol Martin Kavanagh was born in Millicent, South Australia, on 2 July 1944. He enlisted in the RAN in October 1962, and during the following year undertook flying training at Point Cook. Kavanagh then converted to jets at RAAF Pearce, where he was awarded his wings on 4 May 1964. He was then posted to Nowra where he learnt to fly the ungainly Fairey Gannet anti-submarine aircraft which he flew from HMAS *Melbourne* over the next two years.

Errol Kavanagh with a Winjeel trainer during flight training in 1963.

After a period as a flying instructor, Kavanagh was among the first of the RAN's pilots to convert to the A-4G Skyhawk. In 1969, he joined 724 Squadron's aerobatic team – the *Ramjets*. In April 1971, while conducting an instructional flight in a Macchi jet trainer over Jervis Bay, Kavanagh and a student pilot were forced to eject when control of their aircraft was lost after entering an inverted spin.

In August, Kavanagh was selected to serve as an exchange jet instructor with VT22 in the US. During his two-year overseas posting, he flew TA-4J Skyhawks and A-7E Corsairs.

Lieutenant Commander Errol Kavanagh in August 1979 when he became the first RAN pilot to achieve 1,500 hours in Skyhawks while serving as commanding officer of 724 Squadron.

After returning to Australia, Kavanagh spent time at sea in destroyers and in command of a minesweeper. In 1978, he returned to the FAA and was appointed commander of 724 Squadron, where he became the first RAN pilot to log 1,500 hours in Skyhawks. Kavanagh subsequently became commander of VF805, and in 1979 led a 4,000-mile Skyhawk deployment to Malaysia.

After serving with HMAS *Melbourne* during 1980–81, Kavanagh held staff positions in Canberra before resigning from the RAN in 1987 to fly privately operated Learjets in support of the RAN fleet. After two years, he joined Qantas where he qualified as a Boeing 747 pilot and flew internationally around the world.

On 13 March 1993, Kavanagh was killed in the crash of a MiG-15 'warbird' he was flying from Canberra airport. The cause of the crash was subsequently deemed to have been an in-flight fire, and in his last actions Kavanagh was praised for avoiding crashing into a sports oval crowded with school children.

Lieutenant Commander Ray France

Ray arrived at VC724 fresh from No 2 Flying Training School (2FTS) with the exuberance of youth, full of confidence and, as we soon experienced, ability to match. A young man with an infectious self-deprecating humour, he was popular with the entire squadron. At the same time, Ray was joined at the squadron by Gary Osmond and they quickly became known as the 'Mondo Brothers'. Both completed their A-4 OFS together, achieving very high standards.

Ray's transition to VF805 allowed him to perform at the higher level expected and his contribution to the squadron both in the air and on the ground was of the highest order. I shared a cabin with Ray on his initial embarkation with VF805 in 1979 and it was a great experience to see him blossom into an outstanding carrier pilot.

Ray France on graduation from No 13 OFS.

We parted ways on completion of the deployment as I headed off to RAAF Pearce as Senior Naval Officer and Ray continued on with 805. However, in 1983, I headed back to *Albatross* as CO VC724; Ray was my designated Senior Pilot as we readied the squadron for the unhappy task of disbandment. With great assistance from Ray, and also Dave Coote (and Dave Ramsay, CMDR AIR), we managed to achieve all of the fleet and Army tasking prior to guiding 724 into graceful retirement.

After retiring from the Navy, I would occasionally see Ray in Brisbane where, after a stint on the 748 with 'Shep', he was acting as the recruiting officer in Brisbane and living in Wynnum with Beryl and the kids. I was delighted to see him finally accepted into Cathay and, although our paths crossed on the airways, we very rarely got together again.

His death came far too early and to see such a wonderful man taken from his wife and family, not to mention those of us who had the absolute pleasure of his friendship, was indescribable.

RIP Ray.

Miss you, mate.

Hamo (John Hamilton)

> Hamo christened both Gary Osmond and Ray France as the 'Mondo Brothers', as in 'Osmondo' and 'Raymondo', when they arrived from 2FTS. One short and the other tall, one quiet and thoughtful, the other cheeky and infectiously humorous. Even at the beginning of his career, there was an air of professionalism when Ray donned his helmet to fly.
>
> When the fixed wing was shutdown in 1984, Ray went off to fly Mirages with the RAAF. He was successful but opted to return to the RAN and HS748 Flight on 723 Squadron in 1988. It probably appealed to his sense of humour to be flying a spooky turboprop that could shut down the east coast of Australia with the flick of a switch.

In early September 1989, the civil airlines appealed to the government of the day for assistance. A Navy HS748 was the first to arrive on the tarmac of Tullamarine. As the props wound down, the captain's window slid open and Ray let go the best bower anchor, a large red plastic anchor attached to a rope tied to the control column. His first officer held up a sign that read 'The Navy's here,' last heard when HMS *Cossack*'s boarding party raided the German oiler *Altmark* in Norway early in the Second World War. And it was all recorded on national TV. Ray certainly had a sense of history that went with his humour.

In later years, I was based with a large Middle Eastern carrier and Ray was being productive for a large Hong Kong-based airline. On occasions, he would meet up with me in one of the local watering holes and we would spin yarns about the good old days. And then, quite suddenly, he was gone, taken quite suddenly, and far, far too early.

Miss you, Ray.

Purps (Peter Greenfield)

Commander Charles Rex

Charles Robert Richmond Rex, affectionately known as 'Charlie' by most, passed away peacefully on 11 June 2020. He had been frail for many months due to a long illness.

Born in Hobart, Charlie attended Hutchins School, with which his family had a long history. He joined the sea cadets and in 1963 was judged to be the best naval cadet, and the following year he won selection to Jervis Bay.

Charlie entered the RAN College as a Cadet Midshipman in 1964, aged 16. He graduated as a pilot from RAAF Pearce and, in 1968, was posted to the RAN Helicopter Flight Vietnam (2nd Flight) which was integrated into the US Army's 135th Assault Helicopter Company. It operated in the Delta area of South Vietnam in the thick of the fighting, and Charlie was mentioned in despatches during this period.

After returning from Vietnam, Charlie transferred to fixed-wing aviation and completed No 4 Skyhawk OFS in December 1970. He completed a number of operational tours in HMAS *Melbourne* as a member of 805 Squadron and was later appointed Senior Pilot of 724 Squadron.

Charles Rex in 2018 as guest speaker on Anzac Day at his old school, The Hutchins School, Hobart, unveiling an honour board for the school alumni who have died in war.

In the 1980s, Charlie served as the commissioning Commanding Officer of the patrol boat HMAS *Launceston* (II), and later as the Executive Officer of HMAS *Success*. Commander Rex served as the Commanding Officer HMAS *Penguin* from 1992–94 before attending the Joint Services Staff College. He resigned from the Navy in 1995.

Charlie's death represented a very sad and far too early demise of a popular and highly professional FAA Officer. May he rest in peace.

(Courtesy Fleet Air Arm Association of Australia)

Charlie was a complex man. His character, I believe, was moulded by his experiences on the battlefield. He had strong opinions, rarely offered, and was quick to make decisions, which were rarely deliberated on.

In early 1977, Charlie appeared on VC724 for refamiliarisation training on the Macchi and Skyhawk. We looked askance at this young/old lieutenant with salty shoulder boards, did not ask too much and let him get on with it. Towards mid-year, our Senior Pilot, (SP) Clive Blennerhassett, announced his impending departure for the Joint Warfare School at RAAF Williamtown. And the next week Charlie appeared with new lieutenant commander stripes, and the Boss ('Cridge') introduced him as our new SP. All done with no fuss, no fanfare. So Charlie.

The OFS ran to its conclusion. We three students became staff pilots, and the Mayfly continued to be produced with everybody productively working hard. But then, on 31 July, I dropped a rocket pod on the range. I returned shamefacedly and admitted my error to the Boss, who did not make a big fuss; neither did Charlie.

The next day was my second day as a staff pilot and I sat in the front seat of a T-bird monitoring the SP, Charlie, while he did his thing on an instrument flying practice sortie. His final approach was a radar/ground-controlled approach and, as he put the gear down there was a huge bang and the aircraft yawed. I could see the starboard drop tank was skewed about ten degrees to the right. I told Charlie and he promptly gave me control. From his viewpoint he could just see a witness mark on the inboard side of the tank so he told me to land the airplane gently and no heavy braking.

That took longer to write than it took Charlie to make his assessment and decision. So, I landed very gently, and rolled out to the far end of the runway, then taxied in gently. As we crossed Runway 21, we got a utility hydraulics warning which mystified us. At the hot brakes check, the inspector ducked underneath and was there for a longer time than normal. He came out again showing us the nose gear pin and flag, then disappeared again to appear on the other side, giving us the cut sign. So, we shut down, disarmed the seats and dismounted via the wing and port tank. As we looked back down the taxiway, we could see a trail of hydraulic fluid. The inspector said, 'Shit, Sirs, you got to look at this' and led us to the starboard gear leg. He pointed up at the trunnion bearing, and we could see that the top half was missing, and the tank had taken a big blow from something.

It transpired that the cast trunnion bearing had broken when the gear was lowered. The loose bit appeared to have struck the tank a ginormous blow and interfered with the hydraulic lines around the gear leg. Sometime later, I heard that the missing bit was handed in to the main gate by the farmer over whose field we had dropped it. Luckily, we missed all his prize dairy cattle.

A long time later, I made contact with Charlie via Linkedin. He had certainly progressed since his flying days, and I was pleased to see he was the Commissioning CO of HMAS *Launceston*, later promoted to commander and, later still, successful in private enterprise. It was also gratifying to see the respect that former sailors, both naval airmen and seamen, had for Charlie when his death was reported on Navy pages of Facebook.

Vale Charlie Rex.

Peter Greenfield

Lieutenant Commander Peter Marshall AFC

December 3 1969, LCDR PC Marshall was flying a Phantom jet from the Royal Naval Air Station Yeovilton with his observer Flight Lieutenant Jack Haines RAF. They were engaged in mock dogfights over the sea north of Land's End when, at 18,000 feet, their aircraft suffered a heavy blow and began to vibrate severely, with the windscreen covered in thick, dark hydraulic fluid and both engines flaming out.

Peter's immediate instinct was to prepare for ejection; overcoming this, however, he decided to remain with the aircraft. As it turned out, the radar cover on the nose of the aircraft had become detached and it, and parts of the radar, had been ingested by the starboard engine.

Peter found that, although he was experiencing severe buffeting, the jet was still controllable. The starboard engine and intakes were badly damaged by debris that had also punctured the wing's leading-edge flaps and ripped the fuselage skin. Even so, assisted by another aircraft, which joined him in the air, Peter decided to attempt a return to Yeovilton, 130 miles away. It proved an extremely hazardous final approach: forward vision, due to the hydraulic fluid on his windscreen, was

Peter Marshall AFC when serving in the UK. Note the Phantom in the background.

practically nil, while pronounced yaw and buffeting threatened to throw the aircraft out of control.

Nonetheless, Peter managed to land safely, thus saving weeks of speculative investigation and the consequent disruption to the Phantom flying programme, as well as its introduction into front-line service. Peter's version: 'The nose-cone fell off and there was hydraulic fluid all over the place, but I could see the motorway below and knew I could follow that back to base. So, why would I eject from a serviceable aircraft?' He did say, though, that the old maintainers' response to faults – 'ground tested and found serviceable' did not apply in this case. He was awarded the Boyd Trophy 1969 for exceptional skill and personal courage and received an AFC [Air Force Cross].

Peter Charles Marshall was born on January 18 1931 in Birmingham. In 1954, he decided to join the Royal Navy, learning to fly at the US Navy flying school at Pensacola, Florida. He subsequently flew more than a score of aircraft from single-engine trainers to jets and helicopters, and served in the aircraft carriers *Centaur*, *Ark Royal*, *Eagle*, and the Australian *Melbourne*. In 1972, he transferred to the RAN, with which he served for the next 18 years.

Peter commanded 724 Naval Air Squadron from 1975 to 1977. In his long flying career, he logged 4,262 flying hours including 444 deck landings, and by his skill survived several aircraft incidents.

Peter co-founded the *Albatross* Gilbert and Sullivan Society which evolved into the present *Albatross* Musical Theatre Company [AMTC]. In 2012, he shared the stage in a production of *The Boy From Oz* with a daughter and granddaughter, but the cough that stopped him rehearsing for the 2013 production of *Beauty and the Beast* was the first symptom of Mesothelioma. The AMTC turned out in force to sing at his funeral.

LCDR Peter Marshall, born January 18 1931, died August 3 2013.

(via *The Telegraph*, UK)

Peter Marshall was my Boss when I joined VC724 to await the A-4 OFS. When we had completed our Macchi mini-OFS, we were treated as staff pilots and flew a great deal of fleet requirements tasking. One such sortie was a ship strike of four Macchis led by the Boss. Duly briefed, with the invocation of 'always keep me on the horizon', we set off. The weather that day was benign with hardly any wind and no cloud. We formed up in low-level battle formation and, once we went feet wet, the Boss dropped down to not much above the sea. His flying skills were little short of amazing! We knew a heading change was coming up when he precisely lifted us all up 50 or so feet, smoothly rolled in the bank, and once rolled out on heading, lowered us back to the sea.

Later, on the Skyhawk OFS, I was having a great deal of trouble flying the weaponry circuit at Beecroft. My weapons as a result, impacted anywhere but the target, seemingly at random. So it was that I was assigned a T-bird, with the Boss in the backseat. I knew it was a scrub ride and it weighed on my mind. I yanked and banked and the threw the odd bomb to who knows where.

A quiet voice from the back said, 'I have control' and, as if by magic, the aircraft settled down. The Boss then flew the smoothest weapons circuit I had seen, and at the end, as we pitched up in the recovery, he gave me back the aeroplane. His words were, 'You don't need to be aggressive with the aeroplane, just assertive. Make it do what you want to do, without fighting it.'

It was just what I needed; it gave me back my self-confidence, that I could fly. I came back with the best weapons results I had ever had, and thereafter weaponry was never a problem.

Later, on a strike-progression mission, the Boss was riding backseat with me as No 3. Lead (the AWI) called a nav-counter right and rolled into a turn. As I turned to reposition myself, I felt a light forward pressure on the stick and the whispered words 'Whatever you do, don't pull back'. Almost immediately a shadow passed over the cockpit as No 4 crossed over the top, instead of behind. As we regained wings level, the Boss merely said, 'Not your fault, but No 4 needs to be reminded of the right way to crossover.'

The Boss was a very skilful pilot and a very good instructor. He always seemed to know the answers and believed in letting us students learn from our mistakes, up to a point.

RIP Peter Marshall, a good Boss.

Peter Greenfield

Commander Peter Clark DFC

Commander Peter Lloyd Clark DFC was born on 26 April 1947. He joined the RAN in July 1966 as a midshipman. After being assessed as suitable for pilot training, he was sent to Pensacola, Florida, at the end of 1966 to stream though the United States Navy's aircrew training program.

On return from the US, Peter joined 723 Squadron for the Helicopter Flight Vietnam. There, he flew 1,200 hours in his 12-month detachment, was an Air Mission Commander and was awarded the Distinguished Flying Cross.

Back in Australia, he joined 724 Squadron for jet conversion (on the Macchi), a notable event as he and his instructor had to eject on his first flight. Several appointments followed, including to 805 Squadron flying the Skyhawk and, for his final full-time posting, as Commander (Air) of Naval Air Station Nowra.

He left the Navy in 1986 and joined Lloyd Aircraft Jet Charter, flying Learjets out of Nowra. Later, he joined National Jet

Peter Clark as a midshipman in the 1960s.

Systems and rose to senior management positions. After retirement to Queensland, he was diagnosed with a brain tumour (Glioblastoma Multiforme) in October 2005 and succumbed in November 2006. He was only 59 years old.

Peter Clark will be remembered as one of a breed of young Fleet Air Arm officers who returned from active service in Vietnam, battle hardened and not at all interested in the minutiae of bureaucracy. He will always be remembered both in the FAA and in the broader aviation community as a brilliant pilot, a natural leader and a good friend to many.

> When I first joined VC724 in 1975, Peter was the Station AWI, living in an office somewhere near the VC724 Operations Hut. He would appear, in a flying suit with a USN pattern leather flying jacket, cup of coffee in one hand, and a fag in the other. Peter would ask us how we were going and then amble out across to the hangar to talk to somebody in squadron management.
>
> No 2 AWI course was in progress and he, of course, was vitally interested in that. He instructed, but most often was a critical listener at briefs the trainee AWIs were conducting, perhaps flew on a mission, and then settled back in the debrief. And that was where you saw the calibre of the man.
>
> Being one of the people exposed to tragedy and horrors of war at a young age, he was someone who did not bother to call a spade an implement for moving dirt. In other words, there was no BS.
>
> The ejection had left him with a neck injury, and he often complained about a FOV (field of view) problem as he rubbed his neck. But I wondered if he deliberately did that to disarm you, because it was awfully hard to win against him.
>
> I would have loved to have worked for him when he was the CO, but sadly events dictated otherwise. I once called him when I had a troubled period in my life and he gave me his time in the way he had, questions and answers, and then finally his advice. It was sound and set me down a path that ultimately proved happy and successful.
>
> Vale Peter 'Cowboy' Clark.
>
> Peter Greenfield

Chapter 22

THE CASE FOR CARRIER-BASED FIGHTERS

Many readers will no doubt question why this chapter is here. There were many reasons why the Royal Australian Navy had a fixed-wing aviation component, why it lasted as long as it did and why the benefits to the Australian Defence Force (ADF) of returning fixed-wing aircraft to sea far outweigh any apparent disadvantages or perceived 'stealing of thunder'.

Firstly, the senior officers leading the Navy at the end of the Second World War recognised the strategic problem facing Australia. They successfully convinced the government of the day that part of the answer involved forming a Fleet Air Arm.

Secondly, the naval leaders and governments that followed reconsidered the problem at intervals of approximately a decade in the years that followed. They defined that problem as (1) the Air Defence of the Fleet, (2) conducting Maritime Strike and, (3) Close Air Support of troops.

Thirdly, naval aviation since the 1930s has profoundly influenced which power has control of the seas. Small escort carriers helped the Allies win the Battle of the Atlantic. Naval aviation allowed the Imperial Japanese Navy to strike Pearl Harbor, the Philippines, Australia, Ceylon and overpower Malaya and the Dutch East Indies. It took another naval aviation power, the US Navy, to stem those attacks. To finally defeat the Japanese, it took the combined efforts of the naval aviation power of the USN and the RN in a long and bitter battle.

Naval aviation was the first response in Korea; close support was delivered by the USN, the RN and the RAN. During the conflict in Malaysia, RN carriers delivered helicopter support to the troops in contact in Borneo. At the end of that conflict, Exercise *Bersatu Padu* demonstrated the flexibility and power of naval aviation to respond from the sea when land-based forces were out of range.

Further, the *Rimpac* exercise series, in which HMAS *Melbourne* participated, demonstrated the flexibility and capability of naval aviation to project power at long distances from our own shores. The *Kangaroo* exercises demonstrated the flexibility and capability of the Skyhawk force and *Melbourne* to support troops going ashore.

Navy and Air Force leaders have not learnt to co-operate in true joint warfare, to use each other's strengths. Neither can it be said many governments, from 1983 on, have paid due attention to the threats abounding in the region.

The RAN has two very capable Canberra-class Landing Helicopter Docks (LHD), designed by Navantia as power projection ships and very much capable of operating the F-35B Lightning II. A great deal of misinformation has been put about by many self-styled experts. The roles of the F-35 still need to be fulfilled and, despite what the RAAF maintains, they cannot do it with the same assurance as naval aviation embarked on an aircraft carrier. The tyranny of distance works against land-based forces.

It was the original intention of the authors to reproduce the following three papers in this book:

a. *The Particulars of Carrier Operations*, 2009

b. *Forget the Carrier option: an engineer's response*, 2014

c. *Proximity means Capability*, 2016

However, space limitations mean only excerpts and summaries of these papers are given below.

The first paper is a lengthy discussion of aircraft carrier flight operations, and how they differ from those on land. The author, Steve George, is a retired RN commander and Air Engineer Officer. In 28 years of service, he served on all three of the RN's aircraft carriers in both helicopter and fixed-wing squadrons. The paper was written in respect to ongoing debates over the arrangements for operating the new F-35B from the Queen Elizabeth-class aircraft carriers. Steve concluded:

> This essay has sought to illustrate the 'Particular Mechanics of Carrier Aviation', and how they have been developed and perfected by experts in the USN and the FAA to allow the safe and routine delivery of combat capability from the sea. And it has also sought to show that this is an achievable and practical exercise in military organisation and teamwork.
>
> It appears obvious that the management and command of aircraft and carriers must be carried out by a single organisation that has clear accountability for delivering an integrated, effective and safe capability. The inter-relationships between aircraft and people and ship are so close, so potentially hazardous if not perfect, and so vital to delivering the required capability, that they must be under the control of a single responsible 'duty holder'. A single 'ethos', a single aim and a single 'whole ship' way of operating, must be achieved under command of the ship's captain. And that is what all practitioners of naval aviation do.
>
> This is a tried, tested, effective and above all safe way of delivering maritime fixed wing air power. It is the model now applied by all the world's armed forces that deliver this valuable capability. The concept of split command, as briefly tested by the UK with Joint Force Harrier, was ultimately found wanting. It is clear that future UK maritime fixed wing air power should be delivered via the most effective and safest solution – single command at sea.

The second paper is from *The Strategist*, by the Australian Strategic Policy Institute. Steve George was prompted to respond to a paper that stated the purpose of the LHDs was solely for humanitarian assistance and disaster relief, that it was not possible to operate STOVL (short take-off and vertical landing) aircraft from them, and they were intended to be operated for the use of the Army. Steve, as both a serving RN officer and a civilian engineer, was deeply involved in the definition of the F-35B towards its final form. His polite rebuttal is a nice piece of writing and is reproduced here:

> Stuart's piece, 'Forget the carrier option', makes a large and important judgment: that politics and defence funding won't allow the option of deploying F-35Bs on Australia's LHDs. But in making that case Nic repeats erroneous assumptions that are hindering a true exchange of views. It's vital that defence reviews are supported with facts – and some of them bear repetition.

First up, the technical facts. F-35B operations from LHDs are feasible. The F-35B is specifically designed not to drive major ship modifications. The LHD wouldn't need 'conversion' to take F-35Bs, although it would require minor modifications, similar to those being applied to the USN Wasp class. The flight deck is capable of taking an F-35B. The F-35B won't require massive changes to the ships' air traffic control facilities, assuming that they are already up to operating rotary wing aircraft day or night in bad weather. It won't need huge changes to ship structure or facilities.

Those modifications wouldn't 'cost a great deal', as Nic stated. And to repeat, giving the LHD an ability to operate F-35B doesn't mean turning it into a 'mini aircraft carrier'.

Next, remarkable assumptions are being made about what embarked F-35Bs would do. Nic's piece says that their role would be to provide 'intimate air-cover' – a new and intriguing term. With a range of over 300 nautical miles, the most 'intimate' aspect of an F-35B air defence would probably be the effect of an AIM-120 warhead on an incoming threat. But that misses the key point: putting F-35Bs on an LHD would allow more effective use of all the aircraft's capabilities, including precision-strike and ISTAR [intelligence, surveillance, target acquisition and reconnaissance] support, by putting the aircraft closer to the fight. As another article puts it, 'proximity equals capability'. But be in no doubt, air cover will be a requirement for a task group operating anywhere near an enemy air threat. It won't, as the article somewhat dismissively puts it, be a 'nice to have'.

Nic assumes that the RAN would have to buy a third LHD (or a different ship optimised for F-35B) to make the exercise 'worthwhile'. With this leap of logic, he argues that an F-35B option is unaffordable. But this is not a given. The two LHDs are highly capable and flexible assets – their Air Groups will be adjusted to meet the demands of future situations. Yes, embarking F-35Bs will displace some of the planned Air Group. But Tailored Air Groups (TAGs) are a common-place and well-understood way of using small decks to best effect. And be in no doubt, the ADF will have to adjust the LHD Air Groups in the future.

It's almost certain that whatever operational assumptions the LHDs were bought against will change, and change fast. And the way the LHDs will be equipped and operated will need to change. Will amphibious operations be ADF only? Would both LHDs be available? Would they be part of an international task group with USMC participation? Would they be required to go where there might be an enemy air threat? We don't know. But the ADF has to make the best use of the two ships they've got. Sticking to the line that 'we can't do it because that would mean changing our defence planning assumptions' is guaranteed to make it worse.

Nic's article also baldly states that F-35Bs on an LHD would be 'pathetically inefficient'. That's a bold claim, and should be examined against the actual experience of the RN and the USMC's STOVL units over the last 30 years or so. [Actually, it's eerily familiar to the arguments against the Sea Harrier/Invincible-class combination in the late 1970s. Those went away after what happened in the South Atlantic in 1982.] But it's quite true that the issue of 'efficiency' should be considered, particularly for long-range air operations.

Nic asserts that 'our pilots can cope' with long flight times. Yes, of course they can, but that's not the issue. Burning 'more than 10 hours' of flight time to deliver around 25 minutes of 'air power' might not be especially 'efficient'. Critics of the F-35B/LHD option should do the maths on how many land-based aircraft (and tanker slots) are needed to provide continuous, reactive, air support at long range. Do some fuel-usage calculations. Now put 5 or 6 F-35Bs with the task group, on three-minute alert posture, 50 miles from the target and do the maths again. Now decide which option is 'inefficient'. It's a simple effect of geography. Proponents of the F-35B/ LHD option aren't saying it's a replacement for land-based air power. It's for when land-based aircraft, for reasons of pure physics, can't do the job.

Finally, the article says: 'There was…a good argument to be made for incorporating the STOVL version as a part of our original purchase of aircraft'. Agreed. It then says that 'That chance has gone'. Not agreed. There's nothing stopping the ADF making a final buy of 28 aircraft of the F-35B variant. Or even switching some of the existing planned buy from the A variant to Bs. It's a matter of political will.

The divergent views around this debate show just how important it is that the F-35B issue is thoroughly (and independently) investigated so that decisions are supported by facts. The UK's failure to 'get the facts right' in their 2010 SDSR led to an F-35/carrier related mess of epic proportions. Australia now has the chance to do the job properly.

The final paper was a 2015 Defence White Paper Submission: *Proximity Means Capability – Operating F-35Bs from the Canberra-class LHDs*. The prime author is David Baddams, the pilot who had the last Skyhawk catapult shot from HMAS *Melbourne*. He went on to serve in the RN, flying FRS.1 and FRS.2 Sea Harriers, ending his career as CO 800 NAS. Of course, he was helped a bit by his co-authors, Steve George, Peter Greenfield and Ian Hunter. Behind the scenes, we had some advice from a retired submariner who led the team that selected the LHD as the ship of choice.

The executive summary of the paper states:

> The submission argues that acquisition and operation of the F-35B aircraft from the Canberra-class Landing Helicopter Docks (LHD) is affordable, feasible and desirable. Embarked air power would give the Government of Australia (GoA) and the Australian Defence Force (ADF) a significant and necessary increase in their ability to use decisive air power in support of deployed ADF forces and thus assist the prosecution of foreign policy objectives and military tasks.

The paper concludes with an argument for a purchase of 28 carrier-capable F-35Bs to augment the existing fleet of land-based RAAF F-35As. It is argued that F-35B embarked airpower will greatly enhance ADF capabilities, and that this is feasible with the existing Canberra-class LHD designs. The submission concluded with the following:

1. Embarked air power has proven, over many decades, to offer nations in Australia's geographical situation decisive political and military advantages. It would do so for ADF operations in the Pacific littoral areas.

2. A mix of F-35A/F-35B fleet would offer superior air power capability to 100 land-based-only F-35As. F-35Bs could also operate from land.

3. 28 F-35B aircraft would be able to support a viable capability of six to eight aircraft for each LHD.

4. Commonality between F-35A and F-35B would minimise the additional costs of a mixed fleet.

5. Combining the F-35B with LHDs would offer greatly enhanced capabilities to the ADF, is a natural and logical fit to Plan Jericho and offers significant additional options to the GoA.

6. Long range land-based air power projection offers unique political advantages, but it has military limits that constrain its utility and will do so again in future conflicts. Plan Jericho needs to account for these limitations.

7. Total reliance on land-based air power and ship-based missile defences to support ADF operations against emerging threats presents unacceptable risk to ATG assets and personnel.

8. The F-35B has been designed to operate from ships similar to the LHDs, and the LHD design was developed around the F-35B. Integrating the two presents low risk.

Annex A

CONTRIBUTORS

The authors are grateful for contributions of all kinds from a great many people, only some of whom are listed below.

TREV RUTING joined the RAN College in 1968 and then progressed to UNSW where he graduated with a BEng (Naval Architecture). He served on HMAS *Melbourne* (II) on multiple occasions during the 1970s, including for a posting in Flight Deck Engineering during 1976–78. During this posting, he started as Arrestors Officer (also covering LOX and AVFUELS) then moved forward to Catapult Officer. Trev later returned to *Melbourne* as the final Flight Deck Engineer – the last to calculate launch steam pressure for the final fixed-wing (S-2G Tracker) catapult launch in the RAN.

His subsequent postings included several as a naval architect in Design Division, Marine Engineering Officer of Perth, several in Navy logistics, Chief Staff Officer (Technical) to Fleet Commander, then off to Canberra for Joint Services Staff College, Navy policy and a series of Navy project director positions, including Anzac ships (twice). In 1997, he led a Naval Aviation Force Management Review for Chief of Navy. His final Permanent Naval Force posting as rear admiral was as Head Maritime Systems Division in Defence Materiel Organisation. Reserve time followed with seven years setting up, then running, Seaworthiness Boards until 2016.

CDRE John Da Costa. (RAN)

JOHN DA COSTA enlisted in the RAN in 1955 for an initial period of six years as a non-commissioned Naval Airman (Aircrew). He earned his wings at RAAF Point Cook in August 1956 and, following further training at Nowra, joined 805 Squadron flying the Hawker Sea Fury. John subsequently converted to jets and in 1959 was embarked in HMAS *Melbourne* flying Sea Venoms.

In 1960, Lieutenant Da Costa joined 723 Squadron, for helicopter conversion training, to fly utility helicopters, chiefly in a search-and-rescue role. On 2 January 1963, he accepted a permanent commission in the RAN and completed a number of squadron command courses, followed by an RN fighter pilot course in the UK.

After returning to Australia, on 28 April 1966 John was involved in a tragic accident when landing on HMAS *Melbourne*. Piloting Sea Venom 866, and having successfully 'trapped', the arrestor gear parted during the pull out, resulting in the aircraft having neither adequate speed to regain flight or to come to a halt by applying the brakes. Realising the aircraft would ditch, the order to eject was given by the pilot. Although John survived the accident, unfortunately his observer, Lieutenant Ted Kennell RAN, did not.

In 1967, John underwent A-4 Skyhawk training in the US before leading the first A-4 Operational Flying School (OFS) course in Australia. He had the distinction of being the first RAN Skyhawk pilot to complete an A-4 deck landing in Australian waters. During 1968–69, John commanded both VF805 and VC724.

In the 1970s, Commander Da Costa served as both the HMAS *Melbourne* air group commander and Commander (Air) at HMAS *Albatross*. In 1984, he had the honour of flying in Skyhawk 880 on its last flight in the RAN before it was transferred to the RNZAF. John eventually retired from the permanent Navy in 1989 after 34 years of full-time service.

JIM LEE first joined the RAN in 1951 and maintained Sea Fury, Firefly, Tiger Moth, Wirraway and Dakota aircraft before being posted to 816 Squadron on HMAS *Vengeance* to go to the UK to train on the Fairey Gannet. He subsequently held a number of postings: HMAS *Nirimba* for a Mechanicians Course, Aircraft Servicing Unit (ASU), 725 Squadron Wessex, AED Workshop on HMAS *Melbourne* and, upon being promoted to MECHAE 2 in 1963, Jim was posted to Air Training Department at HMAS *Albatross*. In 1966, Jim went to the USA to undertake the first RAN Skyhawk course in both airframe systems and engines. He was promoted to Chief Mechanician in 1969 and posted to VF805 in 1971. In 1973, Jim was posted to VC724, was promoted to WOATA-4 in 1975, and, in 1976, was posted to ASU with a further posting to Air Station Support Section (Salvage) in January 1980. After a posting to HMAS *Melbourne* in 1980 to Air Stores Usage and Control Office, and after a career of 28 years, Jim resigned in 1982 at the expiration of his engagement.

FRED LANE entered naval service in 1947 on the inaugural No 1 Naval Airman Pilots Course. After graduation in 1949, he went to the UK to train on fighters, followed by carrier qualification on HMS *Illustrious*.

On returning to Australia, Fred was hastily converted to Sea Furies and embarked on HMAS *Sydney* in February 1951. He then experienced extended war operations off Korea. Fred subsequently served as Senior Pilot of 817 Naval Air Squadron (NAS) in HMAS *Vengeance* and then qualified as a flying instructor in the mid-1950s. Other appointments in his career progression followed, including Instrument Rating Examiner on Fireflies, Senior Staff Pilot of 808 and 805 NASs, and CO of 805 NAS on Sea Venoms.

Fred was appointed to No 1 Skyhawk OFS in 1968 and appointed to command VF805 in January 1969. He thus became one of the few, and possibly the only pilot, to fly from all three of the RAN's carriers, and to fly all three RAN fighter types (Sea Fury, Sea Venom and Skyhawk).

Fred opted to retire in his early forties 'to get an education'. After undertaking a bachelor's degree at UNSW, he was awarded a PhD in Clinical Psychology at New York State University. Following a period overseas, he became an acknowledged expert in treating dementia, where he ran programmes in NSW for ten years.

IAN SCOTT joined the Navy in July 1970, aged 16, and became an Aircraft Artificer Apprentice at HMAS *Nirimba*. After graduating in 1973, he was posted to VC724. In 1978, Ian was posted to VF805, and then off to sea on HMAS *Melbourne* for *Rimpac 78* and other exercises. Ian was posted to Salvage Section in 1979 where he supervised Bay Servicing on Skyhawk and Macchi Emergency Oxygen systems, and trained Liquid Oxygen Mechanics from VF805 and VC724. He was posted back to VC724 in January 1980, and promoted to CPOATA (Chief Petty Officer Air Technical Aircraft) in September 1980. In September 1983, Ian was posted to the ASU to be in charge of the Skyhawks in storage. In November 1983, he went back to VC724 as the Maintenance Chief until mid-1984. Ian transferred to the RAAF in March 1985 as a flight sergeant and was posted to the Mirages of No 77 Squadron. In 1986, he was appointed Warrant Officer Engineer, and was posted to No 79 Squadron, again on Mirages, in Malaysia. Ian left the RAAF in September 1990 and joined the Royal Australian Naval Reserve as a WOATA.

CPOATA Ian Scott, the picture of suaveness. (Ian Scott)

ROB HALL joined the RAN in 1970 and trained as an Aircraft Artificer apprentice before serving on both VC724 and VF805, as well as the Aircraft Servicing Unit workshops at HMAS *Albatross* where he was authorised to maintain Skyhawk and Macchi aircraft. Rob had the distinction of being the last Maintenance CPO to take VF805 to sea before HMAS *Melbourne* decommissioned in 1982.

In 1984, Rob transferred to the Naval Police Branch and was soon commissioned as a Special Duties officer. In coming years, he was fortunate to participate in many multinational exercises both overseas and in Australia. Following an extensive and satisfying career, Rob retired as a lieutenant commander in October 2017, having served for 47 days short of 48 years in both the Permanent Navy and the Naval Reserve.

ERIC KRENN joined the Navy in Brisbane at 1100 on 11 November 1975. He was posted to HMAS *Albatross* in February 1976 and underwent training to become an Air Technical Weapons Electrical (ATWL) with advancement to Ordinary Seaman ATWL in August 1976. Eric began flight servicing and inspections in January 1977 on the A-4 Skyhawk. On 9 August 1977, he was promoted to able seaman and, in July 1981, leaving the Fleet Air Arm, he changed his category to Meteorology. Eric became a Navigators Yeoman in December 1982 on HMAS *Perth*. In January 1985, he commenced training to become a Chinese Linguist, however, after not completing that course, he was posted to HMAS *Penguin* and was discharged in November 1987.

PETER WELSH enlisted in 1962 and maintained Sea Venoms, Vampires and Gannets with 724 Squadron. In August 1970, he underwent A-4 training and, from October 1970, Peter was a supervisor of A-4 maintenance. In 1974 and 1975, he was in the Air Stores office on HMAS *Melbourne*. On return to *Albatross* in 1976, he was again maintaining Skyhawks and was also responsible for the maintenance on the Delmar Target towing system and the inflight refuelling 'buddy store'. Peter, from 1979 to 1982, spread his time between being the Flight Line CPO, again being responsible for maintenance of the Delmar Target towing system, air-refuelling system and Skyhawk maintenance. He discharged to shore as a chief petty officer in April 1982 after serving 20 years.

(Author Peter Greenfield: Peter is a man of many skills. The best I observed was Peter reskinning CMDR (Air)'s Tri-pacer by hand. I did not know of anybody else capable of that.)

JOHN HETHERINGTON John joined the Navy in 1963 and rose to the rank of Chief Petty Officer. In his last years of service, he was posted to HMAS *Cerberus* to teach marine technical sailors gas turbine engines. After resigning, he attended university to study industrial hydraulics and pneumatics and control engineering. Before retiring, he was teaching those subjects and more to RAN Engineering and Electrical Engineering officers. He lives in Southern Victoria.

PHIL THOMPSON joined the Navy as a Senior Entry to the Royal Australian Naval College at HMAS *Creswell* in 1966. He didn't really know why he joined up but, like most of us, it was an exciting escape to something very different. Subsequently, he undertook flying training and in December 1968 joined VC724 which was in the throes of sorting itself from a Vampire and Sea Venom operator to a Macchi and Skyhawk fleet requirements unit.

Phil successfully completed the OFS in time to start the workup on VF805 in August 1971. He then had that unfortunate ramp strike on the first night of September 1971. Full marks to him for making a successful recovery to Nowra, after what must have been a shocking experience. Phil completed that cruise and was finally posted back to VC724 in April 1972. In 1974, he was posted to a Photo Interpreters Course in the USA, but unfortunately fell ill and, on return to Australia, was discharged medically.

In semi-retirement as a result, Phil took a great interest in compiling the history of the Skyhawk in Australia, and then all things relating to naval aviation in Australia. He developed a huge Adobe file which is now resident on the Fleet Air Arm Association of Australia website.

DAVID COLLINGRIDGE began as a midshipman in January 1962 and then underwent observer training on Malta for two years. On return to HMAS *Albatross*, postings followed to HC725 and HS817 as an observer on Wessex 31A and 31B helicopters.

In 1966, David was trained as a pilot and subsequently joined No 2 OFS for Skyhawk training. This was alongside Errol Kavanagh and Gary Northern, all three destined to command VF805. David then went to sea with VF805 on HMAS *Melbourne*.

Overseas courses in the UK and USA followed, before David was appointed Station Air Warfare Instructor (AWI) at HMAS *Albatross* in 1971–72. In 1974, he was appointed as Senior Pilot with VC724, flying Skyhawks and Macchis. After a stint in the US, he was appointed CO VC724 in early 1977, prior to taking command of VF805 in December.

A variety of staff positions followed. Promoted to Captain, David was appointed Director Naval Air Warfare for 1985–87, and subsequently appointed Director Naval Manpower Planning 1987–89. Now in retirement, he lives in the wilds of Sydney, and fends off unsubtle approaches from younger ex-pilots for articles for books and things.

GRAHAM 'VONDO' WINTERFLOOD joined the RAN in 1966 and was soon posted to NAS Pensacola in Florida for flying training 'up to but not including combat readiness on helicopters.' The initial training was on T-34 Mentors and T-28 Trojans and included deck landings on USS *Lexington*. Graham then converted to helicopters.

In 1968, he converted onto the Westland Wessex at Nowra, and his first cruise on HMAS *Melbourne* was in 1969. In the early morning of 3 June, *Melbourne* and USS *Frank E. Evans* collided.

Graham 'Vondo' Winterflood

At that time, he was co-pilot with Bob Waldron; they had become airborne about five minutes before the collision. They returned to find the bow of the American destroyer had already sunk; all they could do was shine the spotlight on survivors in the water as their Wessex was not fitted with a winch.

In April 1971, Graham was posted to VC724 for conversion onto the Macchi and then the Skyhawk. In 1972, he joined VF805 and flew as No 3 in the *Checkmates* formation team. The following year, Graham embarked on HMAS *Melbourne* for *Rimpac 73*. He left the RAN in 1974 to seek employment in civil aviation.

JOHN 'BOOTS' SIEBERT joined the RAN in 1969 and trained as an A-4G pilot and Landing Signals Officer (LSO). A three-year exchange tour with the US Marine Corps saw him flying the A-4M and qualifying as an AV-8A Harrier pilot. During his time as the V/STOL Project Officer in Canberra, the Defence Department decided to disestablish fixed-wing naval aviation; a career change followed when he transferred to the Royal Navy and qualified as an FRS.1 Sea Harrier pilot. After commanding 801 Squadron in HMS *Ark Royal*, John's final active-duty assignment was at the NATO headquarters in Norfolk, Virginia, on the maritime warfare staff.

John 'Boots' Siebert

After a period of instructing in General Aviation, John returned to Australia to fly Lear 35s at Nowra. In 1996, he transitioned to airline flying and operated the BAe 146 and, later, the Boeing 717. John is now retired in Adelaide.

BARRY EVANS joined the Navy at age 19 as a pilot trainee. After gaining his 'wings', Barry was posted to VC724 at Nowra in September 1971 as a member of No 8 OFS. There he mastered flying Skyhawks, an aircraft he was to have a close association with during a notable flying career in the RAN.

In July 1973, Barry joined VF805 and embarked in HMAS *Melbourne* in preparation for

Rimpac 73. Later that year, he again embarked in *Melbourne* with VF805, deploying to South-East Asia. On 8 November 1973, while the ship was on passage to Singapore, Barry was involved in an incident that saw the Skyhawk he was piloting (889) ditch into the sea ahead of *Melbourne* following a failed catapult launch. Trapped in the aircraft, he passed under the ship before freeing himself from the aircraft and surfacing about 100–150 yards astern of the carrier.

Barry 'Baz' Evans

Further major exercises followed with *Kangaroo I* in 1974 and *Rimpac 75.* On return to Nowra, Barry was selected to fly as a member of VF805's *Checkmate* aerobatic team, before joining VC724 to undertake No 2 AWI course. After attending the 'Top Gun' school in the US, he re-joined VF805 in 1977. During *Rimpac 78*, he was able to cross-deck on the giant nuclear-powered USS *Enterprise.*

Toward the end of his flying career, Barry flew as a maintenance test pilot, and Delmar (towed target) pilot. He finished as Station AWI before resigning from the Navy in 1980. Barry then pursued a successful flying career in civil aviation, including with Cathay Pacific on the Boeing 747, Airbus 330/340 and Boeing 777. He amassed a total of around 16,000 flying hours.

MARK RADISICH joined the RAN in 1976 and trained as an Air Traffic Controller. He then served at HMAS *Albatross*, in the aircraft carrier HMAS *Melbourne* in 1980, on RAAF exchange at Tullamarine airport and for a brief period in the carrier HMS *Invincible* in 1983.

Mark received a Flag Officer's Commendation for firefighting efforts on the night of 4 December 1976 when 12 Tracker anti-submarine aircraft were destroyed or badly damaged by fire at HMAS *Albatross*.

Mark Radisich

He resigned from the RAN in 1986 after the disbandment of fixed-wing elements of the FAA. He subsequently joined the RAAF in 1987 as an Air Traffic Controller. He retired from the RAAF as a squadron leader in 2001 after more than 24 years of combined service.

MICK FLYNN attended medical school at the University of Melbourne before joining the RAN as a doctor. A posting to HMAS *Albatross* opened his eyes to aviation and he wrote an earnest letter requesting approval for a pilots' course so he could better look after the aviators.

Strangely, this was approved; a limited A-4 conversion followed. Mike soon gained a reputation as willing to fly almost anytime and that, combined with a shortage of pilots, meant his experience broadened rapidly. Mike was posted to a USN Flight Surgeons' Course in Pensacola, where his existing qualifications were recognised, and he requalified in TA-4Js.

On return to Nowra, he was welcomed back to VC724 where the CO decided that, on the basis of his experience, the squadron could best utilise him as a spare pilot on both the Macchis and Skyhawks.

When fixed wing disbanded, Doc Flynn went to the dark side and learnt to fly helicopters. Somewhere in all of this, he also managed to go off and do a seagoing job as Medical Officer (MO) on a guided-missile destroyer, was sent to Tarangau as the Base MO, but always returned to HMAS *Albatross*. When the RNZAF came to Nowra on contract, Doc went riding with them, because he also supported them medically.

Eventually, all good things come to an end. After many more adventures in a much wider and more senior capacity, Doc retired as a commodore to live in Sydney.

MICHAEL MAHER joined the RAN as a direct entry pilot in 1975. Joining VC724 for the A-4 OFS in 1976, he graduated in mid-1977, also completing a Forward Air Controller course. After joining VF805, he deployed on the *Rimpac 78* cruise which was followed by LSO training in the US.

Rejoining VF805 on return from the US, Michael embarked on the Indian Ocean deployment in 1980. At the end of 1981, he was posted on exchange to the USMC to fly AV-8A Harriers with VMA213. In the three years serving with the USMC, he completed cruises on USS *Tarawa*, USS *Iwo Jima* and USS *Inchon*. Returning to Australia in 1985, he transferred to the RAAF to fly Mirages and then Hornets, becoming the CO of No 75 Squadron based at RAAF Tindal from 1995 to 1998. He retired from the RAAF with the rank of air commodore. Mike remains an active pilot in retirement.

MARGARET DENNIS joined the WRANS in 1974 and became an ATC in 1977. As her husband, Michael Maher, was posted to fly the Harrier with the USMC, she resigned in 1981; those were the rules back then. On return to Australia, Michael transferred to the Air Force, so they moved to RAAF Williamtown. Margaret volunteered at TS *Tobruk*, before time in Malaysia and Singapore. From 1992, after returning to Williamtown, Margaret did Reserve Service at HMAS *Cerberus*, HMAS *Coonawarra* and HMAS *Manoora*.

Their son was born with Congenital Hyperinsulinism (life-threatening Hypoglycaemia) which, if not properly managed, can lead to a variety of additional conditions. A group of parents started out on a Bulletin Board and have grown to form Congenital Hyperinsulinism International, which has done some amazing things. After moving to Canberra, Margaret rose to become Deputy Director Reserves before completing her service in 2020.

DAVE 'GRAVY' STAINES seemed to have always been a Senior Air Traffic Controller. However, his contribution shows otherwise. He was in fact the Training Officer when Mark Radisich was completing his training. For his sins, Dave took Mark and his colleague to sea as the Carrier Air Group's air traffic control section.

MURRAY COPPINS joined the Naval College in January 1970, straight after finishing school. After some sea time, Murray underwent pilot training and was posted to VC724 for A-4 conversion, which began in July 1977. By December 1979, he was posted to a Qualified Flying Instructors (QFI) course, and from there to the Senior Naval Officer's job at No 2 Flying Training School from May 1980 to May 1983.

A year in Navy Office followed, rewarded with a Macchi refresher course at East Sale prior to appointment as the Naval Liaison Officer at RAAF Williamtown. This was supposedly to ensure the RAAF followed through with its earnest promise to provide all the fleet-requirement sorties the Navy requested. Murray ended up as the last operational jet pilot in the RAN, flying the ex-Navy Macchis, prior to joining Qantas where he flew Boeing 747s for almost three decades.

JOE HATTLEY joined the RAN at age 15 in October 1971. After training, he was posted to HMAS *Albatross* in January 1974 and then joined HMAS *Melbourne* on a cruise to the USA. Upon return to Australia, Joe commenced an ATA Phase 1 course, following which he was posted to VC724 to maintain Skyhawks. In 1976, he joined VF805 and again went to sea on board HMAS *Melbourne*.

In August 1978, Joe completed his technical training and was promoted to leading seaman in 1979, and then to petty officer in 1981, and held various roles with VC724 and the Aircraft Servicing Unit at *Albatross*. Joe was with VC724

Joe Hattley after completing the last engine run and fuel transfer system test prior to Skyhawk 876 flying to New Zealand in 1984. (Joe Hattley)

when the Fleet Air Arm was disbanded in 1984 and prepared the squadron's Skyhawks for sale to New Zealand. In January 1985, he transferred to the RAAF and was posted to RAAF Edinburgh, working as a maintenance supervisor on P-3 Orions. Joe retired from the RAAF in 1993 as a Warrant Officer Engineer, following 21 years in the Australian Defence Force, and joined the Bureau of Air Safety Investigation in Canberra.

COLIN TOMLINSON joined the RAN for No 92 Pilots Course, commencing in May 1974 at Point Cook, before starting A-4 conversion with VC724 and No 11 OFS. Progress thereafter was normal, if the helter-skelter life on VC724 counts. He then walked across the hangar floor to join VF805 but, in January 1979, fate struck. Colin was flying 870 when his aircraft had a major engine failure; he was forced to eject, suffering compression fractures in the rapid ejection sequence at 250 knots.

Colin spent a period grounded before the medical system released him back to active flying. Shortly after that, he attended a Flying Instructor Course at RAAF East Sale and graduated as a QFI. He was then posted to RAAF Pearce as a staff instructor, before returning to Nowra as fixed-wing flying was about to end.

Colin accepted a transfer to the RAAF for a Mirage conversion, but that was unfortunately curtailed when the medical people found out about his back injuries. He was offered, and accepted, a transfer to DHC Caribous, which he really enjoyed flying. At the right time, Qantas called and Colin saw out the rest of his career flying airliners.

ALLEN 'NOBBY' CLARK or, more correctly, Philip Allen Clark, had always had a problem with his name. Fortunately, the Navy provided the solution with 'Nobby' as all Clarks are called.

Nobby joined the Navy from school, eventually finding himself on No 69 Pilots Course. His first posting after graduation was to VC851 for S-2E Tracker OFS with his fellow graduates. After completion, they were posted to VS816.

However, Nobby had a secret desire to fly A-4 Skyhawks. He managed this via a QFI course in Macchis, followed by a two-year posting to RAAF Pearce as a Navy instructor. Subsequently, he was posted to VC724 for Skyhawk conversion, which was completed in July 1978. As he related in Chapter 15, Nobby became the only RAN pilot to operationally qualify on both S-2Es and A-4Gs.

Nobby went on to fly with VF805 during 1979 after which he served as the V/STOL Project Officer in DNAP (Director of Naval Aviation Policy), then returned to VC724 as Senior Pilot. Following the end of fixed-wing naval aviation, Nobby accepted an offer from the Army to be an instructor at Point Cook. After some years doing that, he found himself flying for Jetstar, and doing the job as Recruitment Manager until his eventual retirement from aviation.

JOHN CRAWLEY joined the RAN in 1957. After training as a REM (Air) (Radio Electrical Mechanic, Air) he joined HMAS *Albatross* in September 1959. John had three short postings to HMAS *Melbourne* before being promoted to lieutenant in 1969. He served on both VC724 and VF805 as the Aircraft Electrical Officer/Weapons Electrical Engineering Officer as well as in the Avionics Workshop as the AVO. John was posted to Canberra before leaving the RAN as a commander. One of his many interests was gliding.

Author Peter Greenfield first met John during his gliding course in 1968:

> He came out to check the three of us doing our first solo in the Kookaburra Mk.IV. When I arrived at VC724, he was the ALO about to cross the hangar floor to VF805. He recognised me straight away and asked if had a pilot's licence. When I replied 'yes', he said, 'Great, you can be a tug pilot.' So it was that I went down the first weekend of the next year, John checked me out in the Super Cub and I was busy tugging gliders every second weekend.

MARK BINSKIN arrived at VC724 about two months behind Dave 'Blem' Baddams. He seemed incredibly young but, not surprisingly, he had joined up to fly at his first opportunity, with a burning ambition to fly Skyhawks. That he achieved his ambition was no surprise but, as he told us in his story, he did not get the chance to go to sea. Instead, he was given a surprise opportunity to go on an exchange posting to fly the Mirage. Not surprising was that the RAAF offered him the chance to change uniforms and become a RAAFie. Not surprising, also, was that very capable young pilot went on to rise to the top of the command tree and finish as Chief of the Defence Force.

JOHN 'JB' BARTELS joined the RAN in 1973 for an observer course. He thinks he was talked into it by a recruiter trying to meet his targets, because he had a secret desire to be a pilot. The budgetary cuts meant his 'O' course was delayed, while the paired pilot course was cancelled. The Navy filled in the waiting time by putting him through Basic Seaman Officer Training. And, of course, he was paid!

His first job after 'O' Course was the Wessex Observer OFS on HT723, which obligingly finished just as the Sea Kings arrived at Nowra. The complete OFS was posted to the Sea King Flight for conversion. By devious means, he got himself sent to Canberra while HS817 went to sea, so he pestered the posters for a pilot course.

For his troubles, John was posted to HT723 where he taught navigation to aircrewmen. Eventually, he was given a posting to No 109 Pilots Course, after which he joined VC724 for Skyhawk conversion. However, by this time *Melbourne* was not accepting A-4s any longer. JB flew the A-4 until early 1983 when he became an instructor. Subsequently, Qantas called, where JB finished a second career as a senior A380 captain.

STEVE GEORGE is a retired RN commander and Air Engineer Officer (AEO). In 28 years of service, he served on all three of the RN's aircraft carriers in both helicopter and fixed-wing squadrons. As with most AEOs, he held a very wide range of appointments. He was the AEO of 801 Naval Air Squadron, operating Sea Harriers from HMS *Ark Royal*. On leaving the RN in 2002, he joined the F-35 'Joint Strike Fighter' programme in Fort Worth, Texas, as a specialist engineer.

Steve's MSc in Applied Flight Mechanics was gained at Cranfield in 1984, he was elected a Fellow of the Royal Aeronautical Society in 2003, and his expertise in aircraft weaponry was recognized in 2009 by the award of a Livery in the Worshipful Company of Gun Makers.

In retirement, Steve dwells in 'Zoomerset', near to Yeovilton where he actively supports the Navy Wings Museum effort. He has long been a well-known aviation cartoonist and his works may be seen on the museum's website.

DAVID 'BLEM' BADDAMS dreamed of being a military fighter pilot, growing up listening to stories from his Air Force-trained father, and later from his Navy trained Skyhawk pilot brother, Kim. Following Kim into the Navy, David joined No 105 Pilots Course in 1978.

David then converted to Skyhawks at Nowra before joining VF805 in June 1980 and sailing on HMAS *Melbourne* for the subsequent Indian Ocean deployment during the second half of 1980. The adventures during that deployment are well documented in this book, with the notable event being the last A-4G launch from the flight deck of HMAS *Melbourne* at 1006 local time on 21 October 1980, with 21-year-old David in the pilot's seat.

With *Melbourne* paying off without replacement, David transferred to the Royal Navy in February 1984 where he served as a military pilot for a further 16 years, flying most of the fixed-wing types, predominantly Sea Harriers, accumulating more than 2,000 hours on the type. David was awarded an MBE for leadership in air operations over Southern Iraq in 1998, and retired from naval service in December 1999, returning to Australia with his family that same year.

THE SUNDOWNERS SONG

VF805 was nicknamed 'The Sundowners' by an envious group who shall remain anonymous. We, the squadron members, did not refer to ourselves as such. The reason for the nickname is fairly obvious when you think about it: a, the Skyhawk did not have air-to-air radar, so we could not perform the air-defence role at night; and, b, the aircraft was at the limit of what could be safely operated from the deck of HMAS *Melbourne*. It was 10 knots indicated airspeed faster, and approximately three tons heavier at maximum landing weight, than the Sea Venoms it replaced.

The Sundowners
– as modified by Joe Hattley

We are the Sundowners, so good are we
We only aviate, when we can see,
Moonlight and Stars, you can stick them up your jumper,
Coz' we are the Sundowners

The 816 Tigers think it's a lark
To rubbish us for not getting airborne in the dark
But secretly they wish that submarines were daylight fish,
And they could be Sundowners

The wing-flapping palm trees of HS817
Make out they are happy with the lights of heaven
But after night hovers and ball-dunking bothers
They wish they were Sundowners

As you all know, we're the best in the Fleet
From Colours to Sunset, any threat we'll meet
But when it gets black we say UP YOU JACK,
Coz' we are the Sundowners   Oi!

(Author Peter Greenfield: I never heard this song but am reliably informed it was sung at various gatherings. Both squadrons did fly at night, often, but the flying was mainly from ashore (or always in the case of VC724). We did, however, practise our assigned roles at night, from ashore, and a night maritime strike was one of the 'hairiest'. After the experience of Phil Thompson, night flying from the ship was limited, although there was always a night-flying team.)

INDEX OF NAMES